# Urbanization and Socio-Economic Development in Africa

The main goal of this book is to put urbanization and its challenges squarely on Africa's development agenda. Planned urbanization can improve living conditions for the majority, help in the expansion of the middle class, and create conditions for economic transformation. However, many African cities have developed haphazardly, resulting in the decline of public services, in slum proliferation, and increases in poverty. African cities thrive on activities characterized by easy entry and low productivity, generally referred to as the "informal sector". Indeed, today some urban dwellers are poorer than their cousins in the countryside. In spite of reform attempts, many governments have not been able to create an enabling environment, with adequate infrastructure and institutions to sustain markets for easy exchange and production. This study argues that with careful policies and planning, the situation can be changed. If the recent natural resource-led economic boom that we have seen in many African countries is used for structural reforms and urban renewal, African cities could become centers of economic opportunity. The challenge for African policymakers is to ensure that urban development is orderly and that the process is inclusive and emphasizes the protection of the environment, hence green growth.

**Steve Kayizzi-Mugerwa** is Director in the Development and Research Department at African Development Bank.

**Abebe Shimeles** is Division Manager in the Development and Research Department at African Development Bank.

**Nadège Désirée Yaméogo** is Senior Research Economist in the Development and Research Department at African Development Bank.

# Routledge African Studies

1 **Facts, Fiction, and African Creative Imaginations**
*Edited by Toyin Falola and Fallou Ngom*

2 **The Darfur Conflict**
Geography or Institutions?
*Osman Suliman*

3 **Music, Performance and African Identities**
*Edited by Toyin Falola and Tyler Fleming*

4 **Environment and Economics in Nigeria**
*Edited by Toyin Falola and Adam Paddock*

5 **Close to the Sources**
Essays on Contemporary African Culture, Politics and Academy
*Abebe Zegeye and Maurice Vambe*

6 **Landscape and Environment in Colonial and Postcolonial Africa**
*Edited by Toyin Falola and Emily Brownell*

7 **Development, Modernism and Modernity in Africa**
*Edited by Augustine Agwuele*

8 **Natural Resources, Conflict, and Sustainable Development**
Lessons from the Niger Delta
*Edited by Okechukwu Ukaga, Ukoha O. Ukiwo and Ibaba Samuel Ibaba*

9 **Regime Change and Succession Politics in Africa**
Five Decades of Misrule
*Edited by Maurice Nyamanga Amutabi and Shadrack Wanjala Nasong'o*

10 **The Political Economy of Development and Underdevelopment in Africa**
*Edited by Toyin Falola and Jessica Achberger*

11 **Pan-Africanism, and the Politics of African Citizenship and Identity**
*Edited by Toyin Falola and Kwame Essien*

12 **Securing Africa**
Local Crises and Foreign Interventions
*Edited by Toyin Falola and Charles Thomas*

13 **African Youth in Contemporary Literature and Popular Culture**
Identity Quest
*Edited by Vivian Yenika-Agbaw and Lindah Mhando*

14 **Indigenous Discourses on Knowledge and Development in Africa**
*Edited by Edward Shizha and Ali A. Abdi*

**15 African Culture and Global Politics**
Language, Philosophies, and Expressive Culture in Africa and the Diaspora
*Edited by Toyin Falola and Danielle Porter Sanchez*

**16 Urbanization and Socio-Economic Development in Africa**
Challenges and Opportunities
*Edited by Steve Kayizzi-Mugerwa, Abebe Shimeles and Nadège Désirée Yaméogo*

# Urbanization and Socio-Economic Development in Africa

Challenges and Opportunities

Edited by Steve Kayizzi-Mugerwa,
Abebe Shimeles
and Nadège Désirée Yaméogo

NEW YORK  LONDON

First published 2014
by Routledge
711 Third Avenue, New York, NY 10017

and by Routledge
2 Park Square, Milton Park, Abingdon, Oxon OX14 4RN

*Routledge is an imprint of the Taylor & Francis Group, an informa business*

© 2014 African Development Bank

The right of Steve Kayizzi-Mugerwa, Abebe Shimeles and Nadège Désirée Yaméogo to be identified as the authors of the editorial material, and of the authors for their individual chapters, has been asserted in accordance with sections 77 and 78 of the Copyright, Designs and Patents Act 1988.

All rights reserved. No part of this book may be reprinted or reproduced or utilised in any form or by any electronic, mechanical, or other means, now known or hereafter invented, including photocopying and recording, or in any information storage or retrieval system, without permission in writing from the publishers.

**Trademark Notice:** Product or corporate names may be trademarks or registered trademarks, and are used only for identification and explanation without intent to infringe.

*Library of Congress Cataloging-in-Publication Data*
  Urbanization and socio-economic development in Africa : challenges and opportunities / edited by Steve Kayizzi-Mugerwa, Abebe Shimeles and Nadège Désirée Yaméogo.
     pages cm. — (Routledge African studies ; 16)
  Includes bibliographical references and index.
  1. Urbanization—Economic aspects—Africa.  2. Urban
policy—Africa.  3. Community development, Urban—
Africa.  4. Rural-urban migration—Africa.  5. Africa—Economic
conditions—1960–  I. Kayizzi-Mugerwa, Steve, editor of
compilation.  II. Abebe Shimeles, editor of compilation.  III. Yaméogo, Nadège Désirée, editor of compilation.  IV. Series: Routledge African studies ; 16.
  HT384.A35U7293 2014
  307.76096—dc23
  2013050196

ISBN13: 978-1-138-01681-1 (hbk)
ISBN13: 978-1-315-78002-3 (ebk)

Typeset in Sabon
by IBT Global.

Printed and bound in the United States of America by IBT Global.

# Contents

| | | |
|---|---|---|
| *List of Figures* | | ix |
| *List of Tables* | | xi |
| *List of Boxes* | | xiii |
| *Foreword* | | xv |
| *Acknowledgments* | | xvii |
| 1 | Overview of Urban Development in Africa | 1 |
| | ALBERT MAFUSIRE, NADÈGE DÉSIRÉE YAMÉOGO AND MTHULI NCUBE | |
| 2 | Cities as Drivers of Development | 14 |
| | IVAN TUROK | |
| 3 | Institutions, Decentralisation and Urban Development | 42 |
| | EDGAR PIETERSE AND WARREN SMIT | |
| 4 | Financing Urban Development in Africa | 81 |
| | BEACON MBIBA | |
| 5 | Upgrading Informal Settlements in African Cities | 124 |
| | SOLOMON MULUGETA | |
| 6 | The Way Forward | 156 |
| | NADÈGE DÉSIRÉE YAMÉOGO, ABEBE SHIMELES, STEVE KAYIZZI-MUGERWA AND MTHULI NCUBE | |
| | *Contributors* | 179 |
| | *Index* | 183 |

# Figures

| | | |
|---|---|---|
| 1.1 | Mapping the current urbanization trend in Africa. | 4 |
| 1.2 | Percentage of urban population living in slums. | 7 |
| 1.3 | Infrastructure rural-urban divide. | 9 |
| 3.1 | Dimensions of sustainable urban development. | 63 |
| 3.2 | Functions in relation to development imperatives. | 74 |
| 4.1 | City of Bulawayo expenditure for salaries and capital budgets. | 84 |
| 4.2 | Financing urban development: a holistic view of the financing challenge. | 89 |
| 4.3 | Status of financial and mortgage markets in Africa. | 90 |
| 4.4 | Heuristic models of urban development or utility ownership and management. | 92 |
| 4.5 | The dominance of public utilities in Africa: water and sewerage sector. | 96 |
| 4.6 | Water as main source of revenue: Bulawayo City. | 115 |

# Tables

| | | |
|---|---|---:|
| 1.1 | Percentage of Urban Dwellers in Africa, by Region, with Projections | 4 |
| 2.1 | The Most Distant and Divided Regions of the World | 24 |
| 3.1 | Urban Population by Region, 1950–2010, with Projection for 2025–2050 | 45 |
| 3.2 | Percentage of Slum Dwellers in Three Developing Regions, 2005 | 46 |
| 3.3 | Cost of Water in Accra, Ghana (Approved in October 2012) | 47 |
| 3.4 | Rural and Urban Poverty in Africa | 48 |
| 3.5 | Overall Infrastructure Spending needs for Sub-Saharan Africa (US$ Billions Annually) | 50 |
| 3.6 | Selected African Countries' Governance Index, by Regions (2010) | 52 |
| 3.7 | The Public-Private Sector Model of Urban Management | 56 |
| 3.8 | Functions of Urban Local Government Bodies in Selected African Countries | 58 |
| 3.9 | Sources of Local Government revenue in Selected African Countries | 59 |
| 3.10 | Division of Functions between Local and Provincial Government in South Africa | 72 |
| 4.1 | Availibility and Accessibility of Land Information in Southern Africa | 86 |
| 4.2 | Governance Reforms: Emerging Utility Models in Water and Sanitation | 100 |
| 4.3 | Stratified Tariffs for Water and Sanitation in Senegal—2008 | 107 |
| 4.4 | Stratified Tariffs for Water and Sanitation in Burkina Faso | 107 |
| 4.5 | Customer Group Based Tariffs for Water and Sanitation in Uganda | 108 |
| 4.6 | Fixed and Variable Tariffs for Water and Sanitation in Tunisia | 108 |

xii *Tables*

| | | |
|---|---|---|
| 4.7 | Borrowing from the Market for Service Provision in Africa | 112 |
| 4.8 | Utility Privatisation Structure: The Public-Private Continuum | 123 |
| 5.1 | Average Annual Urban Growth Rates by Major Areas and Regions, 1960–2025 (%) | 135 |
| 5.2 | Distribution of African Countries by Real GDP Growth Rates, 1990–2011 | 136 |
| 5.3 | Population Living Below Poverty Line in Selected Countries of Africa | 138 |
| 6.1 | Income and Urbanisation in Africa—2008 | 158 |
| 6.2 | Shares of Various Modes of Transport in Use in 13 African Cities | 172 |
| 6.3 | Paved Roads in Selected African Cities—2008 | 173 |

# Boxes

| | | |
|---|---|---|
| 3.1 | What is a Slum? | 44 |
| 3.2 | Metroplitan Government in Abidjan | 57 |
| 4.1 | The Challenge of Finance in Post Crisis Zimbabwe | 83 |
| 4.2 | The Salient Role of International Actors in Urban Utility Reforms | 99 |
| 4.3 | Uganda: Setting and Maintaining Real Price Levels for Utility Services | 106 |
| 4.4 | South-South Aid and Harare's Remarkable Turnaround | 113 |
| 6.1 | Tackling Urban Poverty in Ghana | 165 |

# Foreword

Africa has experienced rapid urban growth in recent times, but this is yet to generate any observable structural transformation. In many regions of the world, urban expansion has been associated with structural transformation and improvement in living conditions. For Sub-Saharan African cities, urban growth has instead stretched the existing basic infrastructure, resulting in a decline in the quality of public services, growth of informal settlements and increased urban poverty. It is estimated that more than half of Sub-Saharan Africa's urban citizens live in slums. Several reasons explain the situation.

Firstly, most African cities lack the institutional, financial and political capacity to deal with the growth in their populations. Inadequate urban land markets coupled with informal land tenure systems have also contributed to slum proliferation and increases in urban poverty and inequality. While Africa's future economic success will depend on efficient and productive urban centres, most African governments continue to under-invest in the infrastructure for urban development. Generally, governments have failed to create an enabling environment where economic agents can meet and exchange easily, and workers and productive inputs can move efficiently.

Secondly, contrary to patterns in fast-growing emerging economies, notably in Asia, where economic development has been driven by manufacturing, most African economies have remained basic commodity producers, with low productivity. Yet, it is well known that economic development of cities and towns depends on their efficiency and productivity. While noting the emergence of other factors in explaining the recent growth in the continent, commodities still remain a big part of the story. Manufacturing or services are yet to emerge as dynamic sources of growth. African cities have likewise relied on activities with low productivity, notably in the informal sector, and have not been able to provide sufficient economic opportunities to urban dwellers. This has led to increasing poverty, slum proliferation, and social tensions and instability. The future development and success of Africa's cities and towns will depend on the efficiency and productivity of urban production.

xvi *Foreword*

For the next two decades, this situation could worsen unless urgent measures are taken to reverse it. There is hope in this regard. As highlighted in this report, experience has shown that positive results can be obtained with appropriate efforts, as has been the case in some parts of East Africa. The overarching objective must be to make urbanisation a transformational process that provides economic opportunities and improved quality of life to urban dwellers. The challenge for African policymakers is therefore to ensure an orderly urban development so that cities and towns can become engines of growth. Moreover, the recent unrest in the Middle East and North African countries have demonstrated that it is essential for governments to ensure that development strategies are oriented toward inclusiveness. In addition, as many African countries are dependent on climate-sensitive sectors such as agriculture, tourism, and natural resources, green policies are essential to economic and social progress in African cities. The path to greener cities requires that African governments opt for sustainable consumption strategies while their cities grow richer.

To achieve the objective of sustainable socio-economic development, it is important to understand the factors that have led to the observed underperformance of African cities, and design appropriate strategies that can help cities to become drivers of sustainable and inclusive growth. And this is the goal of this book: *"Urbanization and socio-economic development in Africa: challenges and opportunities"*, motivated by the discussions held during the 2008 Ministerial Round Table of the Annual Meeting of the African Development Bank. This book focused mainly on Sub-Saharan African countries as this region has been facing the biggest urbanization challenges during the last decade, compared to the Northern African region.

Professor Mthuli Ncube
Chief Economist and Vice President,
African Development Bank

# Acknowledgments

This book was prepared from inputs by staff members of the African Development Bank and external contributors under the overall guidance of Mthuli Ncube, Chief Economist and Vice President of the African Development Bank, Steve Kayizzi-Mugerwa, Director of the Research Department, and Abebe Shimeles, Manager of the Research Partnerships Division. The team is also grateful to Louis Kasekende, Léonce Ndikumana, Désiré Vencatachellum, Abdul Kamara, and Peter Walkenhorst.

Special thanks are due to the peer reviewers of the report, Mevin Ndarusigiye, Philip van Ryneveld, John Anyanwu, Barfour Osei, and Barbara Barungi. They carefully reviewed the draft and provided comments and suggestions. The team wishes to thank Joyce Mulama for editorial support, Aymen Dhib, Abdelaziz Elmarzougui, Laureline Pla, and Brodkinson Brennan for research assistance. We would like to thank Rees Mwasambili from the Ghana Field Office for providing data, and Rhoda Bangurah, Abiana Nelson, Josiane Petangui Koné, and Imen Rabai for administrative support. Finally, the book benefited from financial support from the Swedish Trust Fund hosted at the African Development Bank.

# 1 Overview of Urban Development in Africa

*Albert Mafusire, Nadège Désirée Yaméogo and Mthuli Ncube*

## INTRODUCTION

In Africa, the urban population is expected to exceed that of rural areas by 2025 (Tibaijuka, 2010). The rapid population growth in urban locations has stretched the capacity of existing infrastructure and facilities, resulting in a decline in the quality of services in these areas. In some cases, urban infrastructure and services have simply buckled under the unremitting pressure. Moreover, the rapid growth in urban population has not been associated with any observable transformation of the African economies. For many countries, primary commodity production has remained a dominant activity. The high growth rates since the turn of the century and increased foreign capital inflows have done little to change the continent's poverty situation and its economic structure. Attempts to explain what factors account for the less than expected economic contribution of African urban areas have been made. The evolution of the continent's cities and the challenges they face are diverse. These issues need to be carefully understood if practical strategies to addressing underinvestment in urban areas are to be developed.

In spite of the growth in Africa's urban population and in its economies, poverty reduction has been elusive. Between 1981 and 2005, significant poverty reduction was registered, especially in China, East Asia and the Pacific Region. Over this period, these regions experienced a drop in poverty incidence from 78 percent to 17 percent, using the US$1.25 a day poverty line at 2005 prices. In contrast, sub-Saharan Africa (SSA) is the only region that registered almost no change. Furthermore, growth in per capita incomes has been sluggish, with the incidence of poverty and income inequalities worsening in urban areas (Fay & Opal, 1999). In Sub-Saharan Africa, GDP per capita is considered to have fallen by five per cent, with extreme poverty rates rising from 47.4 per cent in 1990 to 49 per cent in 1999. This trend was expected to continue in the early 2000s (World Bank, 2004). Ravallion, Chen and Sangraula (2007) concur, arguing that despite Africa's growth, the number of the poor has increased. Also, the recent African growth is considered to have largely been due to rising oil and natural resource prices (Collier, 2006). Moreover, given the ownership and capital-intensive nature of natural resource extraction, the wealth generated from these activities accrue to a very narrow group of elites and most of it is externalised. As a result, such wealth has no relevance in poverty reduction. Sala-i-Martin and Pinkovskiy (2010), however, refute this conclusion, arguing that between 1985 and 2006, African aggregate poverty rates fell from about 42 per cent to just over 30 per cent.

Despite this less-than-conclusive position with regard to the aggregate poverty in Africa, urban conditions have deteriorated. Deep-seated poverty in Africa's cities has resulted in the rise of unhealthy and overcrowded informal settlements, commonly referred to as slums, which have grown at an average rate of about four per cent annually (United Nations, 2008). This development has been associated with increasing incidents of violent crimes in urban areas. However, rural-urban migration, the main factor behind the growth in urban centres, has persisted in spite of the lack of economic opportunities and deteriorating quality of life. For policymakers, the challenge is how to ensure both orderly development and the transformation of African urban areas into engines of growth. Achieving these two objectives would help in absorbing the growing labour force, while at the same time enhancing the quality of urban life.

The role of cities in economic development is the result of the interplay between exogenous factors that include governance, institutions and public policy, and spatial proximity, which endogenously impacts innovation and technological progress (Henderson, 2005). In addition, literature on economic geography reinforces the importance of agglomeration and clustering in this process (Krugman, 1998). However, the dynamism that is suggested in this literature appears to be absent in the African context. The question that emerges is how African cities could be rejuvenated so that they may play their role in fostering shared growth and development. It is, however, crucial that current trends in Africa's urbanisation processes be reversed. A critical factor in this process is the need to nurture a dynamic entrepreneurial and innovative culture. Yet more has to be done to ensure efficient institutions, appropriate legal and regulatory framework and good governance as prerequisites for engendering the necessary economic dynamism. Such efforts will help in the development of businesses that would provide employment opportunities and increasing productivity, and lead to increasing incomes. The possibilities may not be that apparent, but the good news is that where efforts have been made, positive results have emerged.

Notably, the support provided to family-run, small-income-generating projects has made it possible to upgrade living conditions, with the proportion of urban slum dwellers decreasing by five per cent during the 2000–2010 period (UN Habitat, 2010a). While providing pointers to successful interventions, there are questions regarding the sustainability of such efforts given the low returns to the projects that are being supported. In this context, the debate on how urbanisation could foster growth in Africa remains alive.

The 2008 Ministerial Round Table Discussions of the Annual Meeting of the African Development Bank Group focused on the theme: "Fostering Shared Growth: Urbanisation, Inequalities and Poverty in Africa." The choice of this theme was based on the recognition that towns and cities constitute centres of transformation of the economies around the globe. There is no doubt that African cities could play a similar role, if hindrances to the realisation of such an outcome were addressed. However, such a process would require a clear understanding of the factors leading to observed outcomes. This has to be followed by the design of strategies that could help transform the continent's cities into vibrant economic centres that drive growth through their interaction with the rest of the economy. The African Development Bank's Integrated Urban Development Strategy is part of the efforts aimed at ensuring that urban development harnesses the full potential of all players in this process.

The rest of the introductory chapter highlights urban trends, the current state and experiences with urbanisation in Africa, identifies gaps in policy and suggests responses towards making cities liveable environments and engines for growth and development in the continent.


## URBANIZATION TRENDS IN AFRICA

Between 2005 and 2010, Africa experienced the fastest urban growth in the world with an average annual growth rate of over 3%. Projections also indicate continuing high growth for the next 15 years. Countries which are predominantly urban are in Northern and Southern Africa, whereas the majority of Sub-Saharan Africa's urban population rate is between 25–50% (Figure 1.1). Rapid urbanization is widespread across the entire continent, but not all cities have contributed equally to this rapid growth (Table 1.1). Eastern Africa remains predominantly rural and lags behind the rest of the continent. Only 23.7% of this region's population was urban in 2010 with the less urbanized cities in countries such as Burundi (11%), Ethiopia (17.6%), Rwanda (18.9%) and Uganda (13.3%). Elsewhere, cities such as Abuja, Bamako, Kinshasa and Ouagadougou, for instance, have also registered high annual population growth of over 4%. This suggests that the population of these cities will double in the next 17 years. On the other hand, Maputo and Lusaka are experiencing low annual urban growth rates, with projections pointing to declining trends in the coming years. Also, Rabat and Algiers are experiencing urban population decline (UN-Habitat, 2010b).

In North Africa, except Egypt and Sudan, the majority of the population lives in urban areas. In 2010, the proportion of urban population was about 66.5% in Algeria, 77.9% in Libya and 56.7% in Morocco, whereas in Egypt and Sudan the proportions were below 50%. In these countries, only Egypt registered a decline in its urban population—43.5% in 1990 compared to 42.8% in 2010. By 2030, about 61.3% of the region's population

Table 1.1  Percentage of Urban Dwellers in Africa, by Region, with Projections

| Regions | 1990 | 2010 | 2030 | 2050 |
|---|---|---|---|---|
| Central Africa | 32.5 | 42.9 | 55.3 | 67.4 |
| Eastern Africa | 17.9 | 23.7 | 33.7 | 47.6 |
| Northern Africa | 44.7 | 52 | 61.3 | 72 |
| Southern Africa | 48.8 | 58.8 | 68.8 | 77.6 |
| Western Africa | 33.2 | 44.6 | 56.5 | 68 |
| SSA | 28.2 | 37.3 | 48.2 | 60.5 |
| Africa | 32 | 39.9 | 50 | 61.8 |

Source: Population Division of the Department of Economic and Social Affairs of the United Nations Secretariat.

will be living in urban areas. Projections indicate that Egypt will still have less than 50% of its population urbanized whereas in Sudan, the urban population will more than double (to 60.7%) compared to its level in 1990. The recent urban population growth in Algeria, Egypt, Morocco and Tunisia has taken place in multiple geographically dispersed cities. In Egypt, for instance, Cairo and Alexandria are the main engines of the country's economic growth, accounting for 57% and 22.5% of manufacturing activities, respectively. In Morocco, Casablanca accounts for only 10% of the country's population, but hosts 55% of the country's production units and 60% of industrial workers.

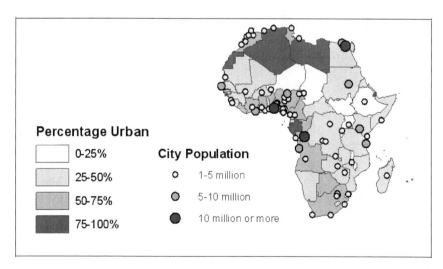

Figure 1.1  Mapping the current urbanization trend in Africa.
Source: UN-Habitat, 2012.

In Western Africa, only 33.2% of the population was living in urban areas in 1990. This number more than doubled to reach 137.2 million in 2010. In the same period, five countries out of the 17 were already estimated to have more than 50% urban dwellers (Cape Verde, Côte d'Ivoire, Gambia, Ghana and Liberia). Projections indicate that the entire region will be predominantly urban by 2020. Unique aspects of this urbanization trend are that in some countries population growth has been much faster than economy growth. These cities include: Lagos (Nigeria), Ouagadougou (Burkina Faso), Lomé (Togo) and Niamey (Niger). As a result, urbanization has been characterized by slum proliferation, crime and high rate of unemployment.

In Eastern Africa, in a period of 60 years, the urban population has been multiplied more than 20 times, from 3.45 million in 1950 to about 78.79 million in 2010. However, only a few countries (Djibouti, Réunion and Seychelles) were predominantly urbanized in 2010. For the next decade, projections indicate that the urban population will increase by another 38.5 million. Yet by 2030, only one-third of East Africans will be living in urban areas, and by 2050, about half of the region's population will still be rural-based, leaving it the least urbanized region in the continent for many years to come. The contributors to urban demographic expansion in the region are mainly urban natural growth and conflicts in some countries such as Somalia. As in Western Africa, urbanization growth has been characterised by slum proliferation, increasing urban unemployment and environmental degradation, among other social and environmental issues.

Central Africa remains the second least urbanized region in Africa after Eastern Africa with about 43% of its population living in urban areas in 2010. But, the region is rapidly catching up with the rest of the continent as its average urban population growth rate has been the highest in the continent since 2005. The situation is likely to remain the same by 2050. In 2010, Gabon was by far the most urbanized country in the region (urban population: 86%), whereas Chad was the least urbanized with only 27% of its population in urban areas. During the last decade, thanks to the fossil fuel boom, Cameroon has been one of the most rapidly urbanizing countries in the region, with an urban population growth rate of 8.5%. Cameroon became predominantly urban before 2005 and accounted for about 58.5% of urban dwellers in 2010. Central Africa is expected to become predominantly urban by 2022, and by 2050, more than 67% of its population will be urban dwellers.

Over the last two decades (1990–2010), Southern Africa has remained the most urbanized region in the continent. In 2010, urban dwellers accounted for almost 59% of its population and projections indicate that this percentage will increase to 69% by 2030 and to 78% by 2050, the highest in the continent. Even though this region has always had the lowest urban population growth rates, Southern Africa has entered a period where these growth rates are expected to slow down further in the coming decades—an average of 1.99% between 2000 and 2005, 1.13% between 2025 and 2030, and 0.74% for the five years to 2050. But, the urbanization process has varied from one country to another. For instance, in 2010, South Africa was by far the most urbanized country in the region with an urban population of 61.7%, whereas Lesotho and Swaziland were the least urbanized with 26.8% and 21.3%, respectively. Yet these latter countries are expected to start catching up from 2020 onwards. However, by 2040, Swaziland will remain the only country which would not have reached the "tipping point" of 50% urban population.

Overall, by 2060, Africa's population is projected to radically shift from rural to urban areas. The proportion of urban dwellers will rise from 40% in 2010 to 65% by 2060. SSA will account for about 60% of urban dwellers by 2050 but Southern Africa will remain the most urbanized in the continent with 77.6% of urban dwellers. The least urbanized part of Africa—Eastern Africa—is projected to remain predominantly rural until after 2050 (UN-Habitat, 2010b).

## THE RAPID URBAN POPULATION GROWTH IN SSA HAS BEEN RATHER PROBLEMATIC

The rapid growth and changes in population structure in the landscape of most African cities have resulted in increasing urban poverty. In Sub-Saharan Africa, it is estimated that 42 per cent of the total population lives in extreme poverty. It has also been observed that 62 per cent of Sub-Saharan Africa's urban population lives in slums (UN-Habitat, 2010b) compared to 35 per cent for South Asia and about 24 per cent for western Asia and Oceania. North Africa, even with its high urbanisation (52 %), has a low proportion (13 %) of urban dwellers in slum conditions. UN-Habitat (2010b) also reports that 22 million people in developing countries have moved out of slums, yet this progress has had limited impact in countering the growth of informal settlements. Even with the deterioration in some urban conditions in Africa, rural–urban migration has not abated. Whether this phenomenon is a result of the neglect of agriculture or the lure of the "bright city lights" is open to debate. However, we posit that the history of a country's socio-economic experiences, and to some extent, its political history, both play an important role in influencing the observed characteristics of urban growth.

These trends are staggering by any account, but they also mask the fact that we are talking about vastly different kinds of urban settlements. Specifically, the vast majorities of African urban dwellers reside, and will continue to reside, in urban settlements, with populations of fewer than 0.5 million people. For example, in 2005, 51 per cent of the urban population lived in settlements with fewer than 0.5 million people, compared

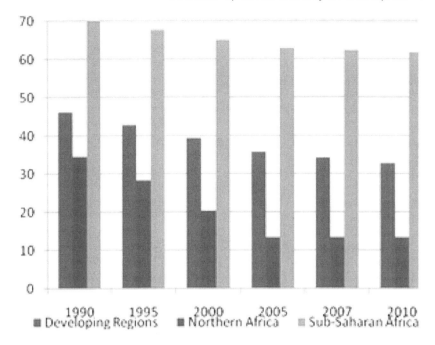

1.2 Percentage of urban population living in slums.
*Source*: Author, based on UN-Habitat (2011) data.

to 10 per cent in cities of between 0.5 and 1 million, 23 per cent in cities of 1–1.5 million, eight per cent in cities of 5–10 million and only nine per cent in cities with more than 10 million people. This is fundamentally different from the typical scenario of mega-city explosions that is popularly associated with urbanisation.

However, Africa is increasingly becoming an urban continent. The continent's average annual urban growth rate of about four per cent in 2008 is the highest compared to the global growth of 3.3 per cent between 1990 and 2000. Whereas this growth was almost always in the form of slum growth, the trend has reversed. However, the proportion of the continent's population still living in slums remains highest in the world (UN-Habitat, 2010a, 2010b; Figure 1.2).

Sub-Saharan Africa's proportion of slum dwellers is higher than in any other region in the world. East Africa, in particular, experienced the highest growth of both urbanisation and the proportion of slum dwellers. On the other hand, North Africa has the lowest proportion of slum dwellers on the continent after having fallen from 34 per cent in 1990 to about 13 per cent in 2010.

Questions have been raised as to whether Sub-Saharan African governments have failed to come up with new urban development systems in the face of rapidly growing urban populations. If this is the case, are there any

8　*Albert Mafusire, Nadège Désirée Yaméogo and Mthuli Ncube*

lessons from this inconsistency? There is a general consensus that North African countries have invested more in infrastructure development than their counterparts in Sub-Saharan Africa. Yet it is also acknowledged that the extent of rural–urban migration after the end of colonialism was beyond what could be sustained by existing urban infrastructure. Colonial cities in Sub-Saharan Africa were especially characterised by the separation of blacks and whites. Very little resources were devoted to the development of African areas. This contrasts with most of North African developments, where more homogenous societies enjoyed more or less similar treatment. In this context, it is argued that a more sustainable way of dealing with slum conditions is to implement slum-upgrading programmes while at the same time taking pro-active measures that would ensure orderly urban development.

Furthermore, it is observed that urban inequality in Africa, measured in terms of the Gini coefficient at 0.54, is the second highest in the world, and well above the international alert line of 0.4. In the larger African economies, such as South Africa, income inequality is far more severely skewed, with Gini coefficients of over 0.7 for all of the largest cities (UN-Habitat, 2008). Based on these trends, it is concluded that urban poverty continued to rise—four times faster than rural poverty—between 1993 and 2002 (See Table 3.4 in Chapter 3). Given the widespread poverty in urban areas, urban management authorities face additional difficulties as the revenue-generation capacity of local authorities is compromised by a real inability to pay. This problem arises due to: (i) Large sections of the population are unable to pay for basic urban infrastructure and facilities, and/or (ii) institutional inadequacies to generate sufficient revenue at the local level.

It is therefore not surprising that basic services backlogs are staggering. Sub-Saharan Africa has only 20 per cent of its population with access to electricity networks; 40 per cent with access to portable water; 27 per cent with access to sanitation; and four per cent with access to fixed or mobile telephony.[1] Moreover, rural and urban disparities are commonplace (Figure 1.3). However, it is generally accepted that the urban and rural populations in Africa without adequate access to water and sanitation are 35–50 per cent and 50–60 per cent, respectively (Tannerfeldt & Ljung, 2006). This suggests better access in urban areas, but the numbers obscure country differences. Countries such as Tunisia and Mauritius have made great strides in providing urban infrastructure, yet on the other hand East African countries are lagging. In addition, intra-city differences exist. The high-income areas are better served when compared to low-income areas, whereas slums lack even the basic infrastructure.

The limited coverage of network infrastructures also means Africans pay much more for access to basic services per unit than those in developed countries, who are better connected to infrastructure systems. For example, Africa's road freight is about 4 times more expensive, power costs 14 US cents per kilowatt-hour versus 5–10 US cents and mobile telephony costs 12 US dollars per month compared to 8 US dollars elsewhere. Similar observations have been made among the poor and rich African urban dwellers.

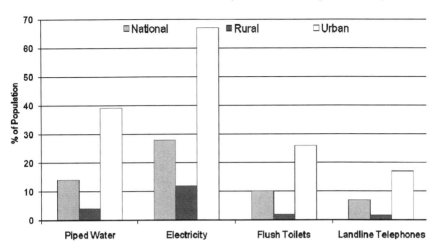

1.3 Infrastructure rural–urban divide.
*Source:* Author's calculations based on the Africa Infrastructure Country Diagnostic data. Banerjee, S., Wodon, Q., Diallo, A., Pushak, T., Uddin, H., Tsimpo, C., & Foster, V. (2008). *Access, affordability, and alternatives: Modern infrastructure services in Africa*. Africa Infrastructure Country Diagnostic.

A specific illustration reinforces this point forcefully. The urban poor of Accra who reside in slums without access to piped water pay exponentially more for access compared to other urban residents in the city as graphically illustrated in Table 3.3 (Chapter 3). This clearly underscores why the lack of basic urban infrastructure and basic services disproportionately impact low-income groups and neighbourhoods that are cut off from networked infrastructure grids. But this is not the only way in which slum dwellers and slum areas are disadvantaged. It is important to bear in mind the differences between economic, household and public infrastructures. They also reflect the relative levels of influence among the different socio-economic classes of urban dwellers. Typically, powerful classes and interest groups who drive the economy have a disproportionate say in determining which kinds of infrastructure are prioritised and where they are provided. To this extent, the continuation of selective under-investment in all categories of infrastructure in low-income locations contributes to the perpetuation of urban poverty, which is increasingly cemented by structural inequality (Parnell, Pieterse & Watson, 2009).

In the short-term, any significant change through rapid and effective provision of urban infrastructure seems unlikely, given the continued under-investment in infrastructure across Africa. A recently published report, *Africa's Infrastructure: A Time for Transformation* (Foster & Briceño-Garmendia, 2010), provides a detailed account of the overall infrastructure trends in Africa, inclusive of both urban and rural areas. Overall, Africa's infrastructure needs are U$93 billion per annum, twice as much as the current spending levels of U$45 billion. A number of questions arise: (i) Is there any potential

10　*Albert Mafusire, Nadège Désirée Yaméogo and Mthuli Ncube*

for areas in Africa to play a transformative role in the continent's economies? (ii) What needs to be done to overcome the constraints to improved investment outcomes and thus achieve economic dynamism in Africa? and (iii) What is the role of International Financial Institutions in this process?

## NURTURING INTERNAL URBAN DYNAMICS FOR AFRICA'S TRANSFORMATION

Whereas the current trends in urban development in Africa are rather depressing, there are opportunities for African cities to become engines of growth and development. It should be recognised that urban and rural development are not mutually exclusive. Rather, they are complementary in a national development context. Turok (Chapter 2) especially notes that benefits of urbanisation flow to rural areas through remittances, investment spill-overs, large urban markets and connectivity to wider national and international networks of information, finance and trade.

On the other hand, Pieterse cautions that the resource extractive model of economic development in Africa limits the spill-over effects of urbanisation, which are critical for creating internal dynamism for sustainable development. This argument is in agreement with the concept of the "enclave economy" (Gallagher & Zarsky, 2007), which suggests that if urban areas are to play the transformative role in African economies, they should generate economic dynamism that exploits economies of agglomeration and innovation. To the extent that such dynamism exists, productivity gains are expected to emerge in a manner that is beneficial to both rural and urban economic activities.

Sound economic and structural reforms are required to ensure that the internal dynamics are realised. This would in turn result in raising the living standards in both rural and urban economies. These reforms must be targeted at:

- Improving institutional efficiency and accountability and centre–local relationships in service delivery by clearly defining responsibilities at each level of governance,
- Creating opportunities for income-generating activities through shared growth,
- Enhancing capacity to mobilise domestic financial resources and attraction of foreign capital, which is complemented by a system that efficiently allocates investments between urban and rural areas,
- Addressing some of the structural factors that hinder risk taking, especially with regard to property rights and land tenure,
- Flexibility in building standards, zoning regulations and urban planning systems that reflects local social and economic power relations, and
- Increasing awareness for community involvement in urban affairs.

But there is even a greater challenge. For many African governments, it is not necessarily the absence of strategies and policies that limits the potential for urban economies to act as engines for growth and development. Rather, it is the lack of practical mechanisms and capacity to implement such strategies. In this context, reforms should focus on addressing institutional constraints to ensure flexible, innovative and responsive urban administrations if the yawning urban infrastructure needs are to be met. These institutional reforms are a primary requirement in the process of addressing structural restrictions to sustainable urban development.

In this context, the conclusions from the United Nations Earth Summit in Rio de Janeiro of 1997, which examined the relationship between human rights, population, social development, women and human settlements, as well as the need for environmentally sustainable development, are informative. Specifically, it is noted that the continuous interaction among the different economic entities produces some internal dynamism that influences the course of development.

According to Turok (Chapter 2) the developmental impacts of urbanisation largely depend on how cities harness knowledge and technology as productivity and income drivers. These two factors are critical for stimulating consumer spending. Mbiba (Chapter 4) goes on to argue that while urbanisation has immense potential as a driver of growth, the attractiveness of cities as investment destinations is also affected by centre–local relations. These relations are important in influencing the structure and content of urban development finance. Consequently, although acknowledging resource constraints faced by many African governments, Pieterse and Smit (Chapter 3) conclude that urbanisation in Africa has failed to bring about growth due to fundamental institutional problems. Among such problems is the rapid urbanisation on the continent. However, this is compounded by the fact that many governments are operating without any explicit urban development strategies. Indeed, controls on rural–urban migration no longer have any legitimacy in independent Africa. Also, rapid urbanisation should not be an excuse for failure to adequately respond to urban development trends. Chapters 3 and 4 identify traditional governance models in Africa as being detrimental to the development of effective centre–local relations. Traditional governance models need to be adapted to ensure meaningful democratic participation mechanisms, which are critical in promoting transparency, accountability and responsiveness.

Mulugeta (Chapter 5), on the other hand, points out that urban development failure intensifies during periods of political crisis. During such times, local government authorities and their enforcement of city by-laws are compromised. With population movements driven by non-economic motives, those involved are not prepared to engage in any meaningful economic activity. The influx of rural populations into Monrovia during the Liberia conflict and more recently political interference with settlement developments in Zimbabwe's urban areas has had similar effects. However,

## 12 *Albert Mafusire, Nadège Désirée Yaméogo and Mthuli Ncube*

in the case of Kibera in Nairobi, the inhabitants could have made rational economic decisions based on their ability to pay for a certain level of services. Yet, even in the case of Kibera, the historical factors[2] and the resultant power relations had important implications on the kind of economic activities that the inhabitants could be engaged in. But we also observe that reorganising these kinds of settlements and the communities to contribute economically to the welfare of the city is normally a challenge, both financially and administratively.

Particularly important, the presumed inability of the slum settlers to pay for services provides no incentive for local authorities to invest in modern and decent infrastructure. This raises the question of who should spearhead the transformation of slums into more organised and economically predisposed places so that they can contribute meaningfully to urban development. While central governments should play an important role in urban development, they should not be the sole financiers, especially in the face of competing demands for available resources. Moreover, sustainable approaches to urban development are those that involve multiple partners, including central governments, multi-lateral and bilateral development partners, the private sector and the urban community. In this context, any efforts to address the deteriorating urban conditions must include improved income generating opportunities that are necessary to ensure enhanced capabilities for the urban poor. Only then are the urban poor able to pay for investments in urban infrastructure and facilities. Furthermore, the role of the private sector, both as a contributor to the current state of urban settlements and its potential in providing solutions to the existing challenges, also needs interrogation. In particular, the institutional, legal and regulatory environment plays an important role in influencing the nature of private sector participation in urban development.

Clearly, there are many challenges to ensuring cities in Africa foster shared growth and poverty reduction. In Chapter 2, Turok discusses the economic underpinnings for urban areas to function as engines of growth. This is followed by a detailed analysis of the role of institutions, good governance and appropriate legal and regulatory frameworks, and the contribution of these factors to orderly urban development. In Chapter 4, Mbiba addresses the issue of urban development financing and how this is related to institutional factors. Details on current financing arrangements, sources of finance and innovations in urban development financing are also provided, with particular attention to inequalities and poverty in the urban areas. Mulugeta's insights on upgrading informal settlements are given in Chapter 5. Having noted the economic, institutional and financing constraints to orderly urban development, proposals and examples of success stories in upgrading slums are analysed. Finally, Chapter 6 provides a synthesis of the issues analysed in this book. It also draws conclusions and lessons for policymakers, and the roles for the various players in urban development.

## NOTES

1. World Bank data quoted in Ajulu and Motsamai, 2008.
2. Original settlers of Kibera are presumed to be Nubians who had fought during the World Wars alongside the British, who then allowed them to settle without title to the land. Over time, other settlers moved in and rented space from the Nubians.

## REFERENCES

Ajulu, C., & Motsamai, D. (2008). The Pan-African Infrastructure Development Fund (PAIDF): Towards an African agenda. *Global Insight, 76.*
Banerjee, S., Wodon, Q., Diallo, A., Pushak, T., Uddin, H., Tsimpo, C., & Foster, V. (2008). *Access, affordability, and alternatives: Modern infrastructure services in Africa.* Washington, DC: World Bank.
Collier, P. (2006). Africa: Geography and growth. *TEN, Federal Reserve Bank of Kansas City* (Fall), 18–21.
Fay, M., & Opal, C. (2000). *Urbanisation without growth: a not-so-uncommon phenomenon.* Washington, DC: World Bank.
Foster, V., & Briceño-Garmendia, C. (Eds.). (2010). *Africa's infrastructure: A time for transformation.* Washington, DC: World Bank.
Gallagher, K. P., & Zarsky, L. (2007). *The enclave economy: Foreign investment and sustainable development in Mexico's Silicon Valley.* Cambridge: MIT Press.
Henderson, J. V. (2005). Urbanisation and growth. In P. Aghion & S. Durlauf (Eds.), *Handbook of economic growth* (Vol. 1). Amsterdam: Elsevier.
Krugman, P. (1998). What's new about the new economic geography. *Oxford Review of Economics Policy, 14,* 7–17.
Parnell, S., Pieterse, E., & Watson, V. (2009). Planning for cities in the global south: An African research agenda for sustainable human settlements. *Progress in Planning, 72*(2), 233–241.
Ravallion, M., Chen, S., & Sangraula, P. (2007). New evidence of the globalization of poverty. *Population and Development Review, 33*(4), 667–701.
Sala-i-Martin, X., & Pinkovskiy, M. (2010). African poverty is falling . . . much faster than you think! *NBER Working Paper Series, 15775.*
Tannerfeldt, G., & Ljung, P. (2006). *More urban less poor: An introduction to urban development and management.* London: Earthscan.
Tibaijuka, A. (2010). *Balanced development for Africa: The cities of the future— Beyond chaotic urbanisation.* Speech delivered at the 1027th Wilton Park Conference, West Sussex, UK.
United Nations. (2008). *World urbanisation prospects: The 2007 revision.* New York: Department of Economic and Social Affairs, United Nations.
UN-Habitat. (2010a). *The state of African cities 2010: Governance, inequality and urban land market.* Nairobi: UN-Habitat.
UN-Habitat. (2010b). *State of the world's cities 2010/2011: Bridging the urban divide.* Nairobi: UN-Habitat.
World Bank. (2004). *World development report 2004: Making services work for poor people.* Oxford University Press.

# 2 Cities as Drivers of Development

*Ivan Turok*

## INTRODUCTION

The conventional wisdom within the international policy community is that urbanisation promotes economic development and raises household incomes. However, there is some debate about the extent to which this applies to Africa, and about the appropriate balance to be struck between urban and rural areas in development policy. The purpose of this chapter is to explore the contribution of cities and towns to the development of African economies and the reduction of poverty. The chapter considers the theoretical arguments for cities as engines of growth, and discusses their applicability to the African context, as far as the available evidence permits. It examines some of the particular challenges and constraints facing African urban economies, and identifies a range of issues that need to be addressed by policymakers if cities are to fulfil their development potential.

The structure is as follows. The rest of this section sets the context for the discussion and introduces the main ideas. The following section examines the general economic arguments for urban growth. It discusses the advantages of agglomeration and the interactions between rural and urban areas. Section three considers the relevance of these arguments to African cities, drawing on an important recent report from the World Bank. The fourth section looks more closely at how dynamic urban economies develop over time, and section five considers the extent to which African cities have followed this trajectory. The sixth section discusses the evidence for a recent recovery in African urban economies, including the role played by foreign investment. The final section discusses some of the ways in which government policy might help to realise the potential of urbanisation to promote economic development and to raise average incomes.

There is a growing consensus among international organisations that urbanisation is a source of prosperity and human progress (HM Treasury, 2006; United Nations, 2007; United Nations Human Settlements Programme [UN-Habitat], 2008, 2010; World Bank, 2009). Cities are believed to foster wealth creation and job generation by harnessing the forces of agglomeration and industrialisation. Dense concentrations of physical, financial and intellectual capital spur economic progress through economies of scale, creative problem-solving and improvements in the division of labour—finding new ways of producing commodities and new items to produce. These changes sometimes involve major structural shifts in the economy. The shift from agriculture to industry and services has historically been accompanied by a transformation in the population geography of nations, referred to as the 'urban transition.' China is widely cited as a vivid contemporary example of how large-scale rural–urban migration can fuel industrialisation and improve living standards (World Bank, 2009; Ravallion, 2009). Average household incomes in Chinese cities are almost three times higher than in rural areas (Bloom & Khanna, 2007).

One of the puzzles about Africa's rapid urbanisation is why it does not seem to have been accompanied by greater economic dynamism (Rakodi, 1997; World Bank, 2000; Davis, 2006; Venables, 2010). Africa is the world's poorest continent and its economies remain heavily dependent on exports of natural resources, rather than processed goods and services typically produced in cities (African Development Bank [AfDB], 2007; Ajakaiye & Ncube, 2010). A recent major study of 90 developing countries around the world found a positive relationship between urbanisation and poverty reduction, except in Sub-Saharan Africa (Ravallion, Chen, & Sangraula, 2007). Similarly, the World Development Report for 1999/2000 stated that African cities were exceptional in failing to serve as engines of growth: "Instead, they are part of the cause and a major symptom of the economic and social crises that have enveloped the continent" (World Bank, 2000, p.130). Another international study also concluded: "There is generally an unequivocal (positive) correlation between urbanisation and economic development and growth, but in Africa, this appears not to apply" (Kamete, 2001, as cited in Njoh, 2003).

This notion of 'urbanisation without economic growth' in Africa is contradicted by at least two other systematic studies that show a positive link between urbanisation and development (Kessides, 2007; Njoh, 2003). Njoh (2003) examined data for 40 Sub-Saharan African countries and found a strong positive correlation between urbanisation and human development. In a wider-ranging study, Kessides (2007) confirmed a connection between urbanisation and growth over the period 1990–2003 in 15 of the 24 African countries she examined. She also showed that national economic growth during this period was derived from urban-based industries, supporting the idea of cities as generators of growth.

Nevertheless, there remains extensive and indeed increasing poverty in African cities. Some 43 per cent of the urban population lives below the poverty line. About 60 per cent earn a living from the informal sector, and 72 per cent live in "slums" (UN-Habitat, 2008). Some have suggested that Africa urbanised prematurely in response to push factors (rural droughts, falling agricultural prices and ethnic conflicts) rather than the pull of economic opportunities (Commission for Africa, 2005; Annez, Buckley, &

16 *Ivan Turok*

Kalarickal, 2010). Indeed, three-quarters of African governments believe that urbanisation is excessive and have policies to reduce rural–urban migration (United Nations, 2008). These governments have strong and increasing anti-urban sentiments because of the social tensions, overcrowding, and physical squalor created in cities, combined with the breakdown of traditional family structures, and the spread of crime and disease (McGranahan, Mitlin, Satterthwaite, Tacoli, & Turok, 2009). There is little doubt that cities are more commonly seen as environmental problems and threats to social order, rather than potential mechanisms for expanding economic opportunities and reducing poverty.

Whatever the stance of governments, independent observers believe that Africa's urban population will continue to grow strongly, both through natural change (births exceeding deaths) and migration from rural areas (McGranahan et al., 2009). Global history shows that urbanisation is inexorable and most attempts to discourage it fail abysmally (Beall, Guha-Khasnobis, & Kanbur, 2010). Todaro's model of migration (2000) has been highly influential in development policy. It has encouraged public investment in rural economies in order to raise rural incomes and thereby reduce the incentive for people to migrate to the cities. However, there is little evidence that this strategy has worked in practice.

UN-Habitat (2008) projects that Africa's urban population will double over the next 20 years, with much of the growth in secondary cities. Rural–urban migration is partly a matter of survival and partly a means of acquiring skills. It is also driven by the need to pursue other assets, especially for people choosing to move away from livelihoods based on natural resources. The evidence suggests that migrants are making economically rational decisions when they move to urban areas (United Nations, 2007; White, Mberu, & Collinson, 2008). There is therefore great danger in governments treating urban problems as symptoms of over-urbanisation, blaming cities for poverty, and responding by trying to stem rural–urban migration. This could make it even harder for people to escape poverty. Government failure to plan for continuing urban growth will also constrain national economic and social development, especially if urban areas are deprived of essential investment in infrastructure and services (Bloom & Khanna, 2007; Kessides, 2007; Venables, 2010; World Bank, 2009).

More organisations are arguing that urbanisation could be a force for greater all-round prosperity if it is properly managed (Kessides, 2007; Martine, McGranahan, Montgomery, & Fernandez-Castilla, 2008; UN-Habitat, 2008; United Nations, 2007). Without suitable conditions, rapid urbanisation could be a recipe for chaos and human suffering. Better functioning cities would foster more enterprising and productive activity, facilitate trade and attract foreign investment. But beyond this broad assertion, there is great uncertainty about how African urban economies might develop over time, and what particular conditions could help cities cope with the profound implications of doubling their population in the next

Cities as Drivers of Development   17

two decades. How will people earn a living? How will the composition of local economies change? And how will revenues be generated to pay for essential services to ensure more liveable, healthier, resilient and productive cities? The informal sector is already important, accounting for some 78 per cent of non-agricultural employment, 93 per cent of all new jobs and 61 per cent of urban employment (Kessides, 2006). However, it operates with minimal capital, low skills, and little added-value. Hence, it does not provide a secure foundation for sustained growth and all-round development.

A general lack of research and robust evidence on African urban economies means there are many gaps in knowledge and understanding. The shortage of statistical evidence enables commentators to make sweeping generalisations and to adopt polarised positions. There is little sensitivity shown to differences between countries across the continent, despite varying levels of urbanisation and diverse economic conditions. Ignorance about the dynamics of economic development in African cities is a specific problem for policy because of growing international evidence that employment is the best route out of poverty, because it can provide a secure livelihood, dignity, meaning and structure to people's lives (Organisation of Economic Co-operation and Development [OECD], 2008a; Turok, 2010a).

The original Millennium Development Goals (MDGs) identified poverty as the top priority but made no reference to employment until the targets were revised in 2007. The MDGs also say surprisingly little about urban areas. For many voters and taxpayers, as well as international donors, government support for job creation and economic development may be more preferable than some forms of welfare spending because the beneficiaries are actively contributing to society. An improved understanding of urban economies should help policymakers to achieve a higher and better employment growth path, and to target pro-poor development programmes in a more cost-effective and sustainable manner than some other types of policy.

## WHY URBANISATION IS IMPORTANT FOR THE ECONOMY

Throughout history, cities have been linked with processes of economic, social and cultural advancement (Beall & Fox, 2009; Castells, 2000; Hall, 1998; Jacobs, 1969). This has been advantageous to the national as well as the local economy. "Urban development is essential . . . for economic and social development. No country has ever achieved significant economic growth in the modern age by retaining its population in rural areas" (Martine et al., 2008, p. 3). Economic progress has often depended on more people living in cities to expand the supply of labour and entrepreneurs and stimulate mutual learning and creativity, which have in turn generated the resources to support continued urbanisation (through essential infrastructure and services). The outcome of this virtuous circle has been a rise in national productivity, higher average incomes and greater all-round prosperity.

18   *Ivan Turok*

The economic rationale for urbanisation is underpinned by two basic concepts—the *division of labour* and *economies of scale*. The former was introduced by Adam Smith. It explains the benefits for productivity that arise from specialisation among producers. It accounted for the great leap forward from craft production to factory production that gave rise to the industrial revolution in the 18th and 19th centuries.

*Economies of scale* are often referred to as *increasing returns to scale*. There are two aspects to this. *Internal economies of scale* relate to the efficiencies that result from larger units of production. Larger firms can spread their fixed costs (rent, rates, R&D, etc.) over a larger volume of output, and buy their inputs at lower prices. *External economies of scale* (or *agglomeration economies*) relate to the benefits that firms derive from being located near their customers and suppliers in order to reduce transport and communication costs. They also include proximity to a large labour pool, and to competitors within the same industry and firms in other industries. Marshall (1920) was the first economist to recognise the benefits for economic agents of having access to a reservoir of information and ideas, skills and shared inputs.

These economic gains from spatial concentration can be summarised as three functions: matching, sharing and learning (Duranton & Puga, 2004; Rice, Venables, & Patacchini, 2006; Turok, 2004; Venables, 2010). First, cities enable firms to *match* their distinctive requirements for labour, premises, suppliers and business services better than smaller towns, simply because there is a much bigger choice available. In a volatile and fast-changing economy, there is a premium on flexibility and adaptability to shifts in markets and technologies, especially as companies tend to be leaner, more focused on core competencies and reliant on buying in goods and services rather than in-house production (Buck, Gordon, Harding, & Turok, 2005; Scott, 2006). Agglomerations enable firms to 'mix and match' their various inputs, access scarce resources and alter their workforce more easily in response to changing business needs. These opportunities and interactions lower costs, facilitate reorganisation and growth and improve corporate resilience. Ease of staff recruitment and replacement are especially important in high turnover and fast-changing activities.

Secondly, cities also give firms access to a bigger and better range of *shared services* and infrastructure. They have a better choice of research and development organisations to assist with product design and improvement, and a wider range of education and training organisations to help with staff development. Cities also have better external connectivity to national and global customers and suppliers through more frequent transport connections to a wider range of destinations, or higher capacity broadband for electronic communication.

Thirdly, firms benefit from the superior flows of information and ideas in cities, promoting more creativity and innovation (HM Treasury, 2006; Jacobs, 1969, 1984; Porter, 1998). Agglomeration is significant for knowledge-intensive functions and technologically advanced activities that differentiate themselves from competitors by continuing to create higher quality goods and services. Proximity is important in facilitating communication and sharing of complex ideas between firms, centres of research and related organisations (Cooke & Morgan, 1998; Scott, 2006; Storper & Manville, 2006). It enables people and firms to compare, compete and collaborate, creating a self-reinforcing dynamic that spurs creativity, attracts mobile capital and talent, and generates growth from within. Brainstorming, mutual learning and exchanging tacit knowledge are more effective face-to-face than remotely through electronic communication. Close contact enables formal and informal networks of technical and scientific staff to emerge, which promotes all sorts of collaborative projects. Cities "epitomise the process of *endogenous* growth, whereby resources are used more productively and in new ways" (Kessides, 2006, p. 13).

Economies of scale also apply to many public services and to consumption. It is cheaper and easier to provide public services such as health, sanitation, power and communications in cities (United Nations, 2007; Martine et al., 2008). The combined spending power of large concentrations of population also stimulates new consumer goods and amenities, such as leisure and recreation activities, which attract further rounds of job-creating investment, tourism and population growth (Glaeser & Gottlieb, 2006).

Cities contain the cultural vitality, social infrastructure and career choices to help regions and nations attract the skills and talent required to generate and exploit knowledge and build dynamic competitive advantage. Some consumer facilities are only viable in large cities, such as major entertainment venues, convention centres, museums, art galleries or specialised centres of education and health. Cities also offer greater choice of shopping, restaurants, hotels, sporting amenities and careers to attract people to visit, study, live and work. New migrants to cities may create new opportunities and new needs. They may offer new skills and new perspectives, and generate new requirements for institutional innovation (Beall et al., 2010).

The benefits of agglomeration can be offset by rising congestion, overcrowding, pressure on natural resources and ecosystems, and higher labour and property costs in cities—*agglomeration diseconomies*. These disadvantages grow if urbanisation is poorly planned and managed, and if cities are deprived of essential public investment in additional infrastructure capacity. The immediate effect may be to deter private investment, reduce urban productivity and hold back growth. Over time, there may be steady decentralisation and dispersal of lower value, land-intensive activities (such as routine production, distribution and warehousing) away from large cities. Provided the congestion and extra costs are not excessive, there could be an upgrading of the economic core to higher value-added industries and higher-skilled functions and occupations, which raises average incomes and living standards. Increasing urban prosperity may also provide the

20   *Ivan Turok*

resources for improved social and cultural amenities, public infrastructure and services, as long as the benefits are not expropriated by urban elites. Improved services and amenities can therefore improve the quality of life and subjective well-being of ordinary people.

The process of de-concentration benefits surrounding towns and rural areas because they gain from the spill-overs of investment, technology and jobs. The hinterland can also benefit from the large markets available in cities, and the logistics systems and shared infrastructure that connect cities to wider national and international markets. Rural areas can supply primary products, energy, water, leisure and recreational amenities, sites for waste disposal, and standardised goods and services for urban consumers. In the foreseeable future rural areas may also be able to raise income by functioning as carbon sinks through reforestation to offset the carbon emissions from cities. The burgeoning climate change agenda and the search for renewable energy sources also provides rural areas with a variety of opportunities to diversify their economies and meet new markets in urban areas, such as the production of biofuels.

Rural workers can commute or migrate to urban labour markets, generating valuable cash remittances for their place of origin. The major international study of poverty by Ravallion et al. (2007) referred to earlier found that urbanisation played an important role in reducing rural poverty, particularly through remittances. This was also because poor rural migrants moving to urban areas increase the proportion of poor people living in cities. In fact, a very striking finding was that the beneficial impact of urbanisation on rural poverty exceeded that on urban areas.

This is an important lesson for Africa, given the widespread concerns about rural–urban migration. Although some migrants are temporary and may be forced to leave rural areas in times of drought or conflict for their own survival, others may save enough money to invest considerable amounts in assets such as land, housing and livestock in their home rural areas (McGranahan et al., 2009). This is just one of a number of "livelihood portfolios" or safety nets that urban activities can contribute to rural households (Ellis & Harris, 2004). Investing in rural assets may enable people to return home later in life, or if their urban jobs, livelihoods or housing prove unstable or insecure. These points illustrate how rural and urban areas can perform complementary functions. Urban and rural development is not mutually exclusive, and it is wrong to think that urbanisation is necessarily harmful to rural areas. Urban–rural interactions should generally be encouraged because they help to promote trade and to distribute resources between groups of people— effectively linking need and opportunity.

There is some evidence that rural poverty is lower and high-value agricultural production more common closer to urban centres (Kessides, 2006). The friction of distance (or costs associated with travel between places) means that peri-urban areas have privileged access to the economic opportunities and educational, health and social facilities in cities. Proximity gives rural producers of agricultural, horticultural, mineral and craft products better and more up-to-date information about markets, including consumer preferences, price expectations and quality standards. They have scope to diversity their activities into other sources of income generation, making them less vulnerable to environmental threats and volatile prices. Tourism is another example of an activity that can connect rural and urban areas by offering packages of different kinds of natural and cultural experiences. It should be possible to use the growing interdependence between cities and their surrounding regions to support wider national goals of rural development and poverty reduction— sometimes described as a process of shared or inclusive growth.

Over time, as cities grow and their influence extends into wider regions, partly through falling transport costs, the functional area of the city-region or metropolitan-region becomes more significant than the city as a continuous built-up area (Neuman & Hull, 2011; Parr, 2004, 2008; Scott, 2001). A range of activities and settlement types become incorporated into the urban system, and it may develop multiple centres to form a 'polycentric' structure. Centres may have different functions, allowing specialisation and a division of labour to emerge between them (Hall & Pain, 2006; Parr, 2005; Turok & Bailey, 2004). Centres with high-level functions of knowledge creation, research and synthesising ideas may develop connections to metropolitan regions elsewhere in the world and become hubs in a wider global system of trade and information exchange (Castells, 2000; Hall & Pain, 2006).

It is very difficult to plan these processes. The most successful polycentric cities seem to have evolved naturally and spontaneously over an extended period. Rather than try to create new urban centres or growth poles from scratch through major new infrastructure or financial incentives to businesses (Parr, 1999), current thinking is to reinforce areas of proven economic success or demonstrable potential through upgrading existing infrastructure and adding extra capacity. This tends to mean a focus on established cities experiencing development pressures and capacity constraints.

## HOW RELEVANT IS THIS TO AFRICA?

The World Bank is one of several international organisations that have advocated for urbanisation in development policy, particularly in Africa. The 2009 World Development Report (WDR) (World Bank, 2009) focused on this theme and marshalled considerable research and historical evidence from around the world to make a strong case for the role of cities in promoting economic development:

> Growing cities, mobile people, and vigorous trade have been the catalysts for progress in the developed world over the last two centuries. Now these forces are powering the developing world's most dynamic places. (World Bank, 2009, p. 13)

## 22  *Ivan Turok*

The WDR focused on three features of territory, which, it argued, play major roles in long-run growth. They are density, distance and division. Density refers to the concentration of activity and people in particular locations. Distance is the gap between economic centres, both within and between countries. Division refers to the obstacles to trade, migration, capital and information flows between places. The WDR argued that higher densities, shorter distances and lower divisions support the transition from resource-based to industrial economies. This generates many formal jobs and large fiscal transfers to support rural areas through cash transfers and improved public services.

The WDR was heavily influenced by the "New Economic Geography" (Krugman, 1991) in maintaining that economic growth is inevitably unbalanced and focused in the major cities as a result of agglomeration forces. It argued that governments should support and not constrain urbanisation. They should do this through improved infrastructure and more efficient land markets. Responsive public services (especially water, sanitation, health and education) in rural areas should equip people with the skills to access jobs in the main urban areas, while preventing forced migration through lack of local facilities.

Lagging regions and rural areas should benefit from urban prosperity through remittances and circular migration, which should be encouraged. Improvements in transport connectivity could facilitate greater 'economic integration' between cities and their hinterlands. The improved flow of goods, investment, people and information would help to distribute income and wealth efficiently. Therefore, although growth will be imbalanced, it can still be inclusive if lagging areas have improved access to the wealth produced in cities. Finally, the WDR stated that efforts should be made to reduce the obstacles to cross-border trade and flows of capital and other resources between countries in order to open up markets and foster accelerated economic growth.

Africa was singled out for special attention. It has the most dispersed and least urbanised populations in the world, the highest transport costs, and the greatest institutional fragmentation and proliferation of national borders because of its colonial legacy (Table 2.1). Consequently, the continent has to promote higher densities, shorten distances and lower divisions between nations to stimulate economic growth. Anti-urban sentiments also need to change: "Urbanisation, done right, can help development *more* in Africa than elsewhere" (World Bank, 2009, p. 285; see also Venables, 2010). Inefficient urban land markets with informal tenure systems and poor basic services obstruct functional urban systems and development. Deficient rural facilities prompt unskilled rural–urban migration, which concentrates poverty in cities and creates squalor, social tensions and instability. Poor transport infrastructure impedes urban–rural interactions and international economic flows (Naude & Matthee, 2007).

Finally, government bureaucracy creates major barriers to trade and resource flows, which also holds back economic development. Nineteen of

## Cities as Drivers of Development  23

Africa's 54 countries have less than five million inhabitants, so their markets are small. The partitioning of the continent by the colonial powers in 1884 created more countries per square kilometre than anywhere else in the world. Each country has four neighbours on average compared with 2.3 in Latin America (World Bank, 2009). Border controls and tariffs impede the movement of goods and people and hold back the emergence of larger regional markets across the continent. Africa's economies often operate in isolation and small countries could benefit far more than at present from their more prosperous neighbours. High transport costs and border delays also complicate the process of exporting and importing for many landlocked countries in Africa.

The WDR's assumption was that economic prosperity would emerge almost inevitably through the growing concentration of population and reduced divisions between places. The state's role was essentially an enabling one to provide public goods, infrastructure and universal basic services. A weak feature of the analysis was its vagueness about timescales and how long this natural process might take to raise incomes above the poverty line and remove hardship. The references to historical experience in Europe and North America suggested that it might take generations. At the end there was a hint that "this Report spotlights the importance of starting small and keeping expectations realistic. Regional integration takes time" (World Bank, 2009, p. 285). More direct measures by local or national governments impatient to accelerate poverty reduction through economic development were not endorsed because that was not viewed as an appropriate role for the state.

The framework of the WDR (the 3Ds) could be interpreted as suggesting there was a universal formula for promoting development in any particular country. Underlying it is a causal model, which holds that urbanisation stimulates or accelerates industrialisation. This creates wealth and reduces poverty. Such an analysis of economic dynamics is rather too simple and the process is far from automatic. It seems to assume that all countries necessarily follow the same development path. It also does not appear to allow for cities being stronger sources of growth in some contexts than in others, despite evidence that urbanisation without economic growth is a fairly common phenomenon around the world (Fay & Opal, 2000).

A recent study examined the relationship between average income and level of urbanisation of some 80 countries at two points in time—1960 and 2004 (Bloom & Khanna, 2007). It found that there was an association between urbanisation and income, particularly at higher levels of urbanisation, but the relationship was not simple or linear. The link had also strengthened between 1960 and 2004. A key conclusion was that the links between urbanisation and income were "relatively weak at low levels of development" (Bloom & Khanna, 2007, p. 11).

The study compared the impact of rapid urbanisation on average incomes in Asia and Africa, concluding that:

*Table 2.1* The Most Distant and Divided Regions of the World

| Region | Trading time across borders for exports (days) | Average transport costs ($ per container to Baltimore) | Population in landlocked countries (%) | Ratio of number of countries to surface area | Road density (km² of road per surface area, 1999) | Estimated number of civil conflicts (1940–2000) |
|---|---|---|---|---|---|---|
| East Asia & Pacific | 24 | 3,900 | 0.42 | 1.44 | 0.72 | 8 |
| Europe & Central Asia | 29 | n.a. | 23.0 | 1.17 | n.a. | 13 |
| Latin America & Caribbean | 22 | 4,600 | 2.77 | 1.52 | 0.12 | 15 |
| Middle East & North Africa | 27 | 2,100 | 0 | 1.60 | 0.33 | 17 |
| South Asia | 34 | 3,900 | 3.37 | 1.67 | 0.85 | 24 |
| Sub-Saharan Africa | 40 | 7,600 | 40.2 | 2.00 | 0.13 | 34 |

*Source:* World Bank. (2009). *World development report 2009: Shaping economic geography.* Washington, DC: The World Bank.

While urbanisation in Africa over the past 45 years has been accompanied by sluggish economic growth, in Asia, where urbanisation has occurred to a nearly identical extent, economic growth has been rapid. (Bloom & Khanna, 2007, p. 11)

Another study focused only on Africa found that 71 per cent of the 32 countries analysed actually had a negative correlation between urbanisation and GDP over the 1985–2000 period (Bouare, 2006, as quoted in White et al., 2008). This would imply that people left rural areas because of poverty and crises, and that migration to urban areas was disruptive to economic performance.

Yet their findings appear to be contradicted by the work of Njoh (2003) and Kessides (2006). The latter concluded that:

Africa cannot simply be characterised as "urbanisation without growth," and the term does not even fit many of the countries. The economic growth that has taken place in the past decade derives mainly from urban-based sectors (industry and services), and this is especially true of the better-performing economies. But cities have clearly not lived up to their productive potential because of widespread neglect and bad management. (Kessides, 2006, p. xxii)

Consequently, there seem to be mixed messages about the connection between urbanisation and economic growth. Yet all studies may be consistent with the conclusion that incomes in Africa may have grown even more slowly without urbanisation. They also suggest that a range of other conditions are at least as important as determinants of income growth. These include the availability of skills, investment capital and supporting institutions, which are obviously more strongly developed in some circumstances than in others. Thus, there are many prosperous cities around the world that aren't growing, just as there are many fast growing cities that are poor. If and when this causal relationship between urbanisation and economic growth does operate, it may take a very long time to make significant inroads into poverty and unemployment. It is unreasonable and unrealistic for citizens facing severe hardship to wait indefinitely for tangible improvements to their living standards.

The WDR considered the urban economy as a black box, with the mechanisms of development underspecified. In assuming a simple linear relationship between urbanisation and growth, no distinction was made between what one might describe as 'extensive' forms of growth (replicating the same kinds of activity and jobs on a larger scale) and 'progressive' growth (developing more valuable activities and better jobs). Significant drivers of productivity were neglected, including enterprise, human resources and technology.

These factors must be important in advancing from predominantly informal, survivalist and basic trading activities to higher value work, and

## 26   Ivan Turok

from simple exploitation of primary products (agriculture and minerals) to resource processing, manufacturing and services. The WDR also treated urban density as an unambiguous benefit, despite evidence that beyond a certain point, density means overcrowding, which increases social tension and conflict over scarce resources such as housing, especially in a context of widespread poverty (Davis, 2006; Turok, 2001).

In addition, in advocating economic integration between territories as a way of promoting inclusive growth, the WDR played down the fact that if places had unequal economic capabilities at the outset, the outcome of linking their economies might be wider rather than narrower spatial inequalities. Regions and nations that are relatively well-endowed may well pull further ahead by drawing skills, capital and other resources from poorer areas. Any compensating flows of income, productive activity and jobs may be insufficient to counter a widening division of labour between the leading and lagging regional economies.

In terms of policy, the WDR took a restricted view of the appropriate role of governments. It was particularly negative about the possibility of spatial development policy in lagging areas. This is not just about 'artificial' spatial incentives to persuade firms to invest where they would not otherwise go. There are many examples around the world of infrastructure investment projects which have generated greater added-value and all-round development because they were carefully planned and embedded in comprehensive economic regeneration programmes, which involved building productive capabilities through enhanced workforce skills, combined with technical and financial support for the start-up and growth of small and medium enterprises (Pike Rodriguez-Pose & Tomaney, 2006; Turok, 2010b).

The WDR's biggest omission was probably its silence on the need for strong city-level institutions (metropolitan governments) to provide the leadership and strategic capacity to guide development, to take a long-term view of problems and potential, and to steer, shape and stimulate the market if and when necessary. Cities are complex systems and national governments are too remote to plan and manage their development effectively, or to cope with the crises that inevitably arise. They need responsive and accountable city-level institutions with the detailed knowledge, revenue-raising capabilities and close relationships with local business and residential communities to make a lasting difference to conditions (Ahmad, 2007; UN-Habitat, 2008).

## HOW DO DYNAMIC URBAN ECONOMIES DEVELOP?

The analytical framework of agglomeration economies and the concepts of density, distance and division are useful reminders of the spatial dimensions of economic development and of the leading role of cities. They also provide some clues as to why economic progress in Africa has been slow, and some suggestions for improving the situation. However, the ideas are too general and lack concrete points of reference to offer more detailed insights into how the structure of urban economies evolves over time. There is an unquestioned assumption that urbanisation is accompanied by industrialisation, which generates economic growth. This offers a very limited explanation for why the economies of African cities stalled or even declined during the 1980s and 1990s.

Urban economies are treated as a black box without unpacking the composition and dynamics. A more elaborate framework is needed to understand the changing economic trajectories of cities, and to uncover Africa's specific challenges. This needs to recognise the significance of the economic base of cities, the role of external trade and moving up the value chain. Subsistence-type activities and those that merely circulate resources locally add limited value and generate low incomes.

Drawing on extensive historical observation and Keynesian regional economics, Jacobs (1969, 1984) identified a series of stages through which city economies typically developed (see also Bryceson & Potts, 2006). The foundation for durable economic growth is basic infrastructure, services and goods, including a stable food supply, water, shelter, security, transport and communications. Once these fundamentals are in place, cities are in a position to grow more rapidly and securely. The second stage (economic dynamism) emerges with the growth of external trade (imports and exports) along with the facilities and services to support this trade, such as storage and distribution (logistics). In the third phase, growth is strengthened by the substitution of imported goods with local production (urban import replacement). This adds diversity and scale to the urban economy, although these goods and services tend to replicate those produced elsewhere rather than being original. According to Jacobs, import replacement builds up local infrastructure, skills, and productive capacity, and can lead to rapid growth when formerly imported goods are produced locally and then exported to other cities.

The fourth stage involves greater ingenuity and innovation through the conception and creation of novel products and services for new markets. This reinforces the vitality and scale of production in the city, and gives it genuine distinctiveness and a differential advantage over other urban economies. One might add that firms can charge premium prices and outperform rivals on the basis of product design and quality rather than cost (Turok, 2009). In a fifth phase of economic revival and renewal, the old skills and activities are refreshed with new ideas and investment, rather than permitting obsolescence and decline. These cities make full use of their productive resources and avoid redundancy, dereliction and social problems through creative problem-solving and entrepreneurial discovery.

This is a helpful account of the growing diversity and complexity of successful urban economies. As they grow and develop, the different activities become more inter-dependent, which increases the city's overall resilience

28  *Ivan Turok*

and adaptability. It emphasises that cities are open, externally-oriented systems in which trade with other places is vital. Subsistence and circulation activities do not generate much growth. Real prosperity (and a strong local multiplier effect) depends on local production of useful goods and services. Cities must use local labour to add value to natural resources and products made elsewhere, and not simply distribute and exchange them. The more efficient, resourceful and ultimately innovative their productive enterprises are, the more wealth and jobs will be generated. Avoiding complacency and 'lock-in' to outdated structures and stagnant markets is also important for increased productivity and robust long-term performance.

## THE ECONOMIC TRAJECTORIES OF AFRICAN CITIES

To what extent have African cities developed along the lines outlined above? If not, why has progress stalled? The phases suggested by Jane Jacobs are not neatly sequential and they overlap in practice, although there is an underlying logic in the shift from simpler local activities to more sophisticated externally-related functions. Have African cities progressed from a basic trading role towards more value-added activities, such as manufacturing, marketing, design, science and technology, and advanced producer services? To what extent has production moved beyond craft-based processes to a fuller division of labour with internal economies of scale, and from mass production of low-value goods to more flexible, small batch and customised production of high-end goods and knowledge-intensive services? In short, how elaborate and productive are African urban economies?

Unfortunately, the detailed analysis required to answer these questions has not been undertaken. Research on the economy of African cities has been seriously neglected for at least the last decade. It is well-known that the overall productivity of most African economies (GDP per head) is very low by international standards. This is the main reason average incomes are also low. An edited collection by Bryceson & Potts (2006) offers some evidence for why most African cities do not have dynamic economies. Urban population growth has out-stripped economic development, having been driven more strongly by rural poverty, conflict, and natural demographic growth than by economic opportunity.

Positioned as coastal ports or major rail depots, most large African cities have good strategic locations to engage in national and international trade. However, productive investment is low by the standards of cities elsewhere in the world. Labour specialisation is also undeveloped, and production processes are rudimentary in the sizeable informal economy. The purchasing power of most urban residents is very low, so consumer demand is a weaker motive force for development and modernisation than elsewhere. "In short, their economic content lacks the dynamism, specialisation, diversity and the economies of scale normally associated with urban life" (Bryceson & Potts, 2006, p. 324).

Looking at each stage of urban economic development, starting with the foundations, there are clear deficiencies in the basic infrastructure and services of many African cities, including a reliable electricity supply, water supply, telephone service and efficient transport systems (World Bank, 2009). This discourages foreign direct investment, because these factors are usually taken for granted in business locations elsewhere. A complete lack of electricity, business premises and poor all-round security are particular problems for enterprises seeking to start up and grow in informal urban settlements.

Available evidence suggests that most informal enterprises are limited to the retail trade (hawkers and spaza shops) (Rogerson, 1997), with no value-added processes and little scope for upgrading without essential infrastructure and facilities. Poor literacy and numeracy skills are additional complications preventing people from breaking out of survivalist activities into more dynamic businesses, or using their experience in the informal sector to progress into formal employment. Imitation seems to be far more common than innovation or experimentation.

The second stage of producing goods for wider markets (tradables) is vital for stronger, sustained growth. Many African cities began to develop manufacturing industries after independence when governments attempted to diversify from exporting basic agricultural products and minerals. However, this was generally unsuccessful, for various reasons including enforced structural adjustment programmes and poor business management (Rakodi, 1997; Bryceson & Potts, 2006). It is also often said that overcomplicated government requirements for starting and operating enterprises impose prohibitive costs on investing and doing business (Wang & Bio-Tchane, 2008; World Bank, 2009). Africa's share of world exports declined from seven per cent in 1970 to two per cent in 2000 (African Development Bank, 2007).

Most cities seem to retain a residual manufacturing sector confined to consumer goods for domestic markets (typically food processing, furniture, soap, beer, textiles, cigarettes, cement and other building materials). Beneficiation (processing) of Africa's abundant primary commodities has been slow to develop because of lack of capital and know-how, and due to high tariffs on value-added agricultural exports to Europe and the U.S. Consequently, 60 per cent of the continent's total exports are still primary products, mainly agricultural and minerals (African Development Bank, 2007).

Trading activities tend to dominate Africa's urban economies, including retail, distribution and import–export services. They do not provide a strong economic base because of their low value-addition, high volatility and low multiplier effects. The jobs are not well-paying and tend to be more insecure than in manufacturing. Many cities have become gateways or depots through which increasing volumes of oil and industrial goods are

30   *Ivan Turok*

imported. Exports have dwindled from most port cities, except for those that handle mineral exports. Mombasa, Mogadishu and Dar es Salaam are good examples of ports dominated by imported goods. Luanda, Beira and Maputo have a better balance of exports, including oil and minerals. Airports have also expanded, bringing in tourism and enabling international travel by business, political and donor organisations. However, Africa's fragmentation means a lack of economies of scale. There are 48 international airports competing for relatively thin air traffic and 33 small ports fighting to capture the meagre freight leaving and entering the continent (World Bank, 2009).

The third phase of replacing imported goods with local production has generally failed to take off. A minor exception is the growth of urban agriculture in many African cities, including cultivation of crops and keeping livestock. Garbage picking and waste recycling could perhaps be placed in the same general category. However, these are very small-scale subsistence activities undertaken in response to inadequate household incomes, with limited scope for expansion (Rogerson, 1997). Reductions in national tariff barriers and falling transport costs associated with containerisation have instead resulted in a flood of cheap imports, particularly from Asia. Chinese textiles, clothing and household goods have eroded the residual local production in many African cities (Southall & Melber, 2009). Deindustrialisation continues in countries such as South Africa, which developed a large and diversified domestic manufacturing sector under Apartheid import protections, but subsequently removed them rather too quickly for many local firms to adapt to global competition (OECD, 2008b).

The fourth and fifth stages of innovation and renewal have also been limited. The most obvious manifestation of this takes the form of improvisation in the informal economy. For example, informal retail enterprises have provided goods unavailable in the formal sector (such as traditional medicines) in smaller quantities, or in locations where formal outlets are sparse (such as informal settlements). Small informal manufacturing enterprises have also emerged following the closure of larger formal businesses where people had acquired relevant skills, such as in the clothing industry. There has also been some outsourcing of work to informal firms in order to circumvent labour regulations and to cut costs, although apparently on a much lower scale than in India.

Unsurprisingly, the rewards and conditions of informal work tend to be inferior, reflecting the lack of capital, skills and technology. Growth takes an extensive character (proliferation of more of the same small-scale units), rather than higher productivity. It is therefore questionable whether this is real progress. It also means that informal enterprises tend to operate in saturated markets and generate low incomes for their proprietors and workers. Consequently, most experts believe that there is little scope for a dynamic informal economy of growth-oriented firms to emerge in Africa without concerted state support in the form of credit, technical assistance and skills training (Bryceson & Potts, 2006; Gill, Kharas, & Bhattasali, 2007; Rogerson, 1997).

In practice, many local and national governments have been unsupportive if not hostile to informality on the grounds that it undermines decent paid work and pays no taxes. Rogerson (1997) argues that there is potential for this sector to enhance urban productivity if a model of "flexible specialisation" can be developed, involving local clusters of small enterprises that form networks and collaborate to recreate a division of labour and scale economies, along the lines of the "industrial districts" in several European countries (Gordon & McCann, 2000).

Considered more generally, the development of a more integrated industrial urban economy with strong multipliers and spill-overs is complicated in contemporary circumstances by the ever-increasing power of multinationals, the vertical disintegration of their production processes, the spread of global supply chains, and the offshoring of selected activities, enabled by Information and Communications Technology (ICT) and cheaper transport (Friedman, 2006; Gereffi, Humphrey, & Sturgeon, 2005).

African cities that manage to plug into the global economy may benefit from opportunities to develop niche functions (such as the processing of specific commodities or the provision of call centres). However, building rounded economies with high-level functions and scope to shape their own destinies is likely to be much more challenging. Urban policymakers are bound to require a better understanding of global value chains and production networks, because city fortunes are increasingly shaped not only by what goes on within them, but also by wider relationships of markets, competition, control and dependency (Gereffi et al., 2005; Coe, Hess, & Yeung, 2008; Yeung, 2009). Selected parts of the urban economy may be linked into international business networks that condition their development paths, depending on the role they perform.

As a result, African urban economies may become more fractured, with weak links between low and higher value activities, giving less scope for upgrading. One part may be technologically advanced and internationally oriented, but with a small economic footprint in most places. Examples are the extraction of oil and mineral resources (Ampiah & Naidu, 2008; Southall & Melber, 2009). Other parts serve domestic markets, with little scope for growth, given constrained demand from low consumer spending and the escalating capabilities required to supply multinationals. Structural inequalities may impede information flows, restrict upward labour mobility, and inhibit indigenous business development. People pursuing basic livelihoods and trading informally may be trapped in marginal product markets by low skills and credit constraints. State policies to control street trading, eradicate shacks and marginalise informal settlements may further inhibit livelihoods (Potts, 2007; Skinner, 2010). Large-scale industrialisation and formalisation of urban employment is challenging in these conditions.

## 32 Ivan Turok

The high end of the urban economy may demand special state support to maintain its global position, including bespoke infrastructure and tax breaks. It may become more decoupled from the rest of the economy through its specialised requirements for technology and talent, often supplied from elsewhere. A concerted developmental agenda from government might require policies to connect the urban economy through stronger backward and forward linkages working through 'demand pull' and 'supply push' events. The former involves supporting successful producers to purchase from local suppliers, whereas the latter concerns building up the all-round capabilities of local enterprises. These should be undertaken together with major investments in public goods—serviced land, premises, electrification, education, and so on. Different industries are bound to offer different possibilities for local development, with different interventions required to realise the potential. The value chain approach may help to understand the linkages between the formal and informal economies, and thus identify the best sites for policy action (Barrientos, Dolan, & Tallontire, 2003; Chen, 2007).

## RECENT IMPROVED PROSPECTS

Commentaries on African urban economies tend to be negative about the past and pessimistic about the future. It is often argued that globalisation has stalled economic progress in Africa. Multinationals are deemed to have exploited the continent's natural resources and bodies such as the IMF and World Bank have dictated unfavourable policy packages (see e.g. Rakodi, 1997; Southall & Melber, 2009). Yet in recent years, there have been some signs of change with brighter prospects than have been seen for decades. The average rate of economic growth across Sub-Saharan Africa increased from 3.5 per cent in 2000–2002 to 5.7 per cent in 2005 (African Development Bank, 2007). Foreign Direct Investment (FDI) increased from $9 billion in 2000 to $62 billion in 2008 (Leke, Lund, Roxburgh, & van Wamelen, 2010). UN-Habitat (2008) estimates that Africa's cities produce 55 per cent of the continent's GDP with only 39 per cent of its population.

The principal cause of the turnaround was strong global demand for primary commodities, especially oil, gas, metals and minerals (such as diamonds and coal). This was reflected in surging commodity prices. For example, oil rose from less than $20 a barrel in 1999 to more than $145 in 2008. However, Africa's four main exports are non-renewable and create few direct jobs. Consequently, the basis of the recovery has been rather narrow. To create and sustain wealth in the long term, national economies have to be diversified by converting these resources into other forms of capital, preferably tradable industries that will outlast the basic commodities (Leke et al., 2010).

Governments (and ruling elites) have gained large revenues from the exports, but they have not reinvested sufficiently in diversification to spread the benefits more widely. Weak institutional capacity and poor governance are partly to blame (African Development Bank, 2007; Southall & Melber, 2009). Export boom has further stimulated urban consumption, inflated house prices, and promoted speculative property development. Nigerian cities have experienced this for some time. Angola's capital Luanda is the latest example.

Booming exports have reflected strengthening economic ties with Asia. Between 1990 and 2008, Asia's share of trade with Africa doubled from 14 per cent to 28 per cent, whereas Western Europe's share shrank from 51 per cent to 28 per cent (Leke et al., 2010). Exports to China grew by almost 50 per cent each year between 1999 and 2004, followed by India. Both countries want access to African raw materials, minerals and fuel, and also to African markets for their manufacturers. It is widely hoped that this will create new development opportunities for the continent, with a fairer "East-South" nexus than the old "North-South" relationships (Ampiah & Naidu, 2008; Murray, 2008).

New kinds of economic relationships may involve governments negotiating multiple long-term deals at once. Africa's cities have a critical role to play in broadening and deepening trade and investment patterns beyond primary products and short-term consumption that sucks in luxury imports to satisfy the lifestyles of local elites and creates macro-economic imbalances. The global commodities boom gives national and local governments more bargaining power to negotiate better deals that capture more value from their natural resources. Buyers are now willing to make upfront payments (in addition to royalties from mineral extraction) and to share management skills and technology.

Foreign investment may help countries to diversify at lower cost and with less risk than starting from scratch. The traditional sources of FDI have been Europe and the U.S., but China, India, Malaysia, Brazil and South Africa itself are increasingly important. India is keen to sell Africa its ICT products, including telephony and mobile internet services. Over the past five years, it has offered lines of concessionary credit to Africa worth $2.5 billion.

China has increased its investment commitments in Africa from less than $1 billion per year before 2004 to $8 billion in 2006 (World Bank, 2008). Over 800 joint Chinese-African projects have been set up, involving large investments in oil, timber, minerals and hydropower in 10 countries. China is also financing the building or rehabilitation of 3000 km of railway lines across the region, including reopening the Benguela railway linking Zambia and the Democratic Republic of the Congo (DRC) to the Angolan port of Lobito. It has bid to access large quantities of copper and cobalt in the DRC in exchange for a $6 billion package of investments in roads, rail, hospitals and schools. In short, China is playing a variety of roles. It is a trading partner, investor, financier, donor, contractor and builder (Wang & Bio-Tchane, 2008).

## 34   Ivan Turok

The challenge with such investments is to ensure that they help with industrial diversification and urban economic development, and that they don't simply accelerate the exploitation of Africa's natural resources for short-term gain, or create narrow enclaves separate from the domestic economy. It is also important to avoid the 'Dutch disease' or 'resource curse,' that is, the situation where increasing external demand for a country's basic commodities strengthens its currency and damages the competitiveness of existing industrial output and jobs, or at least makes the prospect of boosting investment in domestic production and employment more difficult.

A skilful "developmental state" is required to ensure that a reasonable proportion of the value extracted is reinvested in socio-economic development (Edigheji, 2010; Evans, 1995; Robertson & White, 1998). One mechanism may be to create integrated industrial complexes with stronger backward and forward linkages to embed FDI within the region and generate additional business activity and jobs.

The logic partly involves minimising transport costs by concentrating particular value chains in one location, such as export processing zones. Supplier development programmes could nurture indigenous firms to build the skills and capabilities to produce intermediate inputs for the foreign plants, or to attract second-tier suppliers. 'After-care' programmes might persuade inward investors of the overall cost savings from using local suppliers and encourage plant upgrading to higher value functions, superior technologies and better environmental practices over time. FDI might be regarded less as an end in itself and more as a means of harnessing knowledge, techniques and best practices to develop the capacities of domestic firms and workers to sell their products into wider markets (Gallagher & Zarsky, 2007).

South Africa has become a major investor elsewhere in Africa since the early 1990s. Its direct investments have mostly been in consumer-focused businesses in urban areas. It is involved in retailing, hotels, breweries, fast food, mobile phones, banking and construction. The search for markets is a bigger driver than that for minerals and oil (Southall & Melber, 2009). SABMiller (previously South African Breweries) is a good example. It had no operations outside South Africa before 1992, but now has 19 breweries in 10 other African countries, plus additional bottling plants, distribution depots and administrative facilities (SABMiller, 2010). This is in addition to large-scale operations on other continents. The company capitalised on the knowledge it acquired during South Africa's transition in the 1980s and 1990s with an emerging middle class of young consumers aspiring to new brands, and applying these to other economies undergoing similar social changes. It expanded rapidly through the acquisition and modernisation of former state-owned breweries in countries such as Tanzania, Zambia, Mozambique, Zimbabwe, Uganda and Angola.

In such countries, beer consumption is believed to be relatively low compared with South Africa, so there is considerable growth potential: "All you need to do is get cold beer to consumers at an affordable price and they'll buy it" (SABMiller executive, personal interview, 7 July 2009). Growth therefore depends on the fundamentals of efficient production and distribution, unlike the saturated markets elsewhere, where marketing is critical. With beer prices inflated by the costs of imported raw materials and government tariffs, SABMiller has sought to develop affordable products brewed from local African crops and thereby to take costs out of the supply chain. The Eagle brand based on local sorghum is a successful example and is now available in smaller bottles and draught form to make it even cheaper. The company is also working with farmers in several countries to expand production of suitable crops for beer production, including experimenting with maize and cassava.

Affordable products should attract consumers from unregulated home brews to commercial beers produced to higher standards. More formal and regulated brewing will enable governments to benefit from higher taxes and provide economic opportunities for local farmers. Conscious not to be seen as new colonialists, the company has also invested in joint ventures with other brewers and active social responsibility, community development and health programmes for workers. Poor transport infrastructure is an obstacle to growth, both for transporting raw materials to the breweries and finished products to the consumers. The low incomes of consumers and lack of skilled managers and workers are additional constraints in many African countries.

This case illustrates how foreign investment can assist the economic development process by providing vital capital and expertise to raise productivity and facilitate innovation. Consumer-oriented investments tend to focus on the cities, but rural areas also benefit through the stimulus to agricultural production. This may offer a useful example of the benefits of urban–rural integration.

## CONCLUSION

There are polarised views about the economic effects of African urbanisation and the extent to which it is a positive phenomenon. There is also debate about the appropriate balance between urban and rural areas in development policy. Unfortunately, the lack of systematic research and robust evidence makes it difficult to resolve these differences.

There is little doubt that urban population growth in most African countries is likely to continue at a relatively high level for the foreseeable future, both through natural growth (births exceeding deaths) and rural–urban migration. It is also clear that governments are better placed than other bodies to influence whether the consequences are conducive to socio-economic development. Managed carefully, urbanisation could help to reduce hardship and suffering. Managed badly, it could increase poverty and squalor.

## 36   Ivan Turok

Many theories of economic growth and development tend to support the idea that cities are sources of prosperity and human progress. Large concentrations of people, resources and ideas can promote efficiency, stimulate productive activity, and raise incomes. They facilitate useful functions of matching, sharing and learning. Cities also foster new and enhanced consumption, and enable more efficient provision of many public services.

The benefits of agglomeration extend well beyond city boundaries. Rural areas benefit through cash remittances from migrant labour and investment spill-overs generated by cities. Rural enterprises gain from the large markets available in cities, and from the transport infrastructure connecting them to wider national and international markets and suppliers. In thinking about the spatial consequences of urbanisation, it is important for national and local governments and development agencies to recognise the synergies between urban and rural areas. They should be seen as complementary, and not planned in isolation of each other with separate urban and rural policies.

Over time, there is a tendency for urban economies to become more diversified and complex. Prosperous cities have the capacity for creativity and innovation, which increases their resilience and adaptability. Established activities are refreshed and reinvented with new ideas and new investment. Being resourceful avoids being tied into outmoded processes and stagnant markets. Cities become linked into ever wider national and international networks of information, finance, trade and migration. They are active agents of development, harnessing knowledge and technology, rather than passive recipients of external investment.

Available evidence is equivocal about the extent to which African cities function as sources of growth and development. There is a reasonable consensus that they are not fulfilling their potential to generate economic opportunities and reduce poverty. They exhibit less economic dynamism than rapidly growing cities on other continents. The precise reasons for this are unclear. A fairly common view is that it is because of poor urban planning and management and lack of investment.

Further research is required for a fuller understanding of the obstacles to urban economic development and poverty relief. This is also important to identify the specific policies needed to promote stronger growth and improve living conditions. A more differentiated approach to analysis and policy action is important to move beyond generalisations about the continent and to recognise and respond to important sub-continental and regional differences.

## POLICY IMPLICATIONS

Although the current state of knowledge rules out the formulation of detailed policy recommendations, five broad strategic implications emerge from this review. They are high-level policy themes that will need to be applied differently depending on the particular local economic, social and institutional context.

First, there is little doubt that improved physical infrastructure is one of the preconditions for more productive cities. Rapid population growth puts considerable pressure on urban systems. Infrastructure bottlenecks and breakdowns are obvious sources of inefficiency and a cost to the economy as well as to communities. It appears that in many cities, additional investment and improved maintenance are required in transport infrastructure (especially roads and railways), power generation, telecommunications, water and sanitation. The quality of such systems is just as important as the quantity of investment, including issues of reliability, safety, affordability and access. In the case of transport, for example, investment to reduce travel times and delays in moving freight can have valuable productivity benefits (Rice et al., 2006). It would be very worthwhile for the additional funds being generated by Asian investment in the extraction of African resources to be channelled into urban infrastructure improvements.

Second, a more effective supply of land is vital for economic development. Urban land markets are often informal, unpredictable and inefficient. There is confusion over land ownership, complicated procedures for land acquisition and registration, and over-elaborate systems of land-use planning and building regulation (Berrisford, 2010). More predictable, transparent and consistent procedures are required to ensure that businesses, developers and investors can gain access to land needed for development, and that the necessary infrastructure and services will be provided without excessive delay or cost. More proactive and flexible planning procedures would help to anticipate urban growth and cope with the resulting demands from communities and businesses. Governments tend to react to pressure on land and problems of unlawful occupation after they have emerged. They are less good at planning ahead and guiding development towards well-located areas where serviced land and infrastructure could be made available, with a coordinated approach towards transport and land-use regulation.

Third, improvements in education and skills are required to ensure that the potential workforce is equipped for the contemporary urban labour market and can make a positive contribution to business productivity. Rural migrants are often poorly educated and lack the range of skills and competencies required to work in the formal sector. These may include generic skills, such as literacy and numeracy, specific technical skills for particular vocations, and 'soft' skills such as resourcefulness, communication and flexibility. Similar skills are also important for people forced to create their own livelihoods in the informal economy, especially if they are to progress beyond survivalist activities to higher value-added and more productive and dynamic enterprises. A differentiated approach to public support may be important to distinguish between people with the motivation and capabilities to grow more substantial enterprises, and those for whom informal enterprise is undertaken reluctantly, as a last resort.

## 38   Ivan Turok

Fourth, strong and responsive institutions with appropriate strategic, financial and technical capabilities are required to provide leadership and to deliver better public services. City-level authorities have advantages over national departments and state enterprises in their superior local knowledge of problems and opportunities, their closer relationships with business and residential communities, and their greater potential to integrate different functions. A cross-cutting, place-based approach is important to address multi-dimensional challenges, such as poverty, and to embed complex infrastructure projects into the local context. Governance arrangements to coordinate policies across municipal boundaries are also important to manage the growth of extensive city-regions, to facilitate economic interactions with rural areas, and to avoid policy contradictions, duplication of effort and negative spill-overs.

Fifth, there is also an argument for a city-wide policy towards industrial and business development in order to build long-term productive capabilities and promote economic diversification. One element would involve active support for indigenous enterprises, ranging from informal businesses to formal small and medium-sized enterprises. Many of them require access to business advice, training and financial support in order to grow and develop into more viable units that generate a higher income, serve wider markets, and create additional employment. Another element involves the capacity to attract and upgrade FDI in order to absorb external knowledge, techniques and best practices, so as to strengthen domestic firms, enable them to sell their products externally and diversify local economies. Programmes may be put in place to persuade inward investors to help nurture the capabilities of local suppliers to meet their input requirements and to encourage their own plants to be upgraded to higher value functions, superior technologies, and better environmental practices over time.

## REFERENCES

African Development Bank. (2007). *African development report 2007.* Oxford University Press.

Ahmad, E. (2007). Big or too big? *Finance and Development, 44*(3), 20–23.

Ajakaiye, O., & Ncube, M. (2010). Infrastructure and economic development in Africa: An overview. *Journal of African Economies, 19*(Supplement 1), i3–i12.

Ampiah, K., & Naidu, S. (Eds.) (2008). *Crouching tiger, hidden dragon? Africa and China.* Scottsville, South Africa: University of KwaZulu-Natal Press.

Annez, P., Buckley, R., & Kalarickal, J. (2010). African urbanisation as flight? Some policy implications of geography. *Urban Forum, 21,* 221–234.

Barrientos, S., Dolan, C, & Tallontire, A. (2003). A gendered value chain approach to codes of conduct on African horticulture. *World Development, 31*(9), 1511–1526.

Beall, J., & Fox, S. (2009). *Cities and development.* Abingdon, UK: Routledge.

Beall, J., Guha-Khasnobis, B., & Kanbur, R. (Eds.) (2010). *Urbanisation and development: Multidisciplinary perspectives.* Oxford University Press.

## Cities as Drivers of Development 39

Berrisford, S. (2010). *Why it's difficult to change urban planning laws in Africa.* Paper presented to CUBES seminar, Wits University, Johannesburg. Retrieved from https://owa.gla.ac.uk/exchweb/bin/redir.asp?URL=http://ukcatalogue.oup.com/product/9780199590148.do

Bloom, D. E., & Khanna, T. (2007). The Urban Revolution. *Finance and Development, 44*(3), 9–14.

Bryceson, D., & Potts, D. (Eds.) (2006). *African urban economies: Viability, vitality or vitiation?* Basingstoke, UK: Palgrave.

Buck, I., Gordon, I., Harding, A., & Turok, I. (Eds.) (2005). *Changing cities: Rethinking urban competitiveness, cohesion and governance.* London: Palgrave.

Castells, M. (2000). The information age: Economy, society and culture. *Volume 1: The Rise of the Network Society.* Oxford: Blackwell.

Chen, M. A. (2007). Rethinking the informal economy: Linkages with the formal economy and the formal regulatory environment. *United Nations Department of Economic and Social Affairs* (Working Paper 46).

Coe, N., Hess, M., & Yeung, H. (2008). Global production networks: Realising the potential. *Journal of Economic Geography, 8*(3), 271–95.

Commission for Africa. (2005). *Our common interest.* London: Commission for Africa. Retrieved from http://www.commissionforafrica.info/2005-report

Cooke, P., & Morgan, K. (1998). *The associational economy: Firms, regions and innovation.* Oxford University Press.

Davis, M. (2006). *Planet of slums.* London: Verso Books.

Duranton, G., & Puga, D. (2004). Micro-foundations of urban agglomeration economies. In V. Henderson & J. Thisse (Eds.), *Handbook of urban and regional economics* (Vol. 4, pp. 2063–2117). Amsterdam: North Holland.

Edigheji, O. (Ed.). (2010). *Constructing a democratic developmental state in South Africa.* Cape Town: HSRC Press.

Ellis, F., & Harris, N. (2004). *New thinking about urban and rural development.* Keynote paper for DFID Sustainable Development Retreat, University of Surrey, Guildford.

Evans, P. (1995). *Embedded autonomy: States and industrial transformation.* Princeton University Press.

Fay, M., & Opal, C. (2000). *Urbanisation without growth: A not-so uncommon phenomenon* (Working Paper 2412). Washington, DC: World Bank.

Friedman, T. (2006). *The world is flat.* London: Penguin Books.

Gereffi, G., Humphrey, J., and Sturgeon, T. (2005). The governance of global value chains. *Review of International Political Economy, 12*(1), 78–104.

Gill, I., Kharas, H., & Bhattasali, D. (2007). *An East Asian renaissance: Ideas for economic growth.* Washington, DC: World Bank.

Glaeser, E., & Gottlieb, J. (2006). Urban resurgence and the consumer city. *Urban Studies, 43*(8), 1275–1299.

Gordon, I., & McCann, P. (2000). Industrial clusters: Complexes, agglomeration and/or Social Networks? *Urban Studies, 37*(3), 513–532.

Hall, P. (1998). *Cities in civilisation: Culture, technology and urban order.* London: Weidenfeld and Nicolson.

Hall, P., & Pain, K. (2006). *The polycentric metropolis.* London: Earthscan.

HM Treasury. (2006). Devolving decision making: 3—Meeting the regional economic challenge: The importance of cities to regional growth. London: HM Treasury.

Jacobs, J. (1984). *Cities and the wealth of nations.* New York: Random House.

Jacobs, J. (1969). *The economy of cities.* London: Jonathan Cape.

Kessides, C. (2007). The urban transition in Sub-Saharan Africa: Challenges and opportunities. *Environment and Planning C, 25*(4), 466–485.

## 40   Ivan Turok

Kessides, C. (2006). The urban transition in Sub-Saharan Africa: Implications for economic growth and poverty reduction. Washington, DC: World Bank.

Krugman, P. (1991). *Geography and trade*. Cambridge, MA: MIT Press.

Leke, A., Lund, S., Roxburgh, C., & van Wamelen, A. (2010, June). What's driving Africa's growth. *McKinsey Quarterly*. www.mckinsey.com/insights/economic_studies/whats_driving_africas_growth (accessed 6 February 2014)

Marshall, A. (1920). *Principles of economics* (8th ed.). London: Macmillan.

Martine, G., McGranahan, G., Montegomery, M., & Fernandez-Castilla, R. (2008). *The new global frontier: Urbanisation, poverty and environment in the 21st century*. London: Earthscan, Routledge.

McGranahan, G., Mitlin, D., Satterthwaite, D., Tacoli, C., & Turok, I. (2009). *Africa's urban transition and the role of regional collaboration*. London: International Institute for Environment and Development.

Murray, M. (2008). Africa's futures: From North-South to East-South? *Third World Quarterly*, 29(2), 339–56.

Naude, W., and Matthee, M. (2007). *The significance of transport costs in Africa* (Policy Brief 51813–5706). Helsinki: World Institute for Development Economics Research for the United Nations University.

Neuman, P., & Hull, A. (Eds.). (2011). *The futures of the city-region*. Abingdon, UK: Routledge.

Njoh, A. (2003).Urbanisation and development in Sub-Saharan Africa. *Cities, 20*(3), 167–174.

OECD. (2008a). *Growing unequal? Income distribution and poverty in OECD countries*. Paris: OECD.

OECD. (2008b). *Territorial review: Cape Town, South Africa*. Paris: OECD

Parr, J. (2008). Cities and regions: Problems and potentials. *Environment and Planning A, 40*(12), 3009–3026.

Parr, J. (1999). Growth pole strategies in regional economic planning: A retrospective view. *Urban Studies, 36*(7–8), 1195–1215, 1247–1268.

Parr, J. (2005). Perspectives on the city-region. *Regional Studies, 39*(5), 555–566.

Parr, J. (2004). The polycentric urban region: A closer inspection. *Regional Studies, 38*(3), 231–240.

Pike, A., Rodriguez-Pose, A., & Tomaney, J. (2006). *Local and regional development*. Abingdon, UK: Routledge.

Porter, M. (1998, December). Clusters and the new economics of competitiveness. *Harvard Business Review, 77–90*.

Potts, D. (2007). City life in Zimbabwe at a time of fear and loathing: Urban planning, urban poverty and Operation Murambatsvina. In G. Myers & M. Murray (Eds.), *Cities in contemporary Africa*. New York: Palgrave.

Rakodi, C. (Ed.). (1997). *The urban challenge in Africa: Growth and management of its large cities*. Toyko: United Nations University Press.

Ravallion, M. (2009). Are there lessons for Africa from China's success against poverty? *World Development, 37*(2), 303–313.

Ravallion, M., Chen, S., & Sangraula, P. (2007). *New evidence on the urbanisation of global poverty*. Washington, DC: Development Research Group, World Bank. Retrieved from http://go.worldbank.org/AIE683JE90

Rice, P., Venables, A., & Patacchini, E. (2006). Spatial determinants of productivity: Analysis for the regions of Great Britain. *Regional Science and Urban Economics, 36*, 727–752.

Robertson, M., & White, G. (Eds.). (1998). *The democratic developmental state: Politics and institutional design*. Oxford University Press.

Rogerson, C. M. (1997). Globalisation or informalisation? African urban economies in the 1990s. In Rakodi, C. (Ed.), *The urban challenge in Africa: Growth and management of its large cities.* Toyko: United Nations University Press. pp.337–370

SABMiller Corporate Website. (2010). www.sabmiller.com (accessed on May 5, 2010)

Scott, A. J. (2006). *Geography and economy.* Oxford: Clarendon Press.

Scott, A. J. (Ed.). (2001). *Global city-regions: Trends, theory, policy.* Oxford University Press.

Skinner, C. (2010). Street trading in Africa: Demographic trends, planning and trader organisation. In V. Padayachee, *The political economy of Africa.* Abingdon, UK: Routledge.

Southall, R., & Melber, H. (Eds.). (2009). *A new scramble for Africa?* Scottsville, South Africa: University of KwaZulu-Natal Press.

Storper, M., & Manville, M. (2006). Behaviour, preferences and cities: Urban theory and urban resurgence. *Urban Studies, 43*(8), 1247–1274.

Todaro, M. (2000). *Economic development* (7th ed.). Harlow, Essex, UK: Pearson Education.

Turok, I. (2004). Cities, regions and competitiveness. *Regional Studies, 38*(9), 1069–1083.

Turok, I. (2009). The distinctive city: Pitfalls in the pursuit of differential advantage. *Environment and Planning A, 41*(1), 13–30.

Turok, I. (2011). Inclusive growth: Meaningful goal or mirage? In A. Pike, A. Rodriguez-Pose, & J. Tomaney (Eds.), *Handbook of local and regional development.* Abingdon, UK: Routledge.

Turok, I. (2001). Persistent polarisation post-apartheid? Progress towards urban integration in Cape Town. *Urban Studies, 38*(13), 2349–2377.

Turok, I. (2010b). Towards a developmental state? Provincial economic policies in South Africa. *Development Southern Africa, 27*(4), 497–516.

Turok, I., & Bailey, N. (2004). The theory of polynuclear urban regions and its application to Central Scotland. *European Planning Studies, 12*(3), 371–389.

UN-Habitat. (2008). *The state of African cities 2008: A framework for addressing urban challenges in Africa.* Nairobi: UN-Habitat.

UN-Habitat. (2010). *State of the world's cities 2010/11: Bridging the urban divide.* Nairobi: UN-Habitat.

United Nations. (2007). *State of world population 2007: Unleashing the potential of urban growth.* New York: UN. Retrieved from www.unfpa.org

United Nations. (2008). *World population policies 2007.* New York: UN Department of Economic and Social Affairs.

Venables, A. J. (2010). Economic geography and African development. *Regional Science, 89*(3), 469–483.

Wang, J., & Bio-Tchane, A. (2008). Africa's burgeoning ties with China. *Finance and Development, 46,* 44–47.

White, M. J., Mberu, B. U., & Collinson, M. A. (2008). African urbanisation: Recent trends and implications. In Martine, G., McGranahan, G., Montegomery, M., & Fernandez-Castilla, R. (Eds.), *The new global frontier* (pp. 302–316).

World Bank. (2008). *Building bridges: China's growing role as infrastructure financier for Sub-Saharan Africa.* Washington, DC: World Bank.

World Bank. (2000). *World development report 1999/2000: Entering the 21st century.* Washington, DC: World Bank.

World Bank. (2009). *World development report 2009: Shaping economic geography.* Washington, DC: World Bank.

Yeung, H. (2009). Regional development and the competitive dynamics of global production networks: An East Asian perspective. *Regional Studies, 43*(3), 325–351.

# 3 Institutions, Decentralisation and Urban Development

*Edgar Pieterse and Warren Smit*

## INTRODUCTION

Africa had the fastest rate of urbanisation of all regions in the world between 2005 and 2010 (UN-Habitat, 2012). The urban population of Africa is expected to increase from an estimated 441 million people in 2012 to 642 million people by 2025 (UN-Habitat, 2012). UN-Habitat (2010) points out that two thirds of new urban growth in Sub-Saharan Africa is slum growth. In other words, it is expected that significant proportions of urban dwellers in Sub-Saharan Africa will continue to live in slums, as most African cities and towns lack the institutional, financial and political resources to deal with growing levels of urbanisation.

Slum life fundamentally represents a lack of access to a number of essential services and securities that make a productive and modern life possible. It is clearly established in the literature that economic resilience and economic success depend on efficient and productive urban centres, which anchor various economic sectors that span across international boundaries (Kessides, 2006; OECD, 2008; Scott, 2006). If such urban-based systems are non-existent or ineffective, the economy experiences a significant strain, which in turn undermines the national development effort. Yet, despite this relatively widespread consensus, most African governments continue to under-invest in the establishment of the requisite institutional frameworks and systems to enhance the productive functioning of the national urban system. International evidence suggests that at the core of such institutional frameworks is a well-resourced, capacitated, effective, relatively autonomous and democratic local government system that can ensure comprehensive service delivery to citizens and private firms, and also maximise distinctive competitive advantages because of intimate knowledge about local (space-economy) endowments and dynamics.

In this chapter, we explore the institutional dimensions of the urban development crisis in Africa, cognisant of the profound political and policy obstacles that need to be addressed. In the section that follows, we elaborate the scope, scale and dimensions of the urban development challenge in Africa. This is followed by a brief analysis of the institutional dimensions of this crisis. From there, we focus on what we can learn from the uneven

*Institutions, Decentralisation and Urban Development*   43

experimentation and implementation of decentralisation reforms over the past two to three decades across the continent in order to propose an ambitious, but realistic, reform agenda. This discussion is particularly germane in light of the sustained levels of economic growth over the past decade until the global financial crisis in 2008–2009. As discussed in UN-Habitat's *State of the World's Cities 2010/2011*, this economic growth did not really see any shift in the quality of life and environment in most African cities and towns: 'High slum prevalence in many African cities can also be attributed to structural and political failures in the distribution of public goods, as well as to lack of human and financial resources to address urban poverty. Against this background, economic growth in many cases has had little impact on either poverty or inequality, or both' (UN-Habitat, 2010, p. 28).

On this note, it is important to underscore that it is very difficult to generalise across extremely diverse urban and economic conditions in the various regions and territories of Africa. In particular, urban population growth rates vary across Africa. For example, the average urban population growth rate for the 30 low-income countries in Africa was 4 per cent per year during 2005–2010, whereas it was only 2.3 per cent for the nine upper-middle income countries in Africa (UN-Habitat, 2012). In addition, economic conditions also vary considerably. For example, the upbeat economic assessment report on the continent by McKinsey Global Institute suggests that Africa's economies can be divided into four broad categories: oil exporters; pre-transition economies with high levels of poverty and weak macro-economic institutions; transition economies where there is high growth and still a large agricultural sector (up to 35 per cent of GDP) and a strong need for diversification and supporting infrastructure; and finally, diversified economies that need to raise productivity and skill levels (McKinsey Global Institute, 2010). One can segment African countries and regions in other ways as well. Given the scope of the chapter, we cannot fully address how this diversity relates to governance reform, but it is important to note that the significant diversity across the continent is a vital backdrop to what follows.

## SCOPE, SCALE AND DIMENSIONS OF URBAN DEVELOPMENT CHALLENGES

The purpose of this section is simply to draw attention to the scale and rate of urbanisation in Africa, and to contextualise this against some crucial development indicators such as access to basic services, economic infrastructure, environmental performance, poverty and inequality.

The United Nations Population Fund usefully summarises the longitudinal dynamic that sits behind the shifts demonstrated in Table 3.1:

> At the world level, the 20th Century saw an increase from 220 million urbanites in 1900 to 2.84 billion in 2000. The present century will match this absolute increase in about four decades. Developing regions

## 44 *Edgar Pieterse and Warren Smit*

> as a whole will account for 93 per cent of this growth—Asia and Africa accounting for over 80 per cent. (UNFPA, 2007, p. 7–8)

Between 2000 and 2030, Asia's urban population will increase from 1.39 billion to 2.70 billion; Africa's from 288 million to 744 million; and that of Latin America and the Caribbean (LAC) from 394 million to 609 million. As a result of these shifts, developing countries will have 80 per cent of the world's urban population in 2030. By then, Africa and Asia will include almost seven out of every 10 urban inhabitants in the world (UNFPA, 2007). [1]

These trends are staggering by any account, but they also mask the fact that we are talking about vastly different kinds of urban settlements. Specifically, the vast majority of African urban dwellers reside, and will continue to reside, in urban settlements with populations less than 0.5 million people. For example, in 2007, 52 per cent of the urban population in Africa lived in settlements with fewer than 0.5 million people, compared to 10 per cent in cities of between 0.5 and 1 million; 27 per cent in cities of 1–5 million; 4 per cent in cities of 5–10 million; and only 6 per cent in cities with more than 10 million people (UN-Habitat, 2008a). This is fundamentally different from the typical scenario of mega-city explosions that is popularly associated with urbanisation.

What is not in dispute is that Africa is increasingly becoming an urban continent, with the highest levels of urban population growth in the world. The average urban population growth rate in Africa between 2000 and 2010 was 3.3 per cent per year (UN-Habitat, 2008b, 2010). The problem with this growth is that about two thirds of it takes the form of slum growth (UN-Habitat, 2010). Between 1990 and 2000, the average annual urban population growth rate in Africa was 4.58 per cent, whereas the population of urban slums during the same period grew at 4.53 per cent per year (UN-Habitat, 2008a). There are, of course, vast differences in the nature and experience of slum life in different settings. It is for this reason that the UN-Habitat's working definition of slums is useful and instructive to bear in mind (see Box 3.1).

---

### Box 3.1 What is a Slum?

"A slum household is defined as a group of individuals living under the same roof lacking one or more of the following conditions: Access to improved water; access to improved sanitation facilities; sufficient living area (not more than three people sharing the same room); structural quality and durability of dwellings; and security of tenure. Four out of five of the slum definition indicators measure physical expressions of slum conditions. . . . These indicators focus attention on the circumstances that surround slum life, depicting deficiencies and casting poverty as an attribute of the environments in which slum dwellers live. The fifth indicator – security of tenure – has to do with legality, which is not as easy to measure or monitor, as the tenure status of slum dwellers often depends on *de facto* or *de jure* rights, or lack of them." (UN-Habitat, 2008b, p. 92)

*Table 3.1*   Urban Population by Region, 1950–2010, with Projection for 2025–2050

| Major area, region, country or area | 1950 | 1960 | 1970 | 1980 | 1990 | 2000 | 2010 | 2020 | 2030 | 2040 | 2050 |
|---|---|---|---|---|---|---|---|---|---|---|---|
| World | 745 495 | 1 019 638 | 1 352 419 | 1 753 229 | 2 281 405 | 2 858 632 | 3 558 578 | 4 289 818 | 4 983 908 | 5 636 226 | 6 252 175 |
| More developed regions | 441 845 | 555 970 | 670 573 | 757 975 | 827 098 | 881 344 | 957 251 | 1 018 365 | 1 064 290 | 1 099 266 | 1 127 222 |
| Less developed regions | 303 650 | 463 668 | 681 846 | 995 253 | 1 454 307 | 1 977 289 | 2 601 326 | 3 271 453 | 3 919 618 | 4 536 960 | 5 124 953 |
| Least developed countries | 14 562 | 23 194 | 40 702 | 67 571 | 106 912 | 160 599 | 233 802 | 338 163 | 476 971 | 652 038 | 860 316 |
| Less developed regions, excluding least developed | 289 088 | 440 473 | 641 144 | 927 682 | 1 347 395 | 1 816 690 | 2 367 525 | 2 933 290 | 3 442 646 | 3 884 922 | 4 264 637 |
| Less developed regions, excluding China | 235 138 | 351 462 | 531 372 | 791 321 | 1 131 957 | 1 499 423 | 1 916 537 | 2 398 984 | 2 934 704 | 3 510 840 | 4 096 309 |
| Sub-Saharan Africa | 20 069 | 33 180 | 55 643 | 89 709 | 139 414 | 206 322 | 298 402 | 426 522 | 595 544 | 810 152 | 1 068 752 |
| Africa | 33 004 | 53 310 | 86 568 | 134 220 | 203 383 | 288 402 | 400 651 | 551 552 | 744 485 | 983 327 | 1 264 629 |
| Asia | 245 052 | 359 955 | 505 669 | 715 234 | 1 032 275 | 1 392 232 | 1 847 733 | 2 304 715 | 2 702 525 | 3 034 947 | 3 309 694 |
| Europe | 280 602 | 344 397 | 412 199 | 466 318 | 502 983 | 514 545 | 536 611 | 557 585 | 573 494 | 584 494 | 591 041 |
| Latin America and the Caribbean | 69 264 | 108 540 | 163 402 | 232 955 | 311 620 | 393 619 | 465 246 | 531 235 | 585 347 | 625 144 | 650 479 |
| Northern America | 109 667 | 142 856 | 170 691 | 188 118 | 212 088 | 247 911 | 282 480 | 314 905 | 344 444 | 371 234 | 395 985 |
| Oceania | 7 907 | 10 580 | 13 891 | 16 384 | 19 056 | 21 924 | 25 857 | 29 825 | 33 614 | 37 079 | 40 346 |

*Source:* United Nations, Department of Economic and Social Affairs.

## 46  Edgar Pieterse and Warren Smit

*Table 3.2*  Percentage of Slum Dwellers in Developing Regions, 2005

| Regions | % in slums | % moderately/ severely deprived (1–2 deprivations) | % extremely deprived (3+ deprivations) |
|---|---|---|---|
| Sub-Saharan Africa | 62 | 63 | 37 |
| North Africa[a] | 14.5 | 14.6 | 0.6 |
| Latin America & the Caribbean | 27 | 82 | 18 |
| Southern Asia | 43 | 95 | 5 |

[a]Only Morocco and Egypt.

*Source:* UN-HABITAT (2008b). *State of the world's cities 2008/2009: Harmonious cities.* London: Earthscan.

Building on the understanding that slums are identified in terms of five shelter deprivations, the same UN-Habitat report has developed a useful nuance for our understanding of slums by tabulating whether slums are moderately deprived (one of the shelter deprivations listed in Box 3.1), severely deprived (two deprivations) or extremely deprived (three or more deprivations). This work shows that six out of every 10 Sub-Saharan African urban residents are slum dwellers and 37 per cent of slum dwellers live in slum conditions of extreme deprivation. This is an extraordinarily high rate compared to other developing regions, especially North Africa where the rates are the lowest among developing countries (see Table 3.2) (UN-Habitat, 2008b).

It is therefore not surprising that the basic service backlogs are staggering. According to World Bank data cited by Ajulu and Motsamai (2008), only 40 per cent of the population in Sub-Saharan Africa have access to potable water. Only 20 per cent have access to electricity networks. About 27 per cent have access to adequate sanitation, and only 4 per cent have access to fixed or mobile telephones. These are aggregate numbers that include rural and urban deficiencies. However, it is generally accepted that the proportions of the urban population in Africa without adequate access to water and sanitation are 35–50 per cent and 50–60 per cent respectively (Tannerfeldt and Ljung, 2006, p. 60). This suggests better access in urban areas. However, the numbers obscure country differences. For instance, South Africa would have a major skewing effect. The data also under-represents the extent to which available infrastructure has become moribund due to a lack of maintenance. The limited coverage of network infrastructures also means that the urban poor usually pay much more for access to basic services per unit than the wealthy, who are connected to bulk infrastructure systems. One simple illustration reinforces the point forcefully— that the urban poor of Accra who reside in slums without access to piped water pay exponentially more for access compared to other urban residents in the city as graphically illustrated in Table 3.3.

## Institutions, Decentralisation and Urban Development 47

*Table 3.3* Cost of Water in Accra, Ghana

| Water Source | US$ | Users |
|---|---|---|
| Sachet (500 millilitres) | 0.2 | General public, for street purchase |
| 30-pack (sachets) | 5.08 | General public, for house use |
| Water pipe | 0.043–0.064 (Increasing block-tariffs are applied) | Households with pipe connection Households relying on shared standpipe |
| Bucket from kiosk | | |
| 20 liters | 0.75 | |
| 18 liters | 0.56 | |
| Community shower | 0.15/shower (This varies across the city and depends on whether the 'bather' brought his/her soap) | Informal settlement dwellers (bathing only) |

*Source:* African Development Bank: data collected by Ghana Field Office, 2012/2013.

This underscores why the lack of urban infrastructure to provide basic services impacts disproportionately on low-income groups and neighbourhoods that are cut off from networked infrastructure grids. But this is not the only way in which slum dwellers and slum areas are disadvantaged. It is important to bear in mind the differences between economic, household and public infrastructures.

Economic infrastructure refers broadly to connectivity structures such as roads, seaports, airports, stations and other transportation or information and communication network systems. Household infrastructures that address basic needs include water, sanitation and energy. In some countries, such as South Africa, the physical house and the land it is located on is provided for free to the poor. Public infrastructures refer to public resources and spaces such as streets, pavements, squares, parks, community halls, libraries, markets (which can also serve as economic infrastructure). Typically, powerful classes and interest groups who drive the economy have a disproportionate say in which kinds of infrastructures will be prioritised. The continuation of underinvestment in all categories of infrastructure, along with the selective provision of services, contributes to the perpetuation of urban poverty, which is increasingly cemented by structural inequality (Parnell, Pieterse, & Watson, 2009).

Urban inequality in Africa, measured in terms of the Gini coefficient, is the second highest in the world. The regional average Gini coefficient for income distribution in cities in Africa is 0.58 (UN-Habitat, 2010). This is

*Table 3.4*   Rural and Urban Poverty in Africa

| | National poverty line Population below poverty line (%) | | | International poverty line Population below poverty line (%) | | | Gini coefficient | |
|---|---|---|---|---|---|---|---|---|
| | Survey year | Rural | Urban | National | Survey year | Below US$1.25 | Below US$2 | Survey year | Index |
| Algeria | 1995 | 30.3 | 14.7 | 22.6 | 1995 | 6.8 | 23.6 | 1995 | 0.353 |
| Angola | 2001 | 94.3 | 62.3 | 68.0 | 2000 | 54.3 | 70.2 | 2000 | 0.586 |
| Benin | 2007 | 35.1 | 28.3 | 33.3 | 2003 | 47.3 | 75.3 | 2003 | 0.386 |
| Botswana | 2003 | 44.8 | 19.4 | 30.6 | 1994 | 31.2 | 49.4 | 1994 | 0.61 |
| Burkina Faso | 2009 | 52.6 | 27.9 | 46.7 | 2009 | 44.6 | 72.6 | 2009 | 0.398 |
| Burundi | 2006 | 68.9 | 34.0 | 66.9 | 2006 | 81.3 | 93.5 | 2006 | 0.333 |
| Cameroon | 2007 | 55.0 | 12.2 | 39.9 | 2007 | 9.6 | 30.4 | 2007 | 0.389 |
| Cape Verde | 2007 | 44.3 | 13.2 | 26.6 | 2002 | 21.0 | 40.9 | 2002 | 0.505 |
| Central African Republic | 2008 | 69.4 | 49.6 | 62.0 | 2008 | 62.8 | 80.1 | 2008 | 0.563 |
| Chad | 2003 | 58.6 | 24.6 | 55.0 | 2003 | 61.9 | 83.3 | 2003 | 0.398 |
| Comoros | 2004 | 48.7 | 34.5 | 44.8 | 2004 | 46.1 | 65.0 | 2004 | 0.643 |
| Congo | 2011 | 74.8 | - | 46.5 | 2005 | 54.1 | 74.4 | 2005 | 0.473 |
| Congo Democratic Republic | 2006 | 75.7 | 61.5 | 71.3 | 2006 | 87.7 | 95.2 | 2006 | 0.444 |
| Côte d'Ivoire | 2006 | 54.2 | 29.4 | 42.7 | 2008 | 23.8 | 46.3 | 2008 | 0.415 |
| Djibouti | - | - | - | - | 2002 | 18.8 | 41.2 | 2002 | 0.40 |
| Egypt | 2008 | 30.0 | 10.6 | 22.0 | 2008 | 1.7 | 15.4 | 2008 | 0.308 |
| Equatorial Guinea | 2006 | 79.9 | 31.5 | 76.8 | - | - | - | - | - |
| Eritrea | 1993 | - | 62.0 | 69.0 | - | - | - | - | - |
| Ethiopia | 2011 | 30.4 | 25.7 | 29.6 | 2005 | 39.0 | 77.6 | 2005 | 0.298 |
| Gabon | 2005 | 44.6 | 29.8 | 32.7 | 2005 | 4.8 | 19.6 | 2005 | 0.415 |
| Gambia | 2010 | 73.9 | 32.7 | 48.4 | 2003 | 33.6 | 55.9 | 2003 | 0.473 |
| Ghana | 2006 | 39.2 | 10.8 | 28.5 | 2006 | 28.6 | 51.8 | 2006 | 0.428 |
| Guinea | 2007 | 63.0 | 30.5 | 53.0 | 2007 | 43.3 | 69.6 | 2007 | 0.394 |
| Guinea-Bissau | 2012 | 64.7 | 35.4 | 55.2 | 2002 | 48.9 | 78.0 | 2002 | 0.355 |
| Kenya | 2005 | 49.1 | 33.7 | 45.9 | 2005 | 43.4 | 67.2 | 2005 | 0.477 |
| Lesotho | 2003 | 60.5 | 41.5 | 56.6 | 2003 | 43.4 | 62.3 | 2003 | 0.525 |

|  |  |  |  |  |  |  |  |  |  |  |  |
|---|---|---|---|---|---|---|---|---|---|---|---|
| Liberia | 2007 | 67.7 | 55.1 | 2007 | 63.8 | 2007 | 83.8 | 94.9 | 2007 | 0.382 | 2007 |
| Libya | - | - | - | - | - | - | - | - | - | - | - |
| Madagascar | 2005 | 73.5 | 52.0 | 2010 | 68.7 | 2004 | 81.3 | 92.6 | 2010 | 0.441 | 2010 |
| Malawi | 2010 | 56.6 | 17.3 | 2004 | 50.7 | 2004 | 73.9 | 90.5 | 2004 | 0.390 | 2004 |
| Mali | 2010 | 50.6 | 18.9 | 2010 | 43.6 | 2010 | 50.4 | 78.7 | 2010 | 0.33 | 2010 |
| Mauritania | 2008 | 59.4 | 20.8 | 2008 | 42.0 | 2008 | 23.4 | 47.7 | 2008 | 0.405 | 2008 |
| Mauritius | - | - | - | - | - | - | - | - | 2006 | 0.389 | 2006 |
| Morocco | 2007 | 14.5 | 4.8 | 2007 | 9.0 | 2007 | 2.5 | 14.0 | 2007 | 0.409 | 2007 |
| Mozambique | 2008 | 56.9 | 49.6 | 2008 | 54.7 | 2008 | 59.6 | 81.1 | 2008 | 0.457 | 2008 |
| Namibia | 2004 | 49.0 | 17.0 | 2004 | 38.0 | 2004 | 31.9 | 51.1 | 2004 | 0.639 | 2004 |
| Niger | 2007 | 63.9 | 36.7 | 2009 | 59.5 | 2009 | 43.6 | 75.2 | 2008 | 0.346 | 2008 |
| Nigeria | 2004 | 63.8 | 43.1 | 2010 | 54.7 | 2010 | 68.0 | 84.5 | 2010 | 0.488 | 2010 |
| Rwanda | 2011 | 48.7 | 22.1 | 2011 | 44.9 | 2011 | 63.2 | 82.4 | 2011 | 0.508 | 2011 |
| Sao Tomé & Principe | 2009 | 64.9 | 45.0 | 2001 | 66.2 | 2001 | 28.2 | 54.2 | 2001 | 0.508 | 2001 |
| Senegal | 2011 | 57.1 | 33.1 | 2005 | 46.7 | 2005 | 33.5 | 60.4 | 2005 | 0.392 | 2005 |
| Seychelles | - | - | - | 2007 | - | 2007 | 0.3 | 1.8 | 2007 | 0.658 | 2007 |
| Sierra Leone | 2003 | 78.5 | 47.0 | 2003 | 66.4 | 2003 | 53.4 | 76.1 | 2003 | 0.425 | 2003 |
| Somalia | - | - | - | - | - | - | - | - | - | - | - |
| South Africa | 2006 | 55.4 | 24.4 | 2009 | 23.0 | 2009 | 13.8 | 31.3 | 2009 | 0.631 | 2009 |
| South Sudan | 2009 | 57.6 | 26.5 | 2009 | 50.6 | - | - | - | - | - | - |
| Sudan | 2009 | 73.1 | 31.1 | 2009 | 46.5 | 2009 | 19.8 | 44.1 | 2009 | 0.353 | 2009 |
| Swaziland | 2010 | 37.4 | 21.8 | 2010 | 63.0 | 2010 | 40.6 | 60.4 | 2010 | 0.515 | 2010 |
| Tanzania | 2007 | 73.4 | 34.6 | 2007 | 33.4 | 2007 | 67.9 | 87.9 | 2007 | 0.376 | 2007 |
| Togo | 2011 | - | - | 2006 | 58.7 | 2006 | 38.7 | 69.3 | 2006 | 0.344 | 2006 |
| Tunisia | 2010 | 27.2 | 9.1 | 2005 | 15.5 | 2005 | 1.4 | 8.1 | 2005 | 0.414 | 2005 |
| Uganda | 2009 | 77.9 | 27.5 | 2009 | 24.5 | 2009 | 38.0 | 64.7 | 2009 | 0.443 | 2009 |
| Zambia | 2010 | 82.4 | 42.3 | 2006 | 60.5 | 2006 | 68.5 | 82.6 | 2006 | 0.546 | 2006 |
| Zimbabwe | 2003 | - | - | 2004 | 72.0 | 2004 | 61.9 | - | 2004 | 0.501 | 2004 |

Source: African Development Bank, OECD, UNDP, & ECA. (2012). African economic outlook 2012. Retrieved from http://www.africaneconomicout-look.org.

## 50  Edgar Pieterse and Warren Smit

*Table 3.5*  Overall Infrastructure Spending Needs for Sub-Saharan Africa (US$ Billions Annually)

| Infrastructure sector | Capital expenditure | Operation and maintenance | Total spending |
|---|---|---|---|
| Information and communication technologies | 7.0 | 2.0 | 9.0 |
| Irrigation | 2.9 | 0.6 | 3.4 |
| Power | 26.7 | 14.1 | 40.8 |
| Transport | 8.8 | 9.4 | 18.2 |
| Water and sanitation | 14.9 | 7.0 | 21.9 |
| Total | 60.4 | 33.0 | 93.3 |

*Source:* Foster, V., & Briceño-Garmendia, C. (Eds.). (2010). *Africa's infrastructure—A time for transformation.* Washington, DC: The World Bank and Agence Française de Développement.

well above the international alert line of 0.4, beyond which inequality is classified as being unacceptably high (UN-Habitat, 2010). In the larger African economies, such as South Africa, income inequality is far more severely skewed, with Gini rates of over 0.6 for all of the largest cities (UN-Habitat, 2010). We can conclude that urban poverty is likely to continue rising, given that it is growing four times faster than rural poverty (see Table 3.4).

To summarise, 62 per cent of urban dwellers in Sub-Saharan Africa live in slum conditions (UN-Habitat, 2008b, 2010, 2012). Of this group, 37 per cent live in extremely precarious circumstances (UN-Habitat, 2008b). Unsurprisingly, the most recent data on urban poverty demonstrates average growth rates in the numbers of people living below the US$2 and US$1 poverty lines of almost five per cent per year (Ravallion, Chen, & Sangraula, 2007). These alarming trends produce profound patterns of intra-urban inequality, which has resulted in African cities having a higher average Gini coefficient than that of any other region (UN-Habitat, 2010). In the short term, any significant change through rapid and effective provision of urban infrastructure seems unlikely, given the continued under-investment in infrastructure in Africa. In a report published by the World Bank in 2010, a detailed account is provided of the overall infrastructure trends in the continent, inclusive of both urban and rural areas (Foster & Briceño-Garmendia, 2010). The report suggests that Africa needs about US$93 billion per annum to meet its infrastructure needs, but only half of this amount (US$45 billion) is being realized (see Table 3.5).

## INSTITUTIONAL UNDERPINNING OF THE AFRICAN URBAN CRISIS

It is possible to argue that the severe development crisis associated with urbanisation in Africa can largely be attributed to external forces. However, this would be disingenuous because despite the severe resource constraints that mark most African countries, a lot more could have been done to deal with the issue effectively (Pieterse, 2010). The capacity of African states to address the inevitable consequences of increased urbanisation boils down to fundamental institutional problems. First, most African governments have policies that discourage migration into urban areas. This stems from a growing concern that their countries are urbanising too rapidly and that the dynamics need to be restricted through active legislation. In 1996, 45 per cent of all governments in the world had policies to reduce migration to urban agglomerations, and this figure rose to 62 per cent in 2009 (United Nations, 2010). African governments were clearly the most concerned about urbanisation, with 54 per cent having policies to reduce migration to urban agglomerations in 1996, rising to 77 per cent in 2009 (United Nations, 2010).

Secondly, most governments continue to execute their functions without any explicit national urbanisation strategy that can inform and guide strategic investments (Parnell & Simon, 2010). This stems from a broader political sentiment that the economic future of Africa lies with improving its agricultural performance through a so-called second green revolution, which will allow the continent to take its rightful place in the globally connected international economy. It is noteworthy how much of the New Partnership for Africa's Development (NEPAD) policy agenda is taken up by promoting a new agenda for agriculture. It is of course a vital component of a long-term development strategy, but it depends heavily on well-functioning cities and towns to get commodities to market and to absorb the produce. In other words, to plan for agricultural success without planning for connectivity infrastructures and the development of cities and towns is short-sighted.

Thirdly, policy efforts to implement decentralisation measures have on the whole underperformed, mainly due to a lack of fiscal backing and lacklustre political support from national leaders (Mabogunje, 2007; Stren & Eyoh, 2007: p. 28). The reasons for this situation are complex and vary greatly across the different regions of the continent and within countries. In particular, it must be noted that the presence and dynamics of traditional authorities in most African countries create particularly vexing governance challenges which, on the whole, have probably been detrimental to effective democratic decentralisation efforts (JICA, 2008). We explore the modern history of uneven decentralisation and its current manifestations in greater detail in the next section of the chapter.

Fourthly, in most African countries, the division of functions between different levels or spheres of government have been deeply problematic, leading to intergovernmental conflict, misalignment and inefficiency. In most cases, this has been compounded by national fiscal systems that undermine the capacity of local governments to perform their responsibilities (UN-Habitat, 2009a). Lastly, in the absence of sufficient and effective civil society pressure, political leaders have been able to maintain this unsatisfactory urban development and governance situation, which in turn reflects the absence

## 52  Edgar Pieterse and Warren Smit

of meaningful democratic participation mechanisms to induce transparency, accountability and responsiveness. These dynamics are explored at greater length, with an emphasis on policy responses, in the fifth section.

We conclude this section by analysing the recent performance of African countries in terms of governance indicators that could affect cities' and towns' competetiveness. There is a growing consensus that infrastructure has a key role in economic development, especially in cities and towns. According to Calderon (2008), deficient infrastructure has been found to sap Africa's growth by about 2% a year. The lack of adequate physical infrastructure, as well as soft infrastructure, affects productivity and raises production and transaction costs, which hinder growth by reducing competitiveness of firms and the ability of governments to pursue sustainable economic and social policies. Table 3.6 reports the 2011 Mo Ibrahim governance indicators regarding infrastructure provision/maintenance and the institutional dimensions that could affect infrastructure provision, namely (i) public management, (ii) rule of law, and (iii) the business environment. These elements are equally relevant for thinking through the broader institutional agenda that accompanies democratic decentralisation. In terms of infrastructural governance, the continent has made some improvement from 2006 to 2010 (+2.6%), but the average score remains low (31/100). North Africa registered the highest score (54/100), whereas Central Africa performed least well (20/100). The continent's average score regarding public management is about 55, with a slight improvement between 2006 and 2010. Again, North Africa has the highest score (65/100) compared to East Africa which registered the lowest score (49/100). With regard to the quality of regulation, Southern Africa has the best performance regarding the rule of law and business environment.

Table 3.6 clearly demonstrates that institutional decentralisation is not about accruing powers and functions at the lower levels at the expense of national government. Instead, it demonstrates the need to carefully spread out diverse functions and responsibilities across a diversity of government sites, which in turn opens the door for the active enrolment of the private

*Table 3.6*  Selected African Countries' Governance Index, by Regions (2010)

| Regions | Infrastructure | Business Environment | Public Management | Rule of Law |
|---|---|---|---|---|
| Sub-Saharan Africa | 28 | 49 | 54 | 48 |
| North Africa | 54 | 55 | 65 | 47 |
| Central Africa | 20 | 36 | 52 | 36 |
| East Africa | 27 | 47 | 49 | 38 |
| Southern Africa | 44 | 59 | 60 | 63 |
| West Africa | 22 | 50 | 55 | 49 |

*Source:* Mo Ibrahim Index for African Governance, 2011.

*Institutions, Decentralisation and Urban Development* 53

sector and community organisations in various aspects of service delivery and maintenance.

It is important to bear in mind that these indicators come with a particular set of biases about what constitutes an effective institutional framework for infrastructure provision and service delivery. It is of course not clear whether this is the best approach to address the dramatic backlogs in access to services in a context of very high levels of poverty, weak state capacity to regulate and oversee, entrenched rent-seeking practices and growing levels of urban inequality.

Nonetheless, given our claim that an effective decentralisation framework must prioritise the provision of essential network infrastructures to address basic services, economic development and the durability of ecosystem services, it remains instructive to learn from the heuristic tools provided by these indicators to understand the range of institutional reform measures that come into play in sustainable urban development. In the next section, we review where we are presently with regard to decentralisation reforms over the past three decades.

## LEARNING FROM DECENTRALISATION EFFORTS

Almost 40 years ago, Richard Stren wrote the following on African urban policies:

> One of the most widely held criticisms of urban policies in Africa is that they are inconsistent, haphazard, and not coherently articulated. . . . Physical planners rarely work with economists. There are no ministries of urban affairs, and even well-defined problems such as housing and urban transportation run the gamut of intra-governmental negotiations before anything serious can be attempted. The division of function and jurisdiction between local and central government also leaves a great deal of room for manoeuvre, conflict, and overlap in urban policy. (Stren, 1972, p. 505)

Central to these problems was the fact that in most of Africa, urban local governments were unimportant during the colonial era (with a few exceptions), and generally became even weaker and more unimportant in the first few decades after independence. Urban local governments in Africa were generally based on the local government systems established during the colonial era.

In some Francophone countries, for example, urban government was established on the French model. The largest cities had elected councils and mayors, and were responsible for a significant range of local services. However, immediately after independence, the national governments of countries such as Senegal and Côte d'Ivoire took over control of the largest cities, purportedly because of their perceived financial insolvency and

## 54    Edgar Pieterse and Warren Smit

administrative incompetence, but implicitly in order to establish control over potential political opposition (Rakodi, 1997).

Similarly, in Anglophone Africa, elected local councils had been put in place by the end of the colonial period, but their performance fell far short of their responsibilities and growing demands. Their political autonomy and fiscal base were progressively eroded during the 1960s and 1970s. Central governments generally failed to give local government adequate funds or revenue-raising powers or to ensure that they had sufficient decision-making powers and trained staff to address the urban challenges they faced (Rakodi, 1997). For example, in Tanzania, local government was abolished in the early 1970s, and was replaced by direct central government administration (with some decentralisation to regions). This neglect of urban local government had direct impacts on urban management, a notable example being an outbreak of cholera in urban areas in Tanzania (President's Office, United Republic of Tanzania, n.d.).

### Decentralisation in Africa

From the 1980s onwards, there was a shift towards decentralisation in Africa. Decentralisation is any act in which a central government formally cedes powers to actors and institutions at lower levels in a political–administrative and territorial hierarchy. The key theoretical motivation behind the promotion of decentralisation was to bring decision-making closer to people, and by so doing, better address local needs. The three broad types of decentralisation are (Ribot, 2001):

- Political or democratic decentralisation: This is when powers and resources are transferred to authorities representative of, and downwardly accountable to, local populations.
- Fiscal decentralisation: This is where the fiscal resources and revenue generating powers are transferred to lower levels of the state.
- Administrative decentralisation or deconcentration: This is where power is transferred to local branches of the central state.

This wave of decentralisation was all-pervasive. Increasingly, governments and international agencies recognised that improved urban management, decentralisation, and local democracy were interlinked. Thus, there were fresh attempts at decentralisation to the local government level, linked to state democratisation. Local governments were therefore re-established in many countries in an attempt to enhance local democracy and service delivery. In Tanzania, the re-establishment of local government was a direct response to a number of failures in the direct administration system, including the outbreak of cholera in urban areas. The importance of metropolitan government was also recognised, resulting in the establishment of the City of Abidjan in 1980, and a similar body for Dakar in 1983. In Lusophone countries, notably Angola and Mozambique, there was no colonial tradition of elected local government.

Several decades of conflict delayed the decentralisation reforms that occurred in the rest of Africa, but even in these countries there was a move toward the creation of democratic local government, such as the introduction of elected local government structures in Mozambique in the 1990s.

By 2000, it could be claimed that there was not a single country in Africa in which some form of local government was not in operation (Oyugi, 2000). The implementation of decentralisation in Africa has, however, been very uneven and partial. For example, UN-Habitat (2008a) notes of East Africa that "Most of the region's central governments and local authorities claim to embrace good governance, public participation and public–private partnerships. Nevertheless, true decentralisation of powers and resources to the local authorities and participatory urban decision-making is not yet put into effect" (UN-Habitat, 2008a, p. 15). The reasons for the actual decentralisation often lagging behind the related laws and policies include "intergovernmental politics, bureaucratic politics and insufficient capacities in local governments" (Andrews & Schroeder, 2003, p. 31). In some cases, the aim of decentralisation reforms was merely to "reinforce vested interests in existing patterns of patronage and central-local linkage," thus having no impact on furthering a pro-poor development agenda (Crook, 2003, p. 78). At other times, the motivations behind decentralisation were driven by self-interests, such as to shift the responsibility for unpopular structural adjustment programmes from central government to urban local governments that were in many cases controlled by opposition parties (Shah & Thompson, 2004).

Nigeria's case is a good example of a stalled attempt at decentralisation, and the impact of this on addressing urban development challenges:

> Urban governance in Nigeria cannot be fully understood without reference to the three principal levels of power: the local, the state and the federal government. Each of these levels intervenes more or less directly in urban management. Local governments, although saddled with urban governance responsibilities, have never had much autonomy. Reforms have been initiated but the states maintain their holds on local authorities. Local government ability to generate revenue has collapsed, increasing their dependence and reducing their capacities to face the challenges of run-away urbanisation, while lack of co-ordination increases the difficulties of urban management. (UN-Habitat, 2008a, p. 13)

## Shifts in the Role of Government

Simultaneously with increased decentralisation in recent decades, there has been a shift in the way local governments operate. As Ouedraogo (2003) notes, in the "Anglo-Saxon" tradition, decentralisation also includes the devolution of powers and resources to local non-state bodies, such as private companies and non-governmental organisations. In much of Africa, therefore, decentralisation has been accompanied by a strong shift towards corporatisation/privatisation and partnerships. This has been linked to a

## 56 Edgar Pieterse and Warren Smit

global shift to privatisation, corporatisation and public–private partnerships in local government (often under the guise of implementing New Public Management principles). The implementation of Structural Adjustment Programmes in many countries helped introduce these shifts. In Nigeria, for example, since the 1990s, public services that were previously administered by local governments (such as health centres, primary and secondary schools, water supply, road repairs, the management of public facilities and parks) have to a large extent been privatised (UN-Habitat, 2008a). In addition, in many countries in Africa, most urban development and redevelopment projects are now structured as public–private partnerships.

Even in countries that were not subjected to Structural Adjustment Programmes, such as South Africa, global pressures and trends have resulted in similar changes. For example, the City of Johannesburg has been active in restructuring itself and corporatising and privatising service delivery. It now has a large number of 'utilities, agencies and corporatised entities' (UACs), including Johannesburg City Parks, the Johannesburg Property Company, the Johannesburg Tourism Company and Johannesburg Water. There are, however, a number of potential concerns arising out of the corporatisation and privatisation of basic services, most notably the reduction in potential for cross-subsidisation of service charges so as to ensure greater access of the poor to affordable services.

*Table 3.7*    The Public-Private Sector Model of Urban Management

| Actors | Responsilibilities |
|---|---|
| Central government | • Political and administrative control of local governments<br>• Limited provision of grants and loans<br>• More emphasis on coordination |
| Local governments | • Formally more decentralised<br>• Provision and maintenance of basic services<br>• Development control; preparation of coordination plans<br>• Limited direct provision of services |
| Private sector | • Delivery of services: water, sanitation, electricity<br>• Delivery of health and higher education<br>• Urban renewal and housing projects<br>• Public transport<br>• Telecommunications |
| Non-governmental Sector | • Increased local-level interventions (food for work, upgrading)<br>• Social services provision<br>• Focus on poverty, informal activities and access to credit<br>• Rehabilitation and refugees<br>• Defence of land tenure and civic rights |

*Source:* Wekwete, K. H. (1997). Urban management: The recent experience. In C. Rakodi (Ed.), *The urban challenge in Africa: Growth and management of its large cities.* Tokyo: United Nations University Press.

Table 3.7 shows the key characteristics of the "public–private" model of urban management that became prevalent in Africa in the 1990s, and which is defined as an ideal policy approach by the World Bank, as discussed in the third section of this chapter.

## Urban Local Government in Africa: The Current Situation

The status, powers and functions of local government vary considerably across Africa. The nature of local government bodies can range from democratically-elected local governments, with a range of income sources and responsibility for delivering diverse services, to appointed local governments that depend on national government for revenue and which have only limited responsibilities.

Somalia, for example, represents a continuum of the different types of local government found in Africa (UN-Habitat, 2008a):

- In South and Central Somalia, there are no local government bodies (although in some places there are civil society initiatives that attempt to fill the gap).
- In Puntland, there are weak appointed local government bodies.
- In Somaliland, there are democratically elected and functional local government bodies.

In some cases, there are different levels of government. An example is the two-tier metropolitan government in Abidjan, Côte d'Ivoire. This model is explained in Box 3.2.

---

### Box 3.2 Metropolitan Government in Abidjan

In 1980, the government of Côte d'Ivoire created a two-tier political and administrative structure for the metropolitan city of Abidjan. At the lowest level were 10 communes, with elected mayors and councils with the responsibility for functions such as the administration of markets, allocation of plots for public purposes, maintenance of clinics and primary schools, and the operation of social facilities. The major functions of the upper-tier government were waste disposal and management; sanitation, traffic regulation, road and park maintenance; and town planning. The mayor of the upper-tier metropolitan council was chosen by his communal colleagues. Major utilities such as water and electricity were managed by licensed private companies. In 2002 the City of Abidjan was replaced by the District of Abidjan with an appointed Governor (appointed by the President for a five-year term) and District Council (two-thirds of the 61 members are directly elected and one third are selected by the communes). In addition to the original 10 communes, the new District of Abidjan also included three sub-prefectures on the urban periphery. The distribution of functions between the district and the communes is the same as it was between the old 'City of Abidjan' and the communes. (UN-Habitat, 2008a, p. 229–230)

*Table 3.8* Functions of Urban Local Government Bodies in Selected African Countries

| Function | Nigeria (Local Govt. Authorities) | Cameroon (Local Governments) | Uganda (Urban Local Govt. Districts) | Tanzania (Urban Local Govts.) | Mozambique (Municipalities) | South Africa (Metropolitan Municipalities) |
|---|---|---|---|---|---|---|
| Water supply | - | - | ○ | ● | ○ | ● |
| Sanitation | ○ | ● | ● | ● | ○ | ● |
| Refuse collection/ disposal | ● | ● | ● | ● | ○ | ● |
| Urban roads | - | ● | - | ● | ○ | ● |
| Urban rail | - | ● | - | - | - | - |
| Electricity | - | - | - | ○ | - | ● |
| Housing | - | ● | - | ● | ○ | ○ |
| Urban planning | ○ | ● | ● | ● | ○ | ○ |
| Parks & open space | ● | ● | ● | ● | ○ | ● |
| Cemeteries & crematoria | ● | ● | ● | ● | ○ | ● |
| Museums & libraries | - | ● | ● | ● | - | ○ |
| Primary health care clinics | ● | ○ | ● | ● | - | ○ |
| Hospitals | - | ○ | ● | ○ | - | - |
| Pre-school education | ● | - | ● | - | - | - |
| Primary education | ○ | - | ● | ● | - | - |
| Secondary education | - | - | ● | ● | - | - |
| Fire protection | - | - | ● | ▣ | - | ● |
| Police | - | - | - | ○ | - | ○ |
| Economic promotion | - | ○ | - | ○ | ○ | ○ |
| Tourism promotion | - | ○ | ● | ○ | ○ | ○ |

● Sole responsibility for providing servic; ○ Responsibility for providing service is shared with other levels of government
*Source:* : Based on Commonwealth Local Government Forum (2008). *The Commonwealth Local Government*

Only in a few countries, such as in South Africa and Namibia, is the existence of local government enshrined in the constitution. In most cases, local government is created by central government and therefore receives its powers and responsibilities from the enabling statutes or decrees (Wekwete, 1997). The powers and functions of local government can thus vary considerably. Whereas all local government bodies have at least some responsibility for functions such as urban planning and refuse collection, only some local government bodies have responsibility for important functions such as water supply, roads and electricity (see Table 3.8). The responsibilities for core functions such as urban planning may sometimes be shared with other levels of government. For example, many countries rely heavily on centralised agencies to prepare urban and regional development plans (UN-Habitat, 2008a).

The widely varying powers of local governments in different countries are reflected in the proportion of total government expenditure that is spent by local government. For example, local government expenditure forms only 1.3 per cent of total government expenditure in Kenya, whereas it forms 16.9 per cent of total government expenditure in South Africa (UN-Habitat, 2009a).

One of the biggest problems for local governments in Africa is inadequate financial resources. Direct user charges (for example, charging for water provision) is a major source of revenue for local government bodies that provide services such as water and electricity. In addition to direct user charges, the main potential sources of local government revenue are: transfers from central government; property tax; loans; and public–private partnerships.

Table 3.9 compares revenue sources for three countries in Africa. As can be seen, the revenue sources available and the importance of various revenue sources vary considerably between countries.

Government transfers are still the most significant revenue source for local governments in most countries in Africa (e.g. central government transfers form more than 90 per cent of local government revenue in Uganda). This is, however, not ideal, as an over-reliance on transfers from central government can restrict the autonomy of local government.

*Table 3.9* Sources of Local Government Revenue in Selected African Countries

| Type of revenue | South Africa | Kenya | Uganda |
|---|---|---|---|
| Property tax (%) | 16.8% | 15.6% | 2.8% |
| Other taxes (%) | 2.8% | 5.9% | 2.1% |
| Grants (%) | 24.9% | 32.8% | 91.3% |
| Other forms of revenue (e.g. user charges) | 55.54% | 45.7% | 3.8% |
| Total | 100.0% | 100.0% | 100.0% |

*Source:* UN-HABITAT. (2009a). *Guide to municipal finance.* Nairobi: UN-HABITAT.

## 60 *Edgar Pieterse and Warren Smit*

Local property tax is potentially an important tool for raising revenue at the local level and enhancing the autonomy of local government. Property tax can also be used to shape urban development patterns. Property tax is historically associated with local government, partly because real property is immovable—that is, unable to shift location, and partly because of the strong connection between the types of services funded at the local level and the benefit to property values. Property taxes are levied by local governments in most countries in Africa, but generally, they do not provide a significant proportion of revenue. For example, property tax forms only between 15 per cent and 17 per cent of local government revenue in Kenya and South Africa, compared to, for instance, between 37 per cent and 39 per cent of local government revenue in Australia and Canada (UN-Habitat, 2009a).

## Reforms Required

The proportion of Africa's population in urban areas has grown from 23.6 per cent in 1970 to 39.1 per cent in 2008 (UN-Habitat, 2008a). However, many of the problems facing urban management and urban development in Africa are still essentially the same as when Stren (1972) described them almost 40 years ago. For example, UN-Habitat (2008a) notes that:

> The growth, proliferation and persistence of urban slums in East Africa are caused and sustained by: (a) Lack of urban land and planning policy; (b) unrealistic construction standards and regulations; (c) private sector housing mostly catering for high and middle-income groups; (d) lack of strategic positioning by governments and local authorities; (e) lack of public infrastructure; and (f) the politicising of informal settlements and social housing in party lines, current in election years and forgotten as soon as the ballot count is completed. (UN-Habitat, 2008a, p. 14)

Clearly, institutional problems are still an obstacle to addressing the urban development challenges of African cities, and further reforms are required to create enabling policy environments and to create and strengthen democratic local government that can effectively address urban development issues. This includes institutional reform to enhance the delivery of infrastructure as discussed in the third section above, but it also extends beyond that.

With regards to strengthening local government, as UN-Habitat (2008a) suggests, "Deep reforms are still required to ensure: (a) Local autonomy from central government; (b) institutionalisation of real citizen participation; (c) capacity building among councillors and chief officers; and (d) direct election of Mayors by residents to make the function less vulnerable to political manipulation" (UN-Habitat, 2008a, p. 15). In addition, in order to address urban challenges, local governments need to have sufficient financial resources from a range of sources. Local property taxation can be particularly important. In addition to potentially providing access to a reliable source of revenue, it

## Institutions, Decentralisation and Urban Development 61

can help ensure greater autonomy from central government. It can also be a development tool in terms of guiding urban development.

## INSTITUTIONAL REFORM AGENDA FOR AFRICA

In the aftermath of the global financial crisis (of 2008–2009), the rising awareness of the devastating impacts of climate variability and a renewed commitment to systematically eradicate poverty through the Millennium Development Goals, the importance of sustainable urban development has received significant attention across the world. The emerging development consensus on the centrality of sustainable urban development is good news for Africa because it offers an opportunity to address the institutional failures discussed above in a fundamental way.

The first part of this section will therefore spell out the key tenets of a comprehensive approach to sustainable urban development. This agenda must inform the institutional architecture at national and local levels in order to address the prevailing crisis in Africa's cities and towns. Through this discussion, it will become clear that each African country requires an explicit national urban strategy to focus and direct the efforts of a wide ranging number of actors that have a role to play in the urban development agenda. Central to such national policy frameworks is clarity on the appropriate division of powers and functions across the various levels of government, underpinned by an enabling fiscal framework. These elements in turn assume that urban development planning is based on a rigorous and accurate understanding of key trends. In other words, the data platforms in each country and city must allow for well informed and targeted actions, which in turn can be monitored and evaluated to ensure policy implementation and effectiveness.

These various national policy frameworks and local data platforms will then inform a unique infrastructure investment strategy for each city and town in all African countries. City-level infrastructure investment strategies will go nowhere unless they are supported and enhanced by a nationally driven and funded decentralisation strategy and programme. The final aspect of the institutional reform agenda is the question of monitoring and evaluation embedded in a broader consultative process. We will now explore each of these elements of the reform agenda in turn.

## Macro Urban Development Framework

African governments are forced to confront the challenge of sustainable urban development at a very interesting historical and global moment. It is a time in which there is widespread recognition that the resource extractive model of economic development is no longer viable. It will induce a measure of climate variability and instability to the point that it will permanently disrupt societies and infrastructures (Hodson & Marvin, 2009; UN-Habitat,

2010). This heightened degree of risk is forcing a global engagement to redefine the terms of economic development by trying to identify practical measures to internalise the environmental (and possibly social) costs of production and exchange. Unfortunately, the Copenhagen Summit of December 2009 failed to produce a clear outcome, but it does not detract from the fact that the global economy, trading system and national development project will have to be fundamentally re-designed to avoid a human–environmental catastrophe in the not-too-distant future. What is interesting about the climate change debate is that cities have been defined as centre-pieces to any long-term structural response because, while they account for the bulk of greenhouse gas emissions, such as carbon dioxide ($CO_2$), they also hold the most promise to achieve efficiencies in terms of spatial and agglomeration dynamics to create more sustainable ways of habitation and economic reproduction (Local Governments for Sustainability [ICLEI], 2010).

The environmental crisis coincides with a profound social and economic crisis. The latter came into sharp relief with the 2008–2009 global debt crisis, which precipitated a recession in most OECD economies and their trading partners in the global South. This crisis reflected the growing disconnect between economic value and material production. With the growing financialisation of national and global economies, many people of working age are left to fend for themselves in informal (and/or black) economic activities, or fall by the wayside (Borja & Castells, 1997). This is manifested in growing levels of income inequality in almost all regions and countries of the world, manifested most acutely in the growing urban divides (UN-Habitat, 2010).

In the wake of the destruction of wealth, impoverishment of hundreds of millions of people, and the bail-out of the banks with public money, it is clear that mainstream economic activity and measurements need to be redefined. Again, cities and urban centres have emerged as key sites of economic development because the dynamics of globalisation reinforce agglomeration (of firms and workers). Innovation, competitiveness and productivity depend on the milieu advantages that dense settlements offer (World Bank, 2009).

Lastly, with the realisation that globalisation dynamics have been accompanied by rising levels of poverty and inequality (if China is taken out of the equation), the global community of states committed to significantly reduce physical poverty by improving access to basic services and political voice as expressed in the Millennium Development Goals (MDGs) for 2015 (Annan, 3 April 2000). Again, in the context of rising urban poverty, cities are seen as key to making significant progress in attaining the MDGs, without neglecting the profound challenges associated with rural poverty.

This unique global moment has forced a sharpening of our understanding of what it will take to advance and eventually achieve sustainable urban development. Figure 3.1 illustrates the four primary dimensions of sustainable urban development. Domain one denotes the imperative of achieving sustainable urban infrastructure transformations. A key sub-element is the raft of bio-physical network infrastructure systems, such as energy, waste, water,

## Institutions, Decentralisation and Urban Development 63

sanitation, transport, roads and ecological services. Another sub-element is social infrastructure sectors, such as education, health and culture.

Domain two denotes inclusive economies. It is now well established that formal economic metrics are inadequate in capturing the diversity and dynamics of real urban economies. Thus, in addition to conventional formal economic sectors, one has to identify the social economy (Amin, 2009), so-called green jobs (United Nations Environment Programme [UNEP], 2008) and livelihood practices that sustain poor households without access to formal income, social security or government transfers (Moser, 2008). These new economic dimensions need to be considered in addition to the conventional economic sectors and the imperatives to recast these in a low-carbon context (Kamal-Chaoui & Robert, 2009).

In the aftermath of the global economic crisis of recent times, the centrality of urban infrastructure to economic performance has come to the fore. In fact, economic revitalisation was pursued through infrastructure-based investments, especially in the U.S. and South Asia, as poor and fragmented infrastructure networks undermine economic performance (Foster & Briceño-Garmendia, 2010). Domain three indicates efficient spatial form as a key driver of urban development patterns and outcomes. In the wake of the sustainability critique and the worsening of urban inequalities, there is a growing consensus that the spatial forms of cities and towns matter a great deal for the realisation of more sustainable urban development outcomes. Specifically, greater density through compaction is encouraged

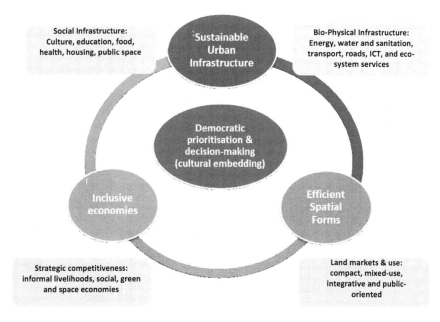

*Figure 3.1* Dimensions of sustainable urban development.

## 64    Edgar Pieterse and Warren Smit

along with a much stronger emphasis on mixed-use land uses to facilitate greater efficiency and pluralism. A public-oriented approach is encouraged in the recalibration of land-uses, which informs a broader agenda to foster greater cultural and social integration (UN-Habitat, 2009b).

At the core of this framework is the democratic work of decision-making over key resources. Public investments are invariably rooted in public decision-making processes. With the spread of democratic local government over the past two decades in particular, there has been an ongoing process of policy and institutional refinement to expand the domain of public influence over decision-making processes well beyond the exercise of one's franchise with every election. It is now taken for granted that urban planning and management should be designed with substantive and ongoing participation in mind for very practical reasons, apart from the normative imperative of political legitimacy. Practically, in a context of limited resources and limited state capacity, it is imperative that local governments work closely with civil society organisations and the private sector to co-produce development strategies and ensure participation in various elements of the service delivery value chain. It is for this reason that decentralised institutional frameworks are so central to how we redefine and activate urban development processes at the local level.

### Tailored National Urban Development Strategy

Very few African states have explicit policies to deal with urbanisation and intra-urban development challenges. According to Parnell and Simon (2010), this stems in part from policy neglect, rooted in a perverse sense of anti-urban bias and confusion about the difference between urbanisation and urban policies. The former refers to explicit government policies that seek to define, understand and shape the national spatial system, including the network of cities, towns and rural settlements. Typically, this understanding informs decisions about where investments should be concentrated in the national territory. National spatial frameworks also inform how migration dynamics are understood and managed. In contrast, urban policies reflect how national governments understand the role of specific cities and towns in the successful execution of national development goals. Typically, urban policies will define what needs to happen with specific cities and towns with regard to various sectorial and higher order development objectives, pertaining to mobility, sustainable settlements, education, connectivity, health and so on. Put differently, urban policies provide perspective on critical issues that need to happen within cities and support the efforts of sub-national levels of government to elaborate more detailed policies and strategies for those places. Urban policies are informative and complementary to more detailed local level development policy processes.

Urban policies are particularly important with regard to the definition and implementation of infrastructure programmes. Depending on the economic

*Institutions, Decentralisation and Urban Development* 65

and ecological function of a particular urban settlement, its relevance for specific aspects of a national logistics system or water management approach will vary. When these urban policies are not in place, most development investments are made in a space-blind fashion, which is highly inefficient and potentially unproductive from a national and regional perspective. It is therefore appropriate to rehash to some extent the insights of Parnell and Simon on the importance of a distinct national urban development policy:

> Today, national urban policy must not only define service nodes and economic corridors, but also facilitate the creation of polycentric city regions that are located in the regional and global economies, and which may themselves transcend national boundaries. With ecological and economic footprints that inevitably exceed even large metropolitan boundaries, and as the sites of critical infrastructural and intellectual investment, these city regions have to assume far greater national and regional policy prominence. Implied in this agenda is a clear understanding of the formal and informal urban space economies that drive African economies. National urban policies should do more than attend to the national urban or settlement system, giving due weight to natural resource constraints and ecological vulnerabilities of cities and towns, especially along the coast. The increasing importance of the urban relative to the rural, and the economic dominance of cities, means that it is imperative that all national policies should work in the urban context, and this entails much more than national spatial planning. (Parnell & Simon, 2010, p. 37)

With this injunction in mind, set against the macro-framework for sustainable urban development as elaborated, we now explore some of the practical steps that are required to institutionalise an effective policy agenda to deal with the complexities of uneven urban development in Africa.

## Sound Data Platforms

Assuming that governments accept that they need to radically adjust their approach and attitude to urban development imperatives, the essential first step is to improve the quality of data, information and analysis about the urban system and particular settlements that play a major role in the national economy. A number of considerations become relevant. Most basic is the need for accurate and reliable data in the form of a periodic national census. A lot of progress has been made with regard to the execution of national censuses in Africa. Onsembe and Ntozi (2006) report that 36 out of 51 countries in Sub-Saharan Africa participated in the 2000 census round, which started in 1995. The 15 that did not participate were Angola, Burundi, Cameroon, Chad, Democratic Republic of Congo, Djibouti, Eritrea, Ethiopia, Liberia, Madagascar, Nigeria, Sierra Leone, Somalia, Sudan and Togo. They observe: "It can be noted that two-thirds of the countries were engaged in conflicts, hence they were not stable enough to plan and execute a census programme" (Onsembe & Ntozi, 2006, p. 13). Apart from undertaking regular censuses that are credible, it is particularly important to ensure that these instruments are premised on enumerator areas that will allow decision makers and citizens to extrapolate meaningfully at the urban scale. Often, surveys that complement the census, such as labour force surveys or firm competitiveness surveys, are not calibrated to allow one to extrapolate meaningfully for the urban areas and more importantly, sub-urban areas. It will be important for national statistical agencies to work closely with local government associations and urban development bodies to develop a shared approach to the collation of data.

A second dimension of the data agenda is local institutional data (Robinson, 2009). Most government departments, local authorities, regional agencies, parastatals, development agencies and large NGOs collect their own data on a range of urban development issues. It is vital to develop some overview understanding of what data exists, its robustness and how it can be related to other data sources. Acknowledging these other repositories of information can also be an effective means of building an inter-governmental and inter-agency awareness of national urban policy goals and strategies.

In recent years, various grassroots organisations, such as members of Slum Dwellers International and Streetnet, have adopted a number of enumeration processes to underpin their claims and strategies. This source of grassroots intelligence and information, typically from neighbourhoods and contexts that the state finds difficult to access, is a vital component of an overall urban data system. It also offers promising opportunities for government officers to better understand (from a different angle) the contexts they are seeking to impact on. Discrepancies between community data sets and official statistics provide an excellent entry point to come to agreements on what the actual local context may be.

Recent advances in geo-spatial representations of various datasets can potentially provide the glue to cohere and relate the various categories of data implied in these data collection instruments. Moreover, geographic information systems (GIS) representations can support administrative decision-making processes to improve prioritising and targeting, and possibly to help to facilitate public engagement with data.

Finally, it is important to recognise and engage with the significant movement to standardise relevant indicators to deal with sustainable urban development. In this regard, the Global Urban Observatory capacity within UN-Habitat and the recently formed Global City Indicators Facility can be useful in providing a framework to facilitate consistent and globally comparative collections of city indicators.[2] In tandem with this trend, many municipalities, with the support of local government associations, are embarking on processes to establish local urban observatories. It is vital that these initiatives are integrated into national urban policy frameworks.

## Infrastructure Investment Strategy and Plan

In the wake of the post-Washington consensus that now dominates development thinking in most development agencies, the central role of the state in development is again recognised. This revalidation coincides with a so-called "infrastructural turn" in policy debates and the broader academic literature. Informed by the experiences of the successful South-East Asian economies, the central role of infrastructure for economic, social and environmental development has taken centre stage during the past few years (Lee, 2007: p. 8–9; World Bank, 2004, 2009). It is also noteworthy that the stimulus packages introduced in many parts of the world (for example, the United States) after the economic crisis of 2009 included large infrastructure investments. These investments aimed to kick-start economies, create a new generation of "green" jobs and form the foundation for a much bigger transition to low-carbon economies. It is further important to note that China, India, Brazil and South Africa are all heavily reliant on national infrastructure programmes to enhance inclusive growth and prepare for ongoing demographic and economic pressures.

It is therefore not surprising that infrastructure is at the heart of urban development policy and strategy at all levels: local, national, regional and to some extent global, in as far as connectivity infrastructures facilitate more efficient interaction with global markets and long-distance value chains. The literature typically distinguishes between infrastructure for meeting basic services of households and connectivity infrastructure to enhance the productivity and competitiveness of economic activity. What is often not highlighted is infrastructure to secure a more resilient and renewable environment, even though this is increasingly coming onto the agenda under the rubric of climate change mitigation and adaptation (ICLEI, 2010).

There is usually an unsatisfactory balance between these categories of infrastructure development. This means that the overall sustainable development effort is constantly undermined. Furthermore, particularly in low-income countries across Africa, there is a real dilemma in that most potential beneficiaries of basic services cannot afford to pay for these services because they simply do not have the requisite income or securities. In such circumstances, governments tend to prioritise infrastructure investments for people and businesses able to pay for the services, in order to ensure financial sustainability.

The financial pressures that accompany infrastructure investment and roll-out in poor countries are compounded by almost three decades of damaging neoliberal urban policies that have sought to reduce the role of the state by focusing only on those "customers" who can pay full-cost for services, and applying market principles to the provision and maintenance of infrastructures (Stren & Eyoh, 2007). The consequences of this have been a heightened manifestation of splintering trends in cities everywhere subjected to neoliberal urban management processes. One of the key authors of

# 68   *Edgar Pieterse and Warren Smit*

this perspective on splintering urbanism, Stephen Graham (2000), explains the dynamic:

> Standardised public and private infrastructure monopolies are receding as hegemonic forms of infrastructure management. We are starting to witness the uneven overlaying and retrofitting of new, high performance urban infrastructures onto the apparently immanent, universal and (usually) public monopoly network laid down between the 1930s and 1960s. In a parallel process, the diverse political and regulatory regimes that supported the 'roll-out' of power, transport, communications and water networks towards the rhetorical goal of standardised ubiquity are, in many cities and states, being 'unbundled' or even 'splintered,' as a result of widespread movements towards privatisation and liberalisation [ . . . ] What this amounts to [ . . . ] is the uneven emergence of an array of what I call 'premium network spaces': new or retrofitted transport, telecommunications, power and water infrastructures that are customised precisely to the needs of the powerful users and spaces, whilst bypassing less powerful users and spaces. (Graham, 2000, p. 185)

These trends are observed in OECD countries and the newly industrialised countries of Asia and Latin America, where there is a considerable history of universal coverage or attempts to do so (Graham & Marvin, 2001). However, in most African countries, especially the low-income ones, there has never been extensive coverage in place, yet the same dynamics have come to shape the urban landscape during the past decade or so, reinforcing the marginalisation of slums and the centrality of wealthy neighbourhoods and prime business spaces.

It is against these trends that African governments need to figure out how they can best address the profound infrastructural deficit in both urban and rural areas, as well as prepare for future growth and demand. This exercise needs to be undertaken with a sober understanding of how economic development, basic services and ecological protection development goals can be integrated, balanced and negotiated. Tough trade-offs will be inevitable, sequenced over various temporal periods. The World Bank's authoritative *Africa Infrastructure Report* (Foster & Briceño-Garmendia, 2010) suggests that it is possible to both deal with poverty associated with basic service deficiencies and improve economic productivity:

> Basic services for households in both urban and rural areas can guarantee sustainable urbanisation and social equity, enhance living conditions, and prevent disproportionate flows of underserved rural people to the city. Investment in infrastructure can improve productivity in the modern sector and connectivity with and across locations. Deficiencies in infrastructure and services, which limit the potential for agglomeration economies, hinder African economies and may explain

*Institutions, Decentralisation and Urban Development* 69

the underperformance of businesses in Africa relative to other continents. (Foster & Briceño-Garmendia, 2010, p. 128)

If the balancing act between basic services and economic infrastructure is not complex and challenging enough, it is now irrefutable that African governments and cities will have to equally factor in how best to adapt to and mitigate climate change impacts. These considerations hinge on managing infrastructural transitions well. For example, smart and strategic infrastructure planning and investment should facilitate:

- greater transport energy efficiency due to reduced distances and greater shares of green transport modes;
- greater heating/cooling energy efficiency in buildings due to lower surface-to-volume ratios of more compact building typologies and urban vegetation;
- more efficient use of grid-based energy systems such as combined heat and power;
- lower embedded energy demand for urban infrastructure due to greater utilisation; and
- greater energy efficiency in operating a range of utilities (LSE Cities, 2010).

On a more practical note, this discussion illustrates that it is simply not possible for African governments to leave infrastructure planning and management in the hands of sectorial interests that benefit from the status quo. A strategic national policy framework on infrastructure is required. Such a framework must spell out how national, urban and rural infrastructural deficits will be assessed, defined, analysed and addressed through short, medium and long-term programmes. Such a framework will have to specify how best to aggregate particular infrastructure sectors into bundles that can enhance the economic potential of certain territories, while forming part of a national and regional whole. Furthermore, such a framework will have to address the institutional modalities of infrastructure provision, maintenance and financing. Traditional privatisation models tended to reinforce a sectoral approach and produce extremely negative social and environmental consequences. In contexts where state capacity is under strain, investment capital is limited and the capacity of citizens to pay for the services restricted, hybrid institutional modalities will have to be developed.[3]

An interesting example in the water and sanitation sector is the Water and Sanitation Urban Programme (WSUP). The mission of WSUP is "is to support local service providers to design and implement water and sanitation solutions that are economically, socially and environmentally sustainable, and which serve the needs of the urban poor in developing countries" (WSUP, 2008). WSUP defines its primary role as that of a broker. It has positioned itself to bring together all the local actors involved in water and

70   *Edgar Pieterse and Warren Smit*

sanitation provision in poor neighbourhoods with the aim of connecting these players with relevant (national) utilities, municipalities, regulators and where possible, relevant national departments. In addition, it brings international water utilities, environmental agencies and international NGOs, such as Water Aid and Care, into the frame as well. Through these partnerships, it seeks to help build the capacity of the local community to undertake detailed water and sanitation planning for their area on a basis that is economically viable, embedded in local practices, but also efficient in order to bring down the costs that poor people normally pay to informal vendors (WSUP, 2008). This model does not necessarily eliminate informal vendors. It brings them into a larger system so that everyone can operate more efficiently. In Africa, WSUP has promising experiments going on in Maputo, Antananarivo, and Kibera in Nairobi.

The WSUP example reflects an attempt to bring the informal delivery systems (which are often very expensive and haphazard) together with actors and elements of the larger water and sanitation system to figure out pragmatic pathways to connect the *status quo* in informal settlements to elements of a bigger, more coherent and efficient system. However, the programme has already been caught up in the problems associated with weak decentralisation systems, which create enormous fragmentation and inefficiency in the division of resources, capacities and energies between different levels of government and their various agencies and utilities. A national infrastructure policy framework must inform and draw on a national decentralisation policy and operational programme.

## Decentralisation Policy and Operational Strategy

In the third section, we intimated that one of the key institutional problems associated with decentralisation efforts in Africa was the problematic division of powers and functions between different levels of government. As demonstrated in the fourth section, in most African countries, the problem is that not enough powers have been assigned to sub-national and, especially, local levels of government. In cases where administrative decentralisation has been instituted, it is often without concomitant powers to raise local revenues to execute the function or inadequate inter-governmental transfers to enable local authorities to fulfil their mandate. This problem is widespread and systemic. However, in a country like South Africa, which has a highly developed democratic decentralised system embedded in the Constitution, a range of other problems crop up. In South Africa, most of the key urban development functions like water, transport, housing, electricity, roads, health and education are awkwardly distributed across three levels of government. For example, in the case of housing, the national government allocates funding for public housing programmes, which are disbursed to municipalities via provinces once provincial governments have approved the municipal housing plans. This division of the function has

## Institutions, Decentralisation and Urban Development 71

created a range of complicated intergovernmental conflicts and very poor outcomes, not least the production of poorly built stock and an exacerbation of urban sprawl (Charlton & Kihato, 2006 p. 254; Pieterse & van Donk, 2008, p.53–60).[4]

The dimensions of sustainable urban development, along with the imperatives of a strategic approach to infrastructure investment and extension, should inform the particular national approach to the division of powers and functions across levels of government. There is no single recipe or formula that can be applied to all African contexts. What is required is a strategic understanding of how limited resources can best be deployed to advance the national development project in the context of specific urban and rural settlements, correlated with (local) state capacity and the institutional modalities of service provision. For example, the national urban policy framework should present a clear description and analysis of the national space economy. This should include where formal and informal economic sectors (and clusters and value chains) are located in space in relation to demographic and resource flow patterns, and the implications of this for various categories of settlement as well as specific urban centres where the national economy is anchored. Such an understanding will provide an indication of how the infrastructure deficits can best be tackled, building on local capacity and responding to key nodes with potential to advance the overall development prospect of the country and its broader region. It would be foolish to undertake this kind of analysis and planning in the absence of sound data or without the active participation of local actors (mayors, local authorities, business interests and civil society organisations). A sensible approach to the division of powers and functions across different levels of government and across diverse institutional forms (e.g. national or local utilities) cannot be achieved without an understanding of what the unique developmental roles are of various local settlements.

The second step in developing a decentralisation policy framework is to define the institutional modalities and configuration of the overall system to give expression to the objectives of the national urban policy and associated infrastructure investment strategy. Given the historical context of institutional reform and the persistent political economy of national control, it is important to be realistic about phasing in decentralisation reforms and creating incentives for all vested interests to maintain the momentum over time.

One of the errors that must be avoided is to create a uniform system of assigning powers and functions to lower levels of government. It is important to differentiate between different categories of local government in relation to their capacity, revenue-raising potential, population size and density.

Table 3.10 illustrates the division of functions between local and provincial government in South Africa in relation to five higher-order development imperatives. What this table does not capture is the fact that metropolitan governments and secondary cities in South Africa can cope with this loading of functions because their local tax bases are large enough, but most

*Table 3.10*  Division of Functions between Local and Provincial Government in South Africa

| Functions | | Allocation of functions in Constitution | |
|---|---|---|---|
| **Primary grouping of functions** | **Secondary grouping of functions** | **Local government** | **Provincial government** |
| Built environment functions benefiting citizens | Planning | Municipal planning | Prov & regional planning |
| | Land for human settlements | | Property transfer fees |
| | Water services | Sanitation; Water (potable) | |
| | Roads | Pontoons and ferries; Municipal roads; Storm water; Street lighting | Prov roads and traffic |
| | Public transport | Municipal public transport; Municipal airports | Public transport; Airports not national |
| | Housing | | Housing |
| | Electricity | Electricity reticulation | |
| | Solid waste | Refuse removal, refuse dumps and solid waste disposal; Cleansing | |
| | Public places | Public places; Municipal parks and recreation; Beaches and amusement facilities, etc. | |
| | Community facilities | Cemeteries, funeral parlours and crematoria; Local amenities; Local sport facilities | |
| Human development | Health | Municipal health services | Health services |
| | Education | | Education |
| | Security services | Traffic and parking; Control of public nuisance | Police (provincial); Road traffic regulation; Vehicle licensing |
| | Emergency services | Fire fighting | Ambulances; Disaster management |
| | Social development | Child care facilities | Welfare services; Population development |
| | Sports, recreation, arts and culture | Recreation included with municipal parks | Libraries, archives and museums, not national; Provincial cultural matters; Provincial recreation; Provincial sport |

| | | | |
|---|---|---|---|
| Built environment functions associated with business development and livelihoods | Land for production | As for land for human settlements | |
| | Access (roads and transport) | As for roads above | |
| | Water supply and electricity | As for water supply and electricity above | |
| | Waste and wastewater | As for sanitation and solid waste above | |
| Other functions related to business development and livelihoods, not associated with built environment | Agriculture | Fences and fencing | Agriculture |
| | Particular business activities: abattoirs and markets | Municipal abattoirs; Markets | Abattoirs |
| | Business promotion (promotion of livelihoods) | Local tourism | Tourism; Industrial promotion; Trade |
| | Regulation of businesses other than environmental | Control of advertising in public places; Trading regulations; Control of liquor undertakings; Food licences | Liquor licenses |
| | Environmental protection (pollution control) | Air pollution; Noise pollution | Pollution control; Soil conservation |
| | Ecosystems and bio-diversity | Municipal parks included under public places | Nature conservation; Environment; Indigenous forests |

*Source:* Palmer Development Group. (2005). Current distribution of powers and functions and impact of devolution to local government sphere with strategy for management of this process. *Unpublished paper.* Cape Town: PDG.

district and rural local governments cannot. Different dispensations should be designed for them. This issue has been recognised as a major policy problem since 2006, but the government has been singularly incapable of addressing it systematically (Pieterse & van Donk, 2008).

The point is that a national decentralisation policy framework needs to clarify government's thinking and intent with regard to addressing basic needs, economic development, citizen empowerment and environmental protection through a sensible division of powers and functions across different levels of government.

This implies a clear policy argument that addresses balances and trade-offs between these different categories of development based on available resources, potential development paths and opportunities for synergy between the government, private sector, civil society organisations and citizens. The Palmer Development Group (2005) proposes a useful conceptual framework in relation to the South African dilemma, but it is arguably informative for most African contexts (see Figure 3.2).

The point of note in this framework is not that it must be neatly applied across Africa, but rather how the discrete functions of the state need to be defined in relation to broad development imperatives, and how that, in turn, can inform a sensible approach to the allocation of local government powers and functions for different categories of settlement.

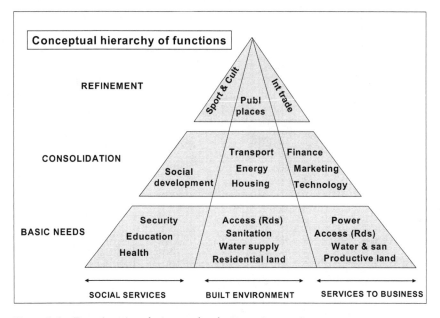

*Figure 3.2* Functions in relation to development imperatives.
*Source:* Palmer Development Group. (2005). Current distribution of powers and functions and impact of devolution to local government sphere with strategy for management of this process. *Unpublished paper.* Cape Town: PDG.

The third step in developing a decentralisation policy is an explicit focus on democratic enhancement tools that foster state responsiveness, legitimacy, accountability and enrolment of civil society and citizens in development programmes. The global experience and the relevant literature are now relatively mature on the range of policy instruments that is available to substantiate democratic decentralisation (Amis, 2009; Fung & Wright, 2001; Gaventa, 2006; Manor, 2004). It is not necessary to rehash all those policy options here, but it is relevant to tabulate the dimensions of democratic decentralisation:

- Local elections: In this regard it is important to decide on the form of elections, and how they will relate to the system of executive power. For example, will Mayors be directly elected or appointed, and so on. In many African countries there remains important foundational work to be done to make local elections transparent, fair and violence-free.
- Traditional authorities: A decision needs to be made about how best to incorporate various categories of traditional authorities that continue to exercise profound influence at the local level. Because these authorities are typically not elected, their interface with the democratic system needs clarity as well as recourse for citizens who nominate to live outside of the jurisdictional claims of these bodies. Most importantly, the role that traditional authorities play in regulating land use and occupancy needs deliberate attention so that it does not impede inclusive economic and social development.
- Citizen voice: It is vital that citizens and civil society organisations have a variety of means to engage with the policy development process, programme and project implementation, and to review or audit dimensions of sound urban management. There are a variety of tools available to facilitate and enhance the quality of citizen engagement with the research and framing dimensions of policy development (Fung & Wright, 2001; Goetz & Gaventa, 2001). In a context of limited resources, vast need and a variety of local compensatory strategies to deal with service deficiencies, it is essential that service delivery—especially in the domain of basic services and social development functions—be undertaken in a partnership framework. Lastly, citizen voice can also be enhanced through various monitoring and review techniques that allow citizens to offer an opinion about the quality and effectiveness of service delivery. The most potent forms of citizen voice and engagement with local development processes are through techniques that allow citizen engagement with the planning and budgeting processes, because this goes to the heart of resource prioritisation. The Municipal Development Programme in Harare, for example, has been building up a significant body of knowledge and experience in working with local authorities and communities across east and southern Africa to explore the potential of particularly participatory budgeting.[5]

## 76  Edgar Pieterse and Warren Smit

The fourth dimension of an effective decentralisation policy and programme is performance. State effectiveness depends on institutional clarity of purpose, effective leadership, capacity, resources, democratic pressure and continuous feedback signals to indicate whether goals are being met or not. This is a tall order in a context where many African state structures have grown out of perverse colonial administrations, followed by manipulations during the post-colonial era, such as erosion or removal of democratic systems, and thereafter denuded during the structural adjustment era of liberalisation and privatisation. These successive waves of institutional disruption and manipulation have left a difficult legacy that cries out for decisive leadership and accountability if state performance is to be improved.


## CONCLUSION

In this chapter we have provided a contextualised discussion of the institutional dimensions of decentralisation in Africa. The discussion started with a confrontation with the negative development trends associated with poorly managed urbanisation—slum growth associated with massive basic service deficiencies, underperforming economies, informalised livelihoods, rising urban inequality and serious environmental degradation, which make these settlements extremely vulnerable to heightened climate variability.

Against that backdrop, the third section explored the institutional underpinning of the urban development crisis in Africa. This provided a platform to review the experience of decentralisation across the continent over the past three decades or so. This is also a disheartening narrative. In most postcolonial contexts, there was a move towards significant decentralisation after colonialism, not least because of the ideological tenets of the some of the liberation parties at the time, but this was soon reversed and replaced with increasing centralisation of power and resources. This is a dynamic that remains by and large the dominant institutional tendency in most African countries, even though there has been widespread re-experimentation with decentralisation models since the 1980s.

The experiments with decentralisation during the height of structural adjustment programmes have not been particularly effective because they often promoted institutional approaches that excluded the majority of urban citizens in Africa. The uneven and problematic history of decentralisation and urban management has produced a very complicated knot of policy problems, which now requires radical and far-reaching reform.

In the fifth section, we put forward a conceptual framework for thinking about the primary dimensions of policy priorities for advancing sustainable urban development. Practically, it implies that national governments need to commit to developing a trio of policy reforms: (i) a national urban policy framework; (ii) a national infrastructure policy agenda; and (iii) a revitalised decentralisation policy framework and operational strategy. The

*Institutions, Decentralisation and Urban Development* 77

African Development Bank, in concert with other pan-African development agencies, can play a key role in supporting national governments and regional bodies to achieve these reforms.

Throughout the chapter, we have been at pains to underscore that for institutional reform to achieve sustainable urban development, it cannot proceed as a top-down endeavour. It must be rooted in genuine bottom-up interventions. There are two dimensions to this.

Firstly, local authorities and governments must be supported to put their agendas and interests into the mix. Moreover, civil society organisations—especially those that champion the interests of slum dwellers—must also be given meaningful opportunities to be part of these processes. When national governments and elites recognise that everyone's long-term interests lie in creating a dynamic institutional framework that allows for an appropriate division of powers and capacities across all dimensions of the governance system, then meaningful progress will be realised.

## NOTES

1. It is important to heed Satterthwaite's caution that urban projections that go too far into the future, e.g. 2030, must be treated with great circumspection because the underlying data sets for many developing countries remain extremely problematic (Satterthwaite, 2007).
2. For more information see: www.cityindicators.org.
3. The SURF-ARUP Infrastructure Framework provides an extremely useful diagnostic framework that all stakeholders in the development landscape can use to arrive at a precise understanding of the national and local infrastructure system, its deficits, and key decisions to be undertaken to move to a more sustainable and resilient footing (SURF-ARUP, 2010).
4. The public housing programme in South Africa entitles low-income households to a free public house. This programme is premised on a subsidy system. The programme exacerbates wasteful sprawl because the subsidy must cover the cost of land, services and the physical top-structure that is the house. In a context where land values are very high, the only place this category of housing can be provided is on the periphery of cities and towns where land is cheapest.
5. For more information, see www.mdpafrica.org.zw.

## REFERENCES

African Development Bank, OECD, UNDP, & ECA. (2012). *African economic outlook 2012*. Retrieved from http://www.africaneconomicoutlook.org (Accessed 19 October 2013)

Ajulu, C., & Motsamai, D. (2008). The Pan-African Infrastructure Development Fund (PAIDF): Towards an African agenda. *Global Insight, 76*. Johannesburg: Institute for Global Dialogue.

Amin, A. (Ed.). (2009). *The social economy*. London: Zed Books.

Amis, P. (2009). *Improving local government: The commonwealth vision*. Background discussion paper for the Commonwealth Local Government Conference, Freeport, Grand Bahama. Birmingham, UK: University of Birmingham.

## 78  Edgar Pieterse and Warren Smit

Andrews, M., & Schroeder, L. (2003). Sectoral decentralisation and intergovernmental arrangements in Africa. *Public Administration and Development, 23,* 29–40.

Annan, K. (2000, 3 April). *We the people.* Secretary General's Statement to the UN Assembly. New York: United Nations.

Borja, J., & Castells, M. (1997). *Local and global: The management of cities in the information age.* London: Earthscan.

Calderon, C. (2008). Infrastructure and growth in Africa. *AICD Working Paper 3, Africa Region.* Washington, DC: World Bank.

Charlton, S., & Kihato, C. (2006). Reaching the poor? An analysis of the influences on the evolution of South Africa's housing programme. In U. Pillay, R. Tomlinson, & J. Du Toit (Eds.), *Democracy and delivery: Urban policy in South Africa.* Cape Town: HSRC Press. 252–282.

Commonwealth Local Government Forum. (2008). *The commonwealth local government handbook 2009.* London: Commonwealth Local Government Forum.

Crook, R. C. (2003). Decentralisation and poverty reduction in Africa: The politics of local–central relations. *Public Administration and Development, 23,* 77–88.

Foster, V., & Briceño-Garmendia, C. (Eds.). (2010). *Africa's infrastructure—a time for transformation.* Washington, DC: World Bank and Agence Française de Développement.

Fung, A., & Wright, E. O. (2001). Deepening democracy: Innovations in empowered participatory governance. *Politics and Society, 29*(1), 5–41.

Gaventa, J. (2006). *Triumph, deficit or contestation? Deepening the 'deepening democracy' debate* (IDS Working Paper No. 264). Brighton, UK: Institute for Development Studies.

Goetz, A., & Gaventa, J. (2001). Bringing citizen voice and client focus into service delivery (IDS Working Paper No. 138). Brighton, UK: Institute for Development Studies.

Graham, S. (2000). Constructing premium network spaces: Reflections on infrastructure networks and contemporary urban development. *International Journal of Urban and Regional Research, 24*(1), 183–184.

Graham, S., & Marvin, S. (2001). *Splintering urbanism: Networked infrastructures, technological mobilities and the urban condition.* London and New York: Routledge.

Hodson, M., & Marvin, S. (2009). Urban ecological security: A new urban paradigm? *International Journal of Urban and Regional Research, 33*(1), 193–215.

ICLEI [Local Governments for Sustainability]. (2010). Cities in a post-2012 climate policy framework. *ICLEI Global Reports.* Bonn, Germany: ICLEI.

JICA [Japanese International Cooperation Agency]. (2008). *Decentralised service delivery in East Africa—A comparative study of Uganda, Tanzania and Kenya.* Tokyo: Research Group, Institute for International Cooperation, Japan International Cooperation Agency.

Kamal-Chaoui, L., & Robert, A. (Eds.). (2009). *Competitive cities and climate change.* Paris: OECD Publishing.

Kessides, C. (2006). *The urban transition in Sub-Saharan Africa: Implications for economic growth and poverty reduction.* Washington, DC: Cities Alliance.

Lee, K. N. (2007). An urbanising world. In L. Starke (Ed.), *State of the world 2007: Our urban future.* New York: W. W. Norton and Company. 3–21.

LSE Cities. (2010). *Green cities.* Summary Report for the UNEP Green Economy Report [Final Draft]. London: LSE Cities.

Mabogunje, A. (2007). Global urban poverty research agenda: The African case. *Urban Update no. 10.* Washington, DC: Woodrow Wilson International Centre for Scholars.

Manor, J. (2004). Democratisation with inclusion: Political reforms and people's empowerment at the grassroots. *Journal of Human Development, 5*(1), 5–29.

McKinsey Global Institute (2010). *Lions on the move: The progress and potential of African economies*. New York: McKinsey & Company.

Mo Ibrahim Index for African Governance. (2011). Retrieved from http://www.moibrahimfoundation.org/fr/interactives/ (Accessed 20 June 2013)

Moser, C. (2008). Assets and livelihoods: A framework for asset-based social policy. In C. Moser (Ed.), *Assets, livelihoods and social policy*. Washington, DC: World Bank, 43–81.

Onsembe, J. O., & Ntozi, J. P. M. (2006). The 2000 round of censuses in Africa: Achievements and challenges. *The African Statistical Journal, 3*, 11–28.

Organisation for Economic Co-operation and Development. (2008). *Cape Town, South Africa*. OECD Territorial Reviews. Paris: OECD.

Ouedraogo, H. M. G. (2003). Decentralization and local governance: Experiences from francophone West Africa. *Public Administration and Development, 23*(1) 97–103.

Oyugi, Walter O. (2000). Decentralisation for good governance and development. *Regional Development Dialogue, 21*(1), 3–22.

Palmer Development Group. (2005). *Current distribution of powers and functions and impact of devolution to local government sphere with strategy for management of this process* (Unpublished paper). Cape Town: PDG.

Parnell, S., Pieterse, E., & Watson, V. (2009). Planning for cities in the global south: An African research agenda for sustainable human settlements. *Progress in Planning, 72*(2), 233–241.

Parnell, S., & Simon, D. (2010). National urbanisation and urban policies: Necessary but absent policy instruments in Africa. In E. Pieterse (Ed.), *Urbanisation imperatives for Africa: Transcending policy inertia*. Cape Town: African Centre for Cities.

Pieterse, E. (2008). *City futures: Confronting the crisis of urban development*. London: Zed Books.

Pieterse, E. (2010). Filling the void: Towards an agenda for action on African urbanisation. In E. Pieterse (Ed.), *Urbanisation imperatives for Africa: Transcending policy inertia*. Cape Town: African Centre for Cities. Retrieved from www.africancentreforcities.net (Accessed 19 August 2013).

Pieterse, E., & van Donk, M. (2008). Developmental local government: Squaring the circle between policy intent and outcomes. Chapter 3 in M. van Donk, M. Swilling, E. Pieterse, & S. Parnell (Eds.), *Consolidating developmental local government: Lessons from the South African experiment*. Cape Town: University of Cape Town Press. 51–75.

President's Office, United Republic of Tanzania. (n.d.). *History of local government in Tanzania*. Dar es Salaam: United Republic of Tanzania. Retrieved from www.pmoralg.go.tz (Accessed 19 February 2013)

Rakodi, C. (1997). Conclusion. In C. Rakodi (Ed.), *The urban challenge in Africa: Growth and management of its large cities*. Tokyo: United Nations University Press.

Ravallion, M., Chen, S., & Sangraula, P. (2007). New evidence on the globalisation of poverty. *Policy Research Working Paper Series 4199*. Washington: World Bank.

Ribot, J. C. (2001). *Local actors, powers and accountability in African decentralisations: A review of issues*. Paper prepared for International Development Research Centre of Canada Assessment of Social Policy Reforms Initiative. Washington, DC: World Resources Institute.

Roberts, P., Ravetz, J., & George, C. (2009). *Environment and the city*. London: Routledge.

80  *Edgar Pieterse and Warren Smit*

Robinson, J. (2009). *State of cities reports: Briefing document* (Unpublished paper). Cape Town: African Centre for Cities, University of Cape Town.

Satterthwaite, D. (2007). The transition to a predominantly urban world and its underpinnings. *Human settlements discussion paper. Theme: Urban change no. 4.* London: International Institute for Environment and Development.

Scott, A. J. (2006). *Geography and economy.* Oxford: Clarendon Press.

Shah, A., & Thompson, T. (2004). Implementing decentralised local governance: A treacherous road with potholes, detours and road closures. *World Bank Policy Research Working Paper 3353.* Washington, DC: World Bank.

Stren, R. (1972). Urban policy in Africa: A political analysis. *African Studies Review 15*(3), 489–516.

Stren, R., & Eyoh, D. (2007). Decentralisation and urban development in West Africa: An Introduction. In D. Eyoh & R. Stren (Eds.), *Decentralisation and the politics of urban development in West Africa.* Washington, DC: Woodrow Wilson International Centre for Scholars. 1–20.

SURF-ARUP. (2010). *The SURF-ARUP framework for urban infrastructural development.* Manchester: University of Salford and ARUP.

Tannerfeldt, G., & Ljung, P. (2006). *More urban less poor: An introduction to urban development and management.* London: Earthscan.

Turok, I., & Parnell, S. (2009). Reshaping cities, rebuilding nations: The role of national urban policies. *Urban Forum 20*(2), 157–174.

UNEP [United Nations Environment Programme]. (2008). *Green jobs: Towards decent work in a sustainable, low-carbon world.* Nairobi: United Nations Office.

UNFPA [United Nations Population Fund]. (2007). *State of the world population 2007.* New York: United Nations Population Fund.

UN-Habitat (2008a). *The state of African cities 2008: A framework for addressing urban challenges in Africa.* Nairobi: UN-Habitat.

UN-Habitat (2008b). *State of the world's cities 2008/2009: Harmonious cities.* London: Earthscan.

UN-Habitat (2009a). *Guide to municipal finance.* Nairobi: UN-Habitat.

UN-Habitat (2009b). *Planning sustainable cities: Global report on human settlements 2009* (Abridged version). London: Earthscan.

UN-Habitat (2010). *State of the world's cities 2010/2011: Bridging the urban divide.* London: Earthscan.

UN-Habitat (2012). *State of the world's cities 2012/2013: Prosperity of cities.* London: Earthscan.

United Nations. (2010). *World population policies 2009.* New York: Department of Economic and Social Affairs.

United Nations, Department of Economic and Social Affairs. (2011). *Population division: World urbanization prospects, the 2011 revision.* New York: United Nations office.

Wekwete, K. H. (1997). Urban management: The recent experience. In C. Rakodi (Ed.), *The urban challenge in Africa: Growth and management of its large cities.* Tokyo: United Nations University Press.

World Bank. (2004). *World development report 2004: Making services work for poor people.* Oxford University Press.

World Bank. (2009). *World development report 2009: Reshaping economic geography.* Oxford University Press.

WSUP [Water and Sanitation Programme]. (2008). *Quarterly project report: March 2008.* London: WSUP. Retrieved from http://www.wsup.com/ (Accessed 20 February 2013)

# 4 Financing Urban Development in Africa

*Beacon Mbiba*

## INTRODUCTION: ORGANISATIONAL STRUCTURE AND PURPOSE

This chapter highlights the centre–local relations that influence the structure and content of urban development finance in Africa. It also identifies enduring challenges in the funding of urban development, and assesses the potential role of private sector participation and that of both multi-lateral agencies/donors and community organisations.

We draw attention to urban finance, as it relates to land development and the outcomes of decade-long reforms in the management of Africa's urban water and sanitation utilities. Furthermore, we note that financing urban development is intrinsically about strengthening local government, irrespective of whether the local government is a decentralised state department, elected local government or public corporation, or privatised utility. Centre–local relations and the statutory framework for local government operations in terms of asset ownership and disposal, operational and management independence, degree of freedom to borrow and political interference, are central to the organisational structure and limits to financing models possible in any given context.

This chapter first highlights the distinguishing features and nature of centre–local relations, and emphasises the prominence of diversity in practice. These differences are illustrated in subsequent sections with reference to land development finance and the water and sanitation sector. The second section presents a holistic view of the urban finance challenge. In particular, we posit that attention on cost-recovery in services such as water, sanitation, and electricity may not yield enough surpluses unless addressed in the context of broader local government reform and the development and management of land. Hence the perspective to utilise the management models presented is useful not only for a discussion of utilities such as water, but also for the development of land and housing.

The chapter assesses reforms of the past decade, especially in the urban water and sanitation sector, where commercialisation and use of performance management contracts has created 'institutional turn-around.' Crucially, there is an attempt to identify and emphasise linkages and lessons

## 82  Beacon Mbiba

across local authorities and international development organisations, including the leading work of UN-HABITAT in this sector. We lament the dearth of urban development finance information (UN-HABITAT, 2009; WSP, 2009) and call for collaborative efforts to improve access to this information for use by decision makers in the effective management of cities.

The material presented illustrates the importance of improving operational and management cultures in the short term. However, it underlines that the primary condition for improved urban development finance is inclusive and growing urban economies (UN-HABITAT, 2008a). There is also the need for practitioners and policymakers to better understand the linkages between urban development and urban economies (Tibaijuka, 2009).

## THE CHALLENGE OF URBAN FINANCE: CENTRE–LOCAL RELATIONS AND URBAN GOVERNANCE REGIMES

Mbiba and Ndubiwa (2009, pp. 88–90) reaffirm that national and urban political economy and statutory regimes impact directly on centre–local relations as well as the degree of freedom enjoyed by local authorities and utilities in the delivery of services and management of land. In particular, we posit that settler colonialism and urban apartheid in Southern Africa created the need for urgent reform towards more inclusive urban governance (UN-HABITAT, 2008a, 2010). But the challenge is equally urgent in Central, West and East Africa, where until recently, conflicts and collapsing economies created an African urban crisis (Stren & White, 1989) that spawned neo-liberal reforms from the 1980s. In addition, most national governments have weak electoral mandates in urban areas and among the youth, who form the majority in cities (UN-HABITAT, 2008a, p. 156).

The question of centre–local relations in the context of urban, municipal or local government finance is high on the Habitat Agenda. It is best appreciated by considering the delivery of public services (waste removal, water and sanitation, street lighting, road upgrading, electricity, ambulance services, etc.) (UN-HABITAT, 1997). Traditionally, central government departments or local governments delivered these services. This remains the case in many countries depending on the service considered. But there are huge changes taking place in some countries (see Box 4.1). For instance, in Zambia, 90 per cent of water and sanitation services are now provided by commercial utilities, seven per cent by local authorities, and one per cent by private schemes (National Water Supply and Sanitation Council [NWASCO], 2008).

As discussed later, the trend has been to transfer responsibilities to local authorities and commercialised entities. In contrast, in Namibia and the Republic of South Africa, municipalities make bulk purchases of water and electricity from public utilities for distribution to households, whereas in Angola, Botswana, Lesotho, Mozambique, Swaziland, Tanzania

## Financing Urban Development in Africa 83

and Zimbabwe, some of these services are provided directly to consumers by the relevant public authorities (state or local government). Some large municipalities also run their own police service independently from national forces, with variations in how criminal cases and traffic offences are handled. In the context of recent reforms, Suleiman and Cars (2010, pp. 273–274) describe how in Ghana, the Public Utilities Regulation Commission (PURC), formed in 1997, took over regulation of tariffs and quality control of services for electricity, water and sanitation. Water and sanitation services are provided by a range of institutions, including Ghana Water Company Limited, which is responsible for most urban settlements. The continental patterns for water provision are captured in Map 4.1 below.[1]

---

### Box 4.1 The Challenge of Finance in Post Crisis Zimbabwe

The challenge of urban development finance is illustrated in Zimbabwe, once an African leader in water and sanitation (with its well-managed cities and Blair toilets and bush pumps for rural and peri-urban areas). Now emerging from a decade-long political economic crisis, the country needs US$215 million per year for the next five years to rehabilitate its infrastructure and operations and bring them to pre-1999 levels. But only about US$45 million was available for 2010 (Government of Zambia [GoZ], 2010a). Consequently, a recent change of direction to give priority to infrastructure refurbishment, especially electricity generation and urban water, in the 2011 national budget, is a welcome development for economic recovery and improvement in welfare conditions (see GoZ, 2010b).

---

In Africa, the problem of urban, local government or municipal government finance has often been perceived as the gap between financial resources or revenues on the one hand, and expenditure needs on the other (UN-HABITAT, 2009, p. 3). This fiscal gap arises from lack of elasticity of municipal income. In other words, revenues do not grow in tandem with urban populations and economic needs. As in many regions of the world, most local authorities derive the bulk of their income from central government transfers or grants. Considered in the context of centre–local relations, central governments end up having disproportional influence on local governments. Thus, local governments become less responsive to local needs.

A related problem in centre–local relations is the question of jurisdictional conflicts and "unfunded mandates" (UN-HABITAT, 2008a, p. 158), whereby urban authorities perform functions on behalf of higher order governments (state, regional, provincial) and bear the costs of delivering these functions from their own revenue without receiving the commensurate compensation from the higher order governments. Often when the money is paid, it is late and inflation and time-related costs are not factored in. Third is that the bulk of the revenue to local authorities is taken up by personnel costs, leaving little for improvement of systems or capital investments.

Generally, salaries take up between 30 and 40 per cent of the expenditures of local authorities (UN-HABITAT, 2008a, p. 158). However, even for a well-managed city like Bulawayo, this figure rises to as much as 80 per cent when economies are in crisis (Figure 4.1)—a pattern repeated for Harare. As the component of personnel costs rises, the actual expenditures for capital developments declines (Figure 4.1), and has never been above 10 per cent for Zimbabwean cities since 2003.

A further problem has to do with allocation of responsibilities and co-ordination of policy actions among different state departments or ministries, especially in the water sector, where agriculture and land/natural resources (for dams and irrigation), energy and transport (for generation of electricity), local government and urban development (cities and governance) and health are examples of ministries with a stake in water management. Where countries aim to boost hydro-electric power, the energy sector will take the lead and issues concerning health may not be a priority. Until recently in Southern Africa, the development of water infrastructure and the allocation of water and tariffs structure gave priority to agriculture and water for irrigation, not urban water supply and

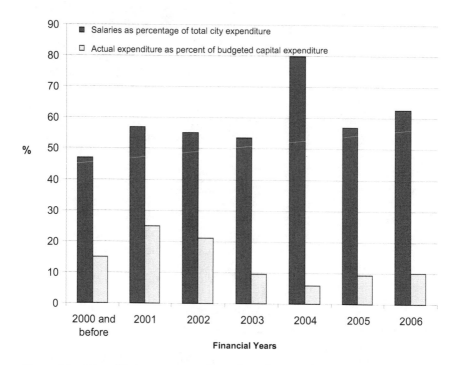

*Figure 4.1* City of Bulawayo expenditure for salaries and capital budgets.
*Source:* Audited Annual Accounts, Bulawayo City, Zimbabwe.
GoZ. (2010b). *Zimbabwe: The 2011 national budget—Shared economy, shared development, shared transformation—Creating the fair economy.* Harare: Zimbabwe Ministry of Finance.

*Financing Urban Development in Africa* 85

sanitation.[2] Similarly, in Burkina Faso, the state corporation that provides water and sanitation to urban areas, Office National de L'eau et de L'assainissement (ONEA), is regulated by the Ministry of Agriculture, Water Supply and Fishery Resources.

In Zimbabwe, it is only after the health crisis (2008–2009 cholera epidemic) in urban areas that the government returned water management responsibilities to cities and a broadening of stakeholders and efforts to seek new institutional structures and finance mechanisms emerged (GoZ, 2010a; UN-HABITAT, 2010). In 2006, the government had transferred all urban water management and resources to Zimbabwe National Water Authority (ZINWA). This created institutional conflicts and contributed to the rapid collapse of urban water and sanitation services. Only Bulawayo City resisted all government political, legal and financial pressures to enforce this transfer of responsibilities for the four years ZINWA managed urban water.

The key is how statutory provisions in each country define the fiscal and organisational autonomy of local authorities, especially the power to raise revenues in their area of jurisdiction and to manage urban development with minimum interference from the state. The major sources of income outside government grants ought to be land-based revenues (land or property taxes, rates, rents, land fees). But these generate between 10 and 40 per cent of local authority revenues in Southern Africa (UN-HABITAT, 1998, 2009, 2010; City of Johannesburg, 2010, p. 3). Consequently, electricity in South Africa and water in Zimbabwe are the main sources of revenue generated by local authorities. They provide over 40 per cent of incomes.[3] With regard to land taxes in the rest of Africa, the situation is not expected to be any better. Administrative challenges to keep updated land records and poor collection efficiency (UN-HABITAT, 2010, pp. 219–211) result in lower land taxes in the rest of Sub-Sahara Africa compared to South Africa.

As captured in Table 4.1, lack of adequate information about land availability means that local authorities are not able to levy rates on all properties in their areas of jurisdiction. And when they do, the rolls are out-dated and the formulae used do not yield full potential from the land. Also, the income from rates has declined instead of rising in line with growing urban areas. This is due to capacity problems (UN-HABITAT, 1998).

The position typical of the African urban finance crisis is illustrated by Kenya's data from 1980 to 1997. In that period, the national average default level on land rates was 30 to 35 per cent (UN-HABITAT, 1998, p. 10), with that for Mombasa being 68 per cent in 1996. For Nairobi, whereas the city collected 90 per cent of rates due in the 1991–1992 financial year, the collection dropped to 63 per cent by 1995–1996, hence the plummeting contribution of land rates to Nairobi's revenue from a peak of about 70 per cent to 77 per cent between 1985 and 1988 to as low as 51 per cent to 55 per cent in the 1991–1997 period (Mbiba & Njambi, 2001, p. 88). Clearly,

86  *Beacon Mbiba*

these patterns were at the peak of the urban crisis in Africa prior to recent reform efforts. But we lack comprehensive and updated national, regional and continental data that is sorely needed for monitoring and analytical comparisons over time.[4]

*Table 4.1*  Availability and Accessibility of Land Information in Southern Africa*

|  | Country | Availability of land information index | Accessibility of land information index |
|---|---|---|---|
| Southern Africa | Angola | 60.0 | 36.8 |
|  | Mozambique | 62.5 | 33.3 |
|  | South Africa | 85.0 | 47.4 |
|  | Zambia | 75.0 | 37.5 |
|  | Regional Average | 75.5 | 37.26 |
| Eastern Africa | Ethiopia | 2.5 | 0.0 |
|  | Kenya | 85.0 | 22.2 |
|  | Tanzania | 62.5 | 36.8 |
|  | Uganda | 77.5 | 25.0 |
|  | Rwanda | 50.0 | 38.5 |
|  | Sudan | 30.0 | 30.8 |
|  | Regional Average | 51.25 (or 61.0 without Ethiopia) | 26.88 (32.26 without Ethiopia) |
| Western Africa | Burkina Faso | 50.0 | 31.6 |
|  | Cameroon | 55.0 | 52.6 |
|  | Ivory Coast | 75.0 | 47.4 |
|  | Ghana | 85.0 | 30.0 |
|  | Liberia | 15.0 | 28.6 |
|  | Mali | 5.0 | 28.6 |
|  | Nigeria | 67.5 | 50.0 |
|  | Senagal | 75.0 | 50.0 |
|  | Sierra Leone | 30.0 | 26.3 |
|  | **Regional Average** | 50.8 | 38.3 |
| Sub-Saharan Average |  | 58.5 | 41.3 |
| Global Average |  | 70.6 | 33.9 |

*Source:* World Bank. (2010). *Investing across borders 2010.* Washington, DC: The World Bank.
*(Based on main cities)  (100 = fully available or fully accessible)

However, the quest to improve, innovate and overcome capacity constraints in the rates sector is illustrated by Temeke Municipal Council in Dar es Salaam, Tanzania. Temeke has demonstrated that innovative methods to update and manage valuation can yield higher land-based incomes ahead of the traditional methods. Franzsen and McCluskey (2005) report that over a two-year period and using in-house capacity, the Temeke Municipal Council managed to add about 80,000 properties to its flat tax property register at a cost of less than US$1.00 per property. This compares extremely favourably to the mere 5,000 properties added to the valuation roll by private consultants at a cost of approximately US$17.00 per property over a similar period.

Urban local authorities also have other non-land revenue sources, depending on context; for example, user charges, tax on income, licence fees (for vehicles, businesses), service charges and income-generation ventures. In South Africa where local authorities retain mandates to distribute electricity, they generate surpluses of between four and 14 per cent, hence their resistance to have this responsibility taken away from them as has happened in most of Africa (UN-HABITAT, 2008a, p. 158). UN-HABITAT (2009, p. 7) records that income-generating ventures are another source of local government revenue especially in Tanzania, Nigeria, Kenya, South Africa and Zimbabwe. In Zimbabwe, for instance, marketing of opaque beer is a monopoly of the local authority in its area of jurisdiction. Local authorities also engage in peri-urban livestock breeding and sales (Mbiba, 1995).[5] The national legal context is variable but critical.

A last but major issue relates to borrowing. Few local authorities (for example those in South Africa, Namibia, Zimbabwe, Uganda) and utilities have the legal authority to borrow. Where they do so, they need approval from the government for amounts above certain levels. In other cases, borrowing is completely prohibited, such as in Kenya and Botswana. The 2010–2011 capital budget for Johannesburg was to be funded from a combination of 64 per cent cash and loans, 29 per cent national and provincial grants and seven per cent from other sources (City of Johannesburg, 2010). The ability to borrow is also undermined by poor credibility and eroded creditworthiness. Lack of competent senior managers weakens both strategic and operational activities, including the ability to negotiate loans or contracts with external partners. These issues will be pursued in detail following conceptual discussions in the next section.


## FINANCING URBAN DEVELOPMENT: A HOLISTIC VIEW AND THE FINANCE CHALLENGE

For most urban actors and residents, the question of urban finance arises when it comes to paying for frontline services, such as water, electricity, refuse removal, health and education fees. These services are key elements of well-being and development as rightly captured in the MDGs and cities without slums campaigns.[6] However, a holistic view generated in the build-up to the 1996 Istanbul Conference and underscored in the subsequent Habitat Agenda[7] revealed that the provision and financing of these services was highly intertwined with the urban development activities that preceded service provision, namely the land development process (Adams, 1994; Harvey, 1996; Healey, 1991; Rakodi, 1996).

The land development process is a chain of value-adding events. Triggered by the decision to provide a service or facility, the process involves land identification and site selection, land acquisition, land use planning, sub-divisions and layout designs, cadastral surveys, infrastructure designs and construction engineering, architectural and building designs, construction, long-term operation and management (Adams, 1994; Healey, 1991). At the core of this urban development process is the provision of housing, commercial, industrial and recreational spaces—all fully serviced with roads, electricity and sewers. The point to make here is that while operation and management of local governments and utilities is important, it has to be understood as an integral part of this complex process (see Figure 4.2). The 'lubricants' of this process are governance and finance at every stage with tenure, property regimes and know-how as other critical determinants of opportunities in any given context.

Developers involved in the land use process are entrepreneurs who take risks hoping to earn an income. The higher the risks and costs encountered in the process, the higher the costs of the final product (housing) or service (water, sewer) available to the public. Urban development regulatory audits of the 1990s in Sub-Sahara Africa reveal that the median length in months to obtain approvals, permits and titles for a medium-sized residential development (between 50 and 200 units) in an urban fringe where development is permitted was about 23 months compared to a world average of 13 months (GoZ/United States Agency for International Development [USAID], 1995, p. 83). More recently, investment data confirms that access to land information in African cities is extremely difficult even for cities where this data is available and collected as part of administrative processes (World Bank, 2010). This lack of access to information compounds the delays in subdivision, layout planning, infrastructure design and construction, cadastral surveying, building and plan preparation noted above. The consequences are that:

- The risks to investment are increased, especially in an inflationary and politically unstable economic environment.
- Few developers, investors and service providers are prepared to withstand such delays or information-poor scenarios. But if they participate, they charge higher and punitive fees and prices for the services and products, which become unaffordable to the majority poor.
- Developers and investors 'cherry-pick' projects and services where risks are lowest, particularly the high income groups, and shun areas where the poorest reside.

- Delays and poor information also create opportunities for inefficiencies, corruption and other 'rent-seeking behaviours' among decision makers along the value chain.[8]
- In rapidly urbanising Africa, the delays lead to backlogs in housing and services.
- The poor who cannot afford services resort to the informal economy. Growth of informal economies erodes the revenue base of local authorities.

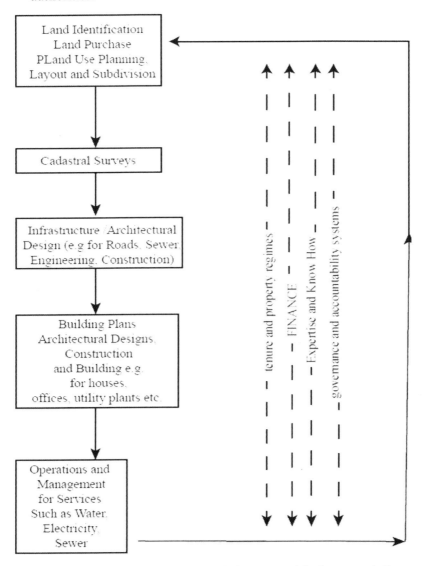

*Figure 4.2* Financing urban development: a holistic view of the financing challenge.
*Source:* The author.

Housing finance may be a useful sub-sector to help illustrate the conditions in the land development process and the implications to lending institutions of the delays, bottlenecks and constraints identified. For housing finance to be sustainable, lending institutions like building societies expect to earn a reasonable return to investment in mortgages. For this, the building society lend rates should be higher than deposit rates in commercial banks. However, in most African countries, the prime interest rates and lending rates are already very high, leading to unaffordable mortgage rates.

For instance, in Ghana in early 2010, the prime rate for Bank of Ghana was 16 per cent. Lending rates for many banks 'hovered' at about 30 per cent. Whereas banks paid interest rates of 10 per cent and below for deposits, they charged up to 27 per cent for mortgages (Yeboah, 2010, 27 April). While this ensures the lenders stay in business, mortgages become unaffordable to the majority. The cost of a typical formally produced house in Africa becomes so unaffordable that even in South Africa, one of the countries with an advanced mortgage system, only 13 per cent of the population can afford it (FinMark Trust, 2010, p. 49). Other than for South Africa and Mauritius, FinMark Trust (2010) data shows that the percentage of people that can afford such a formally constructed house on the market in Africa is below five per cent. Further, those excluded from financial markets altogether are as high as 78 per cent in Mozambique, 55 per cent in Malawi, 54 per cent in Tanzania, 33 per cent in Botswana, 63 per cent in Zambia, 53 per cent in Nigeria and 52 per cent in Rwanda.

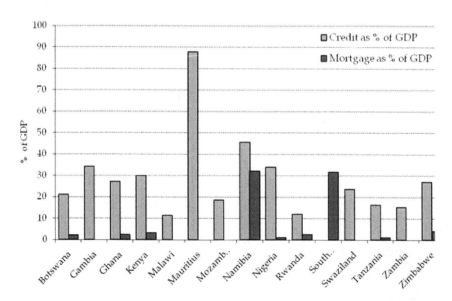

*Figure 4.3* Status of financial and mortgage markets in Africa.

*Financing Urban Development in Africa*  91

As captured in Figure 4.3, the formal markets for housing are weak in large parts of Africa as indicated by the contribution of mortgages to GDP. The chart highlights a dearth of mortgages and mortgage information in most African countries, even though some of this is available as 'grey materials' in local institutions. An urgent intervention is that, working in collaboration with research institutions, national statistical offices, national banks and professional associations, development institutions such as the World Bank, AfDB and UN-HABITAT should promote and expand the collection of information necessary to compile robust urban development and finance indicators as was done in the lead-up to the UN-HABITAT II.[9]

In countries like The Gambia, only 18 per cent of buildings are of a durable material (FinMark Trust, 2010, p. 26) making it difficult for mortgage markets to grow. Prohibitive borrowing costs, volatile economies, barriers and bottlenecks in the land development process result in urban infrastructure, houses and services that are not affordable to the poor, who constitute the majority of the population. The financing of urban development is dependent on key aspects in the national political economy, namely: organisation of various sectors, centre–local relations, constitutional standing of local government and governance, the economic model in terms of the degree to which markets operate, human capital in the economy,[10] land tenure and rule of law. Countries where building societies operate and where undeveloped urban land has a market value offer different challenges and opportunities for urban financing, compared to those that do not. In particular, this will affect the range and mix of developers and investors, and the development, operational and management models (Harvey, 1996).

The implication of the preceding section is that weak formal urban land and housing markets lead to poor local authority incomes available from rates. Overall, the subsequent revenues are pitiful. There is need for a holistic understanding that links the land development process to the institutional arrangements for management as suggested in the next section.


## HEURISTIC MODELS OF URBAN DEVELOPMENT AND UTILITY OWNERSHIP AND MANAGEMENT

A standard and traditional institutional approach to urban development, utility management and service provision is one where the public sector (state, central government or local government) acts as owner, developer, manager and service provider to communities in a given area. In Figure 4.4, it is located at the bottom left hand corner.

However, the performance in terms of output, efficiency of delivery and results has been unsatisfactory, leading governments to seek other approaches to organise, finance and manage urban development. Figure 4.4 sketches the spectrum of potential public, community and private sector partnerships.[11] The extreme top right hand corner would be those

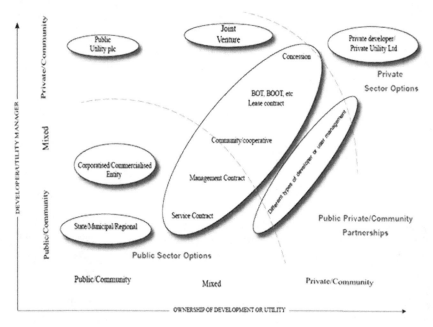

*Figure 4.4* Heuristic models of urban development or and utility ownership and management.

circumstances where private sector or community entities have full ownership of the development process, management and services as well as the land and other associated physical assets. In practice, most African countries are in the early stages of public–private partnerships characterised by commercialised public sector service and management contracts. Also, there are attempts and expressions of interest to explore lease contracts, concessions and fully flagged private sector models.

The role of the private sector and the complexity of the development process and utility models increase the more we progress towards the top right hand corner of Figure 4.4. Sansom, Franceys, Njiru and Morales-Reyes (2003, p. 1) observe that service and management contracts are the two most common forms of private sector participation (PSP) and public–private partnerships (PPP), especially in the water sector. Complex forms of PSP and PPP arrangements, such as leases, concessions and Build Operate and Transfer (BOTs), have potential to offer substantial benefits. However, their success depends on conditions that do not fully prevail in most African cities. BOT contracts require high tariffs to meet operator costs. Contract periods normally last for over 20 years to enable the contractor to pay off loans and achieve return on investment (Sansom et al., 2003a). However, few countries in Africa have had enduring political and economic stability to support such contracts. Other conditions that are not fully developed include robust information and management systems, competitive procurement and bidding processes, local expertise to manage complex contracts, local markets that allow for competitive PSP and impartial dispute resolution and adjudication structures (Schwartz, 2009; Sansom et al., 2003a, 2003b).

A model complementary to both Figure 4.2 and Figure 4.4 is one that incorporates a spatial dimension to development and finance, such as:

(a) off-site capital projects like reservoirs, highways, and regional distributor networks,
(b) on-site development and investments, such as access roads, water, sewer and electricity lines, and
(c) on-plot infrastructure and services to each property or plot.

Financing (a) and (b) is the major gap in large parts of Africa, with households, communities and the informal sector only able to make a difference in (c) and to some extent (b). The work by Tremolet, Kolsky and Perez (2010) is a recent confirmation of household willingness to invest in on-site sanitation, especially among low-income groups.

In the face of rapid population growth, diminishing revenues and weak public capacity to offer services, PPP and other interventions have been used in different contexts.[12] But questions remain regarding their effectiveness and sustainability. To address these questions, it is therefore important to identify and learn from experiences where such interventions have been made. The following sections will identify and illustrate first financing models in the land development process and then utility management, focusing particularly on the urban water and sanitation sector. These sectors are key for the achievement of the MDGs, and are a top priority for improving the well-being of residents. As underlined in section eight of this chapter, water and sewerage services have the potential to generate surplus revenues.

## FINANCING URBAN DEVELOPMENT: FURTHER INSIGHTS FROM LAND AND HOUSING DELIVERY

This section considers examples of how private sector participation can contribute to urban development finance when property rights and contract conditions are favourable, particularly in countries where private individuals have title to urban and peri-urban land. This offers problems and opportunities. As witnessed in South Africa and Zimbabwe, landholders hold on to their pieces of land for as long as possible (land speculation) inhibiting the supply of land when and where it is needed most (Rakodi, 1996; UN-HABITAT, 2008a). When the land is eventually released, it comes in small, disjointed and expensive pieces. The cost of land becomes the most significant component in the urban development process. Governments elsewhere have responded through raising land taxes. In the past, they resorted to

94   *Beacon Mbiba*

land nationalisation (e.g. Mozambique, Zambia and Tanzania) and setting limits on land holdings that private individuals can hold. Still, this may not release the required land. Hence a range of options have been attempted that entail involving the private sector and landlords in the development process. These are characterised by versions of land pooling and land re-adjustments (Doebele, 1983).

## VERSIONS OF LAND POOLING AND ADJUSTMENT: NORTON TOWN LANDLORDS[13]

Land pooling is when a group of land owners come together to consolidate their pieces of land for urban development in partnership with the local authority. For example, in the 1990s, a group of farmers in peri-urban Norton Town, 40 miles south west of Harare, gave up a portion of their farming land for urban development because of demand for housing land from middle class residents of the capital city, Harare. The local authority prepared the land-use plans from which the farmers computed the size of land needed for infrastructure and the parcel (Part A) that if sold would provide an income equal to the cost of providing the required infrastructure (roads, drainage, sewer, water and electricity mainlines). The profit margins were based on keeping this Part A as low as possible. Profits would come from the sale of the remainder of the serviced land (Part B) with each owner getting income proportionate to the share of land they contributed to the main pool (Part A + Part B). A portion of this land (Part B) was reserved for low-income groups.

In practice, the attraction for the local authority was that the land-owners were going to provide fully serviced land. The deal was that the local authority would be responsible for the administrative costs: selecting and allocating land to the low-income beneficiaries. Plots for the middle and upper income groups were sold first at market price so that landlords could realise income from their investments, and also so as to generate the income to subsidise subsequent phases for the low income group. The mix of income groups ensured the development of a fully inclusive project where the middle classes subsidised the poorer groups from land purchase through use of utility services. On our model in Figure 4.4, this would be a mixed-type PPP.

### Private Sector-Led Development: OMPIC
### Westgate Development, Harare

By the early 1990s, Harare's liberalised economy was experiencing a boom and rapid growth. However, resources for the local authority to provide housing and infrastructure continued to diminish. The Westgate project was a response by the pension fund managers Old Mutual Properties

*Financing Urban Development in Africa* 95

Zimbabwe. They negotiated the purchase of 550 hectares of Bluff Hill Estate, then a peri-urban farm holding off Lomagundi Road to the west of Harare city centre. Although Old Mutual Properties were the project owners, they brought in other private sector actors to manage activities such as land use planning, surveying, infrastructure development, marketing, selection of clients and collection of fees. The planned development (now complete) has an urban commercial core (a prestigious shopping centre incorporating shops, cinemas, doctor's suites, a post office, banks and satellite police, etc.), light industrial zones and residential areas for upper, middle and low middle income groups with residential plot sizes of 800m$^2$ to a maximum of 4,500m$^2$ for the upper income group.[14]

To finance the development, the implementation proceeded in phases, with plots sold off-plan to prospective clients and blocks of stands allocated to different building contractors for development. Each phase was designed to sell and raise resources to finance the next. The Building Society, CABS (Central Africa Building Society), had the linch-pin role of selecting clients, collecting deposits and managing mortgages where applicable. Phasing also allowed the developers to adjust for inflation in the plot prices for subsequent phases. All properties were developed to strict Harare City Council standards in terms of Section 27 of the Regional Town and Country Planning Act, Zimbabwe.

Westgate added a total of 2574 residential units to the stock of properties in Harare (OMPIC, 1995). As with the Norton development, Westgate provided housing to thousands of middle and upper income households who otherwise would have raided projects meant for the poorest of the poor in areas like Kuwanzana, Budirio and Dzivarasekwa. Crucially, both developments were able to use private resources and innovations to finance on-site infrastructure provision at no cost to the local authority. What remained unresolved, however, were issues of post-development provision and management of services and the broader financing of off-site capital projects, such as dams, water and sewage works and upgrading of 40-year-old water pipes in the rest of Harare (and other cities like Bulwayo and Gweru).[15] On our model, OMPIC's Westgate is a typical private sector joint venture development. Such high value real estate and commercial developments with quality on-site infrastructure provide enhanced revenue bases (rates) for local authorities. Manda Hill (Lusaka) and the Village Market (Nairobi) are similar developments that are now a feature of most major cities in Africa.

Such developments are possible even where land is in public ownership or community hands. Particularly in West Africa, huge trading markets that are located on public or community land are economic cores of cities such as Accra, Ibadan, Abidjan, Kumasi.[16] In Ghana, Accra Metropolitan Authority (AMA) has taken the redevelopment of these markets as a central feature of urban economic development and regeneration. Using the national social security and insurance authority (SSNIT) to create a private entity, AMA has developed New Makola Market II as a partnership whose operation and management incorporates aspects of traditional community social capital and the private sector.

In this and similar markets, operations seek to cover costs of infrastructure and maintenance. A key point to reiterate from these cases is that different private sectors can play different roles in the development process. Also important, particularly in Southern Africa, is the role of pension funds (mining industry, railways and local government), whose resources can contribute significantly to infrastructure and urban development.

## URBAN UTILITY MODELS IN AFRICA: PROVISION AND OVERVIEW OF WATER AND SANITATION

### From Public Sector to Private Sector Participation

Public sector ownership and management of water utilities remains the dominant model despite encouragement from donors to reform and introduce PSP in this sector (Schwartz, 2009). Figure 4.5 captures the broad ownership and management of water at the turn of the century.

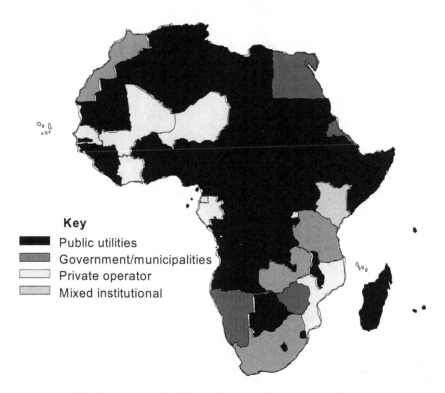

*Figure 4.5* The dominance of public utilities in Africa: water and sewerage sector.

But most of these public utilities are bedevilled by a lack of capital investments and operational inefficiencies. These result in high unaccounted for water[17], low-cost recovery, low tariff levels, high staff per 1000 connections, high labour costs, low productivity, low and erratic supplies, poor quality water, low coverage, problems of accountability and autonomy, poor institutional arrangements and lack of effective regulatory frameworks (Mwanza, 2006). Also, public utilities are heavily subsidised, yet in some cities, they benefit the middle class and wealthy groups more than the majority poor (Kjellen, 2006; UN-HABITAT, 2008a).

The results of these failures include stunted economic investment and growth, poor quality of life, water-related diseases and general ill-health for the majority poor (UN-HABITAT, 2008a, 2010; Tremolet et al., 2010). In Ghana, for instance, water-borne diseases account for 70 per cent of all diseases (Mills-Tettey & Adi-Ado, 2002; Suleiman & Cars, 2010, p. 272). That the poor are affected disproportionately when utilities collapse was well illustrated by the cholera epidemic in urban Zimbabwe 2008–2009 (UN-HABITAT, 2010, p. 210–211). Consequently, agreement regarding the need for reform has been unanimous although there is no consensus on how this should be done. Early reforms of these public sector utilities in the water sector were driven by a desire to improve revenue collection, to expand coverage and inject capital into the utilities and improve governance (Sansom et al., 2003b; Schwartz, 2009; Suleiman & Cars, 2010; WSP, 2009). These reforms involve commercialisation of services within the public sector framework or introducing private sector participation in some aspects of utility management.

Key features and outcomes of these reforms are revealed in a comprehensive review of six African case studies of PSP in urban water utilities (Sansom et al., 2003b, pp. 110–146), several erudite studies (Joffe et al. 2009; Kjellen, 2006; Schwartz, 2009; Suleiman & Cars, 2010; Tremolet et al., 2010) and reports of on-going privatisation programmes (NWASCO, 2002, 2010; WSP, 2009). Within the PSP context, the state, or some statutory body like NWASCO in Zambia, retains the core functions of planning, regulation, emergency services, compliance monitoring, community and customer care. The PSP takes up service contracts (e.g. for billing and meter reading), and then progresses to handling management contracts for part- or whole-city water distribution networks, with the ultimate intention to move towards concession, as in the case of Johannesburg Water—moving diagonally from left to right on Figure 4.4.

According to Sansom et al. (2003b, p. 112):

> . . . key reasons behind selection of these types of contracts included the potential to improve operational management with better incentives and also to generate better quality management information and systems to possibly allow the implementation of more complex/comprehensive contracts, such as lease and concessions in the future.

## 98   Beacon Mbiba

The outcomes have been varied, and are dependent on quality of contract, expertise and contextual conditions in the political economy:

- According to Sansom et al. (2003b), only the Johannesburg Water Management Contract used full procurement and bidding processes to select the management operator for the management of water and sanitation services. In the other cases for Kampala[18] and Malindi, the services and management contracts were awarded to an engineering firm without going to tender. The selected international firm, already working on other projects in the region, had no experience of such management roles, but was picked because of the previous construction work it had done. In Ghana, following highly protracted and contested attempts at reform and privatisation, the management contract for Ghana Water Company Limited was awarded to foreign private operator, Aqua Vitens Rand Ltd (AVRL), owned by Vitens from the Netherlands (51 per cent) and Rand Water from South Africa (49 per cent) (Suleiman & Cars, 2010, p. 284). Operations commenced in 2006, but whether the tendering process was open remains contested.
- For the Kibera case (Kenya) where a community organisation was the operator, and for Tongaart (Durban, South Africa), it was the contractors who approached the authorities about taking over water management services in their respective areas. There were no tenders (Sansom et al., 2003a, 2003b). Fortunately, these performed much better than the Kampala and Malindi PSP contracts.
- Donor funding from the World Bank and GTZ was a trigger for the Kampala and Malindi initiatives. It partly explained the limited success in that there were no internal drivers of change to sustain reforms once the donor funding expired (see Box 4.2). The management and operations relapsed to pre-PSP situations once the external support expired.
- Sansom et al. (2003a, 2003b) and Schwartz (2009) have also revealed that where operations and management improved, the PSP transformations did not bring in or attract any investment finance for source works, bulk transmission pipelines, treatment works, storage, residential pipe connections and meter installations—the off-site and on-site infrastructure.
- Further, although revenue collection improved, funds collected were insufficient for new investments; hence tariff increases did not appear a sufficient basis for financial capacity (Schwartz, 2009, p. 408) to support capital investments.
- Lack of competitive bidding for contracts weakened the potential benefits to both parties.
- Crucially, the local expertise to manage water contracts and local market conditions to allow competitive PSP is weak, with foreign companies playing a pivotal role in the management of contracts, such as that of Johannesburg Water. Elsewhere, in Senegal, the ultimate parent company of SDE (a privately owned water sector operator) is Buoygues Group, one of France's largest industrial conglomerates. Joffe et al.

(2009) suggest that this has proven to be a strong source of support in terms of technical support and systems. Within the 'corporatised' utilities, organisational culture change to improve performance has been slow, while transfer of expertise from foreign contractors to local staff is not always effective as in the case of Kampala.

---

### Box 4.2 The Salient Role of International Sctors in Urban Utility Reforms

International donors and lending agencies introduced the International Drinking Water Decade (1980–1990) and continue to fund flagship water and sanitation initiatives in Africa such as:

→ USAID – Sustainable Water and Sanitation for Africa
→ The World Bank Water and Sanitation Program (WSP)
→ United Nations Water Decade 2005–2015.

The World Bank has 'pushed' privatisation of urban utilities in Ghana and has a presence in Zambia, where China, Irish Aid, Germany and Denmark are other key players in the water and sanitation sector (NWASCO, 2008, p. 3). However, while very welcome, the sustainability of PSP initiatives is locally contested and there are structural barriers in the local political economy in which conditions for competitive local market players do not exist.

---

Reforms have also been initiated in broader governance of utilities. State boards, corporations, and water and sanitation companies have been established to pursue commercialisation of services. But in most countries, governments retain many powers over these boards and corporations. The water and sewage utilities do not have full financial autonomy and remain heavily dependent on central government finance. Given that funding comes in the form of loans from international finance institutions (e.g. World Bank), it is important to improve the creditworthiness of urban utilities and ensure that PSP improves credit rating, actual revenue collection and the ability to repay loans.

### Governance Reforms and Emerging Utility Models—The Water and Sanitation Sector

Over the past 10 years, one can identify emerging trends engendered by the reforms: a mix of ownership and operational models. First is continued direct central or local government ownership of assets, through to public properties owned by holding companies as in Senegal and the seven asset-holding water boards in Kenya, or councils in Zambia. There are also cases where the government is the only shareholder in public utilities, such as the Uganda National Water and Sewerage Company (NWSC), SONEDE of Tunisia, ONEA in Burkina Faso, Johannesburg Water in South Africa and Nairobi Water and Sanitation Company in Kenya.

## 100 *Beacon Mbiba*

Recruitment of non-governmental board members drawn from customers and business communities as in the case of Johannesburg Water and NWSC helps to promote commercial approaches and responsiveness to customer needs. The structure in itself does not say much about operational and management practices.

*Table 4.2* Governance Reforms: Emerging Utility Models in Water and Sanitation

| *Type of Strucure and Contract* | *Examples* |
|---|---|
| *Performance Contract:* | Nairobi water and Sewerage Company |
| • For senior staff and performance targets for all employees | Etekwini Municipality (Durban) |
| | Tunisia |
| | In Senegal, the public asset holding company (SONES) has a performance contract with a private contractor or operator (SDE) for service delivery |
| *Performance Contracts* | Zambia, South Africa and Uganda (see text above) |
| • Between asset holder and private operator/ contractor | The government of Uganda has a three-year contract with the National Water and Sewerage Company. That has enabled NWSC to suspend debt service obligations |
| | Also Tunisia and Burkina Faso |
| | Nairobi Water Services has a management contract with the Ministry of Water and Irrigation, and has in turn entered into a service provider agreement with Nairobi Water and Sewerage Company, which is wholly owned by Nairobi City Council. |
| Service Delivery Agreement | Johannesburg City Council and Johannesburg Water (the 'corporatised' sewage and water utility) |
| Management Contract | Johannesburg Water and JOWAM |
| Concession Contract | In Senegal, SONES has a 30-year concession from the Ministry of Water. |
| Leasing Contract | In Senegal, both SONES and the government have leasing contracts with the private operator, SDE. Ivory Coast* has an operational leasing contract. |

*Source:* Various reading sources and Web sites.
*Sansom, K., Franceys, R., Njiru, C., & Morales-Reyes, J. (2003a). *Contracting Out Water and Sanitation Services: Vol. 1.* Guidance notes for service and management contracts in developing countries. Leicestershire, UK: Water, Engineering and Development Centre (WEDC), Loughborough University.

The reforms are dominated by performance and management contracts between governments and utilities and between asset owners and private contractors. Continuing from the heuristic models in Figure 4.4, the key features and examples of models in practice are presented in Table 4.2. In some cases, the use of management contracts is short-term. Once turn-around has been achieved in terms of improved systems, revenue collection and support to the poor, the operational management can be brought back in-house to the asset holder.

For instance, the management contract between Johannesburg and JOWAN from 2001–2006 reverted back to Johannesburg Water after capacity building and improvements had been achieved. From 2002–2004 in Uganda, NWSC used a management contract with ONDEO Services (an international water operator), after which the operations and management reverted to NWSC. Now NWSC uses internal contractors to 'mimic' private operational practices. In countries like Kenya, Uganda and Tanzania, performance contracts for staff and organisational units are now part of a broader culture of results-based management (RBM) that has been mainstreamed into local government and the public sector.[19] A similar culture was gaining ground in Zimbabwean cities, but stalled with the inflationary crisis and manpower exodus of 2004–2009.

## Ingredients of Successful Utility Models and Reforms

A review of the key studies reveals that economic and technical models are a necessary but not sufficient condition for success. Instead, successful utility models and reforms depend on a mix of 'ingredients,' especially the removal of structural barriers in the institutional and political economy of the respective country or urban areas (Sansom et al., 2003b; Schwartz, 2009; Suleiman & Cars, 2010). In specific terms, action areas include:

- strengthening capacity or localising 'know-how' through joint work with external partners, exchange visits and extensive training programmes;
- changing institutional, political and consumer cultures within the sector broadly so as to foster market conditions for competitive investment and service provision. Tremolet et al. (2010) provide further insights into lack of funding and lack of political will in the sanitation sector;
- positive use of opportunities engendered by 'key moments' (a disaster like cholera in Harare, 2008–2009, or an innovation) and external input from donors or international finance institutions;
- presence of 'prime-movers' or 'drivers of change' for example in the form of competent committed and charismatic leadership at both the technical and political levels (See Joffe et al., 2009, pp. 14–15).

## 102    *Beacon Mbiba*

*Zambia Good Practice: Benchmarking and*
*Key Performance Indicators (KPIs)*

Good information, benchmarking and release of regular KPIs is a critical aspect of management, irrespective of the utility model. With statutory muscle and consensus among stakeholders, NWASCO, the Zambia water and sanitation regulatory authority, has completed a decade of regular data collection and monitoring. Reports and programs are posted on the internet. The KPIs compiled include those for unaccounted-for water, connection and coverage, production, metering ratios, water quality, hours of supply, collection efficiency, billing and staff efficiency and costs structures including those associated with personnel.

Although the provision still has major gaps and the investment is donor-dependent, the benchmarking and monitoring data is of high quality and is a basis for targeted interventions whenever resources become available. Together with credit ratings, benchmarking provides corroboration of creditworthiness that is the basis for use in market finance. It has created conditions for improved market financing in the sector. Further, the Zambian case confirms the presence of a yet to be tapped 'niche market' in the provision of utility support and instruments in the local authority and utility sector, namely:

- Credit rating for local authorities and utilities;
- Project development; and
- Benchmarking and KPI compilation and monitoring.

This niche market is an extension of the broader 'urban indicators' where major gaps exist (FinMark Trust, 2010; IAB, 2010). Previous comprehensive efforts to compile 'urban indicators' supported by USAID in the build-up to HABITAT II fizzled out once donor funding disappeared, largely because no complementary changes took place to enrich demand or a local market for these services and data. Other than for South Africa, there is neither a market for nor the presence of private firms that compile these indicators. The same weak local market conditions seem to afflict UN-HABITAT's urban observatories. There is need for these observatories and the urban indicators, but until local institutions begin to factor these as part of their operational activities, little will remain once the donors disappear.

## Water and Sanitation: Informal and Community Models

In Africa, utility services from the public sector and formal private sector, whether individually or in partnerships, do not fully cover all urban communities. Downsizing the role of the state has also left gaps in service provision. These gaps, arising from either unaffordable service costs or lack of coverage, are filled in by informal and small scale or independent providers (ISSPs), the civil society and the community sector (Suleiman & Cars, 2010). There is a high degree of entrepreneurship in ISSPs as well as linkages with the public and private sectors.[20] In water and sanitation, community organizations are also potential owners and providers of services highly linked to ISSPs.

In Luanda, where only 25 per cent of the population has access to piped water, the poor in peri-urban settlements depend on informal providers. The water is brought by tankers to dealers who re-sell water to households at up to US$16.90/m³, such that the poor end up paying multiple times more for water compared to the well to do, who are connected to the formal water system (UN-HABITAT, 2008b, p. 146). Similar tankers provide water to areas that are not covered by piped water in Accra. But the cost to consumers is 10 times more than for those with direct access to public piped water (Suleiman & Cars, 2010, p. 278).

In Accra, some households with piped water earn an income by packing water in plastic sachets and using networks, such as *kayayo* girls, to sell the ice-cold 'clear water' on the streets.[21] Unregulated private sector operators, individuals and households sell bottled water or operate tankers, most of them drawing from public water reservoirs or pipes, to sell to those who are not connected to the public system. In cases where such water is obtained illegally, the practices contribute to high levels of unaccounted-for water.[22] Even in better-equipped cities like Johannesburg, the level of unaccounted-for water is over 25 per cent, while that for electricity is 14 per cent. The unpopular prepaid meters continue to be viewed as the best management solution to reduce the unaccounted-for service.[23]

## Community and Diaspora Organisations' Involvement

Sansom et al. (2003a, p. 19) observe that community and co-operative contracts for delivery of infrastructure and services are becoming more common, especially in informal settlements. For instance, reforms of urban water services saw a community organisation emerging to act as a contractor to operate services in Kibera slum in Nairobi (Sansom et al., 2003b). The service entailed managing some water distribution pipes and water kiosks. In Nairobi's Mathare low-income area, 'community cleaning services' have become an effective form of cleaning public areas and shared community facilities that are in deplorable conditions (Thieme, 2010). As far back as the 1990s, a community model was used to construct and manage standpipes in peri-urban Luanda, Angola (Kirkwood, 1997), with positive outcomes on maintenance and user fee collections. Using community approaches reduces labour and travel costs, and enables poverty reduction interventions to proceed where government and the private sector would not make much progress on their own.

In south west Nigeria, Lambert (2009) reports of self-help urban development initiatives coordinated by traditional local authorities, which rely on communal efforts from citizens of each area and its associations. Of note is the growing significance of home town associations and diaspora organisations whose collective remittances are channelled into public services, infrastructure and micro-credit schemes. Restoration of piped water, regular electricity supply, connection to a telephone network and provision of health and education services are some of the key projects that have been completed through communal efforts in Ayege town, Nigeria (Lambert, 2009). In Bali, Cameroon, a water-by-gravity project and a mortuary are among the projects completed by the Bali Cultural and Development Association (BANDECA) using resources from national and international diaspora (Mercer, Page, & Evans, 2009). Yahya (2008) describes the significant role of faith-based organisations in organising communities and raising funds for development. Community organisations and faith groups have also acted as effective interlocutors between communities, donors and the government in the on-going redevelopment of Nairobi's Korogocho informal settlement.[24]

This community involvement in the design, financing and implementation of urban development in Africa has not received as much research and policy attention when compared to participatory budgeting and urban governance in Latin America (Cabannes, 2004). There could be several reasons for this. Community involvement has often been perceived as a crisis response indicative of public sector failures. Thus, to concentrate on such involvement would amount to celebrating failure. Crucially as noted by Mercer et al. (2009, p. 151), projects completed by communities and diaspora associations tend to be small. They also take years to complete. Much of this involvement is via informal geo-ethnic, regional and family formations that do not conform to normative methodologies of governments and donors. Lemanski (2008) also points to instances in Cape Town where community problems prevail, ranging from "lack of community" within some poor neighbourhoods to lack of expertise.

Strong grassroots and social movements have been a feature of urban development for centuries. However, they perform better only at key moments, working as critical and complementary actors rather than as substitutes to mainstream providers of large scale urban infrastructure and services.

## Financing On-Site Infrastructure and the Role of Targeted Subsidies

Two critical points concerning finance have been noted in previous sections, namely that households are prepared to invest in on-plot infrastructure, but that these investments and the market conditions for competitive private sector participation (PSP) in the provision of off-site and on-site infrastructure do not exist. This raises the question of how limited public and donor funding can be used to leverage households, whether to promote demand or to support the supply side of the market; whether to give subsidies directly to households (as in the case of South Africa's housing subsidy); or whether

*Financing Urban Development in Africa*    105

to promote production of materials and to support credit schemes (Tremolet et al., 2010). Conditions in each context should guide when and where to intervene and the support to be aimed at. As shown in the housing sector (Bovet, 1993), the sector-wide approach, although more complex and expensive, appears to be the most effective.

But given that most urban residents are prepared to invest in better services and on-plot improvements, the limited subsidy could target wider on-site and off-site infrastructure and the supply side aspects of hardware, such as production of building materials. When cement, bricks, tiles, electricity, timber and equipment are widely available at competitive prices, both service providers and households are better placed to address water, housing and sanitation problems. Reducing the price of a 50kg bag of cement from the current US$10 to US$15 (FinMark Trust, 2010: 2) to below US$10 would have a significant impact on building and construction investments. The fact that national and local conditions determine the success or impact of finance interventions is illustrated by results from a study of water and sanitation in Senegal and Mozambique (Tremolet et al., 2010). A range of possible interventions emerged. They included the start-up of revolving funds and credit schemes, demand stimulation through community mobilisation and education and output-based hardware subsidies of up to 75 per cent capital costs. Such output-based subsidies stimulate demand and also leverage private sector investment.

## IMPROVING PRICING AND REVENUE COLLECTION AS PRECONDITION FOR MARKET FINANCING

There is a general consensus that tariffs for utility services have been set at levels that do not cover operations and maintenance costs (Schwartz, 2009), let alone provide for sorely needed investment. In most countries, utility providers do not have power to set prices. Such power is retained by the state. Joffe et al. (2009) show that operational efficiency has broadly improved. However, NWASCO (2008) data confirms that despite these improvements in collection efficiency, funds are absorbed by personnel costs (50 per cent), leaving little for needed spare parts and infrastructure maintenance.[25] Given the dilapidated nature of this infrastructure, the gains made are at risk. In some cases, collection of fees and user charges have been very low, and therefore is in need of urgent review (GoZ, 2010a).[26]

The tariffs also remain constant or decline in value *vis-à-vis* inflation. Raising them is always unpopular with consumers and politicians. However, improving revenue collection and setting competitive prices remains central to reforms and new urban developments and utility management levels. But there is in-built institutional and political inertia among professionals (e.g. engineers), worker trade unions and politicians that acts as a major barrier to economic tariff setting and broad reforms. In Ghana, for

106    *Beacon Mbiba*

instance, a coalition of trade unions and civic organisations mobilised successfully to stall privatisation efforts and to fight for a "rights aware" water provision (Suleiman & Cars, 2010). UN-HABITAT (2010) notes that similar protracted struggles for rights-based approaches to water and electricity provision in Johannesburg ended up in the Constitutional Court.[27]

---

**Box 4.3 Uganda: Setting and Maintaining Real Price Levels for Utility Services**

Between 1994 and 2000, the tariff charged by National Water and Sewage Corporation (NWSC) of Uganda remained unchanged, leading to real value decline of 55 percent in revenue collections. Since 2002, however, as part of political commitment to support NWSC reforms, the government supported annual tariff indexation linked to the domestic price index, exchange rates, foreign price index and electricity tariffs.

---

Although Box 4.3 and the WSP (2009) paint a positive picture of political support, other messages from the field are often contradictory. For instance, Uganda's NWSC is subject to restrictions regarding borrowing. Joffe et al. (2009, p. 23) note that the "corporation's credit policy does not allow for disconnection for non-payment of water services, thus directly affecting both operating performance and overall liquidity." Joffe et al. (2009) claim that political interference and bureaucracy in Uganda's NWSC and Nairobi City Water and Sewage Company (NCWSC) undermine the operations and full commercialisation and privatisation of the respective water utilities, even though the regulatory framework appears sound on paper. The policies of water and electricity disconnections in Harare and Johannesburg are not a feature of provision in most other cities.

### Price Setting and Tariffs in Practice: The Water and Sewage Sector

In theory, the setting of prices for services should seek to cover costs of providing the services. The production costs could include both capital investments as well as operational costs, with prices set on the basis of incremental costs. In practice, computing the marginal costs in economic, financial and accounting terms is complex and leads to prices well above affordable levels for the majority. Hence setting prices is largely based on political and social considerations, and not solely on financial accounting and economic computations. Examples of tariffs from water and sewage will be used to highlight patterns and features of current practices. The practice is dominated by multi-part or stratified tariff structures, where different prices are set for blocks of units of service used and applied to different consumer groups and levels of consumption.

Senegal has a typical stratified tariff structure (there are variations of this in Kenya and Burkina Faso) with a social tranche and a deterrent tranche as key features (Table 4.3). The social 'tranche' is equivalent to the 'life-line' block pricing, where a basic amount of service (water, electricity) is priced at below cost for distributional and social reasons, that is, to ensure that everyone has access to a minimum amount needed for basic consumption.[28]

The state sets the tariffs and provides for asset financing. It also makes collections from government entities. The right to increase tariffs rests with the Minister of Water. While there is a commendable social and deterrent tranche, there is no clear inflation indexing to make this tariff more sustainable. Burkina Faso also has block tariffs, but the country has higher charges than Senegal for the same amount of water (Table 4.4).

For Burkina Faso, a tariff review is conducted every five years. But ONEA lacks the financial autonomy to set tariffs and can only make proposals for consideration by a council of ministers (Joffe et al. 2009, p. 17). Different tariffs apply to different consumer groups based on consumption, with larger consumers subsidising smaller consumers and larger centres subsidising smaller centres. What is not clear, however, is whether the same tariffs apply for commercial, residential, and industrial sectors and public institutions.

The disparities by consumer group are more glaring in Nairobi, where the NCWSC is forced to charge less for its water than what the government charges. Where no water metres are installed, a monthly flat fee of KShs 200 is charged for government schemes compared to KShs 120 for

*Table 4.3*  Stratified Tariffs for Water and Sanitation in Senegal—2008

|  | Consumption (m3) | Tariff (CFA/m3) |
| --- | --- | --- |
| Social Tranche | 0–20 | 191.3 |
| Full Tranche | 21–40 | 629.9 |
| Deterrent Tranche | > 40 | 788.7 |

*Source:* Joffe, M., Hoffman, R., & Brown, M. (2008). *African water utilities: Regional comparative utility creditworthiness assessment report* (Revised 2009). Report of the Water and Sanitation Programme in Partnership with African Water Association, Private Public Infrastructure Advisory Facility (PPIAF) and the African Development Bank.

*Table 4.4*  Stratified Tariffs for Water and Sanitation in Burkina Faso

| Consumption (m3) | Tariff (CFA/m3) (at 2008) |
| --- | --- |
| 0–8 | 188 |
| 9–15 | 430 |
| 16–30 | 509 |
| > 30 | 1040 |

*Source:* Joffe et al. (2008).

108   *Beacon Mbiba*

NCWSC. Bulk water for kiosks and private vendors are charged at a subsidised flat rate of KShs 15/m$^3$ for government schemes compared to KShs 10/m$^3$ for NCWSC. There are separate tariffs for schools. The metered connection also has these variations, starting with a 'lifeline' supply of 10m$^3$ that is charged a flat rate of KShs 200 for Government schemes compared to KShs150 for NCWSC. These block charges for the lifeline tariff (the first 10m$^3$) are paid irrespective of whether the consumer uses substantially less than 10m$^3$ (Joffe et al., 2009, p. 19). The government schemes have five further tariff blocks between 10m$^3$ and 300m$^3$, whereas NCWSC has three further blocks from 10m$^3$ to 60m$^3$.

Compared to Senegal and Burkina Faso, the Kenya tariff system is more complex. Joffe et al. (2009, p. 20) reported that on average, the 2008 tariffs needed to go up by at least 75 per cent to reach a sustainable level. Furthermore, the tariffs are not inflation indexed, and had not changed for 10 years before 2008.

As highlighted in Box 4.3, neighbouring Uganda has incorporated inflation indexing. Its tariffs are based on different socio-economic consumer

*Table 4.5*   Customer Group Based Tariffs for Water and Sanitation in Uganda

| *Customer Group* | *Fixed Tariff per m3 (UShs /m3)* |
|---|---|
| Public Stand Pipes | 688 |
| Residential/Domestic | 1064 |
| Institutional/Government | 1310 |
| **Industrial/Commercial** | |
| 0–300m$^3$/month | 1716 |
| 501–1500m$^3$/month | 1716 |
| > 1500m$^3$/month | 1496 |

*Source:* Joffe et al. (2008).

*Table 4.6*   Fixed and Variable Tariffs for Water and Sanitation in Tunisia

| *Consumption (m3)* | *Tariff (TD)* |
|---|---|
| 0–20 | 0.14 |
| 21–40 | 0.24 |
| 41–70 | 0.30 |
| 71–150 | 0.55 |
| >151 | 0.84 |

*Source:* Joffe et al. (2008).

Financing Urban Development in Africa   109

groups, not just on consumption quantities. Table 4.5 shows that the industry tariff is more responsive to quantities consumed, but unlike in Senegal, there is no explicit use of 'deterrent' in the charge. The fixed tariff in the other groups has no deterrent factor and encourages wastage. The government sets policy and determines tariffs, and NWSC policy does not allow disconnections for non-payment of water.

The role of government in setting tariffs in all the above cases is also the case in Tunisia, where the Ministry of Water revises the tariffs twice every five years and applies the tariffs uniformly across the country. The tariff structure has a fixed and a variable component that is proportional to consumption (Table 4.6). The first bracket of $0-20m^3$ quarterly consumption provides low-income households with 40 litres per person per day, and offers them a subsidy of 30 per cent of the cost of supply.

Clearly, there is wide variation in pricing of services according to the following: fixed and variable structures, 'lifeline' basic blocks, inflation indexing, stratification by socio-economic group and the amount of service consumed. Political and social consideration and the development status of each country appear to determine the pricing of water and sanitation services. Similar principles and patterns apply for the electricity sector.

## ENHANCED ACCESS TO FINANCING FOR LOCAL AUTHORITIES AND URBAN UTILITIES

### The Finance Gap

The preceding sections have exposed the finance gap in urban development; namely that local authorities and utility service providers are dependent on unreliable central government grants, and that such transfers are not adequate to finance new capital projects or the needed refurbishment of dilapidated infrastructure (see Figure 4.2). Secondly, even where operational performance has been improved to register surplus income, such revenue is 'gobbled' up by wages and other recurrent expenditures, leaving little for capital investments.[29]

This section considers local market conditions and the extent to which local authorities and utilities can raise loans from local banks and credit institutions. It reinforces the view that donor funding can and should be used as a catalyst to leverage market finance and stimulate broader sector-wide reforms that will enable local competitive markets to grow. The section advances the already noted pre-conditions to be met if market finance is to be a reality. These include: reducing political risks and encouraging centre–local relations that offer independence to operational managers; government support with debt such as debt to equity in Uganda; reforms and track records of improved performance; creditworthiness; operational surpluses; local capacity and 'know-how'; consumer awareness and choice.

## 110  *Beacon Mbiba*

### Mobilizing Local Market Finance for Urban Utilities

Studies concur that the establishment of good management systems, business plans, manpower and skills improvements, improved governance structures, performance and management contracts benchmarking, and government commitment to reform witnessed in recent years augur well for tapping into local market finance. Of the 14 water and sewage utilities surveyed by WSP (2009, p. 22) that include those in Kenya (Nairobi), Uganda (Kampala), Tunisia, Senegal, Burkina Faso and South Africa (Johannesburg and Durban), 80 per cent had operations that could cover operating costs through income, while more than 50 per cent were generating a surplus. The successes noted largely hinged on the use of management and performance contracts to address local challenges. WSP (2009, p. 18) records that the Senegal concession, leasing and performance contract arrangements have resulted in improvement in operational performance and tariffs gravitating towards cost recovery levels while maintaining a social policy to ensure affordability for the poor. These improved and stable conditions have led to success in the mobilisation of local market resources:

- In 1998, Citibank and Compagnie Bancaire de L'Afrique Occidentale (CBAO) extended a line of credit for US$24.1 million over six years, at 9.75 per cent interest rate as a structured arrangement with an escrow account for debt services and mutually contingent on donor financing being effective.
- Successful Citibank/CBAO line of credit was followed by a US$7 million direct loan by CBAO to Societe Nationale des Eaux Senegal (SONES)[30] for a design and build finance contract to which an extra US$16 million was provided by Banque Ouest Africaine de Développement (West African Development Bank) (BOAD). The government provided guarantees and a comfort letter to cover political risk (WSP, 2009, p. 18).

Similarly, improved conditions in Johannesburg enabled Johannesburg Municipality to source funds from local markets, mainly from Development Bank of Southern Africa (DBSA), and through issuing municipal bonds. The initial bonds were guaranteed by USAID's Development Credit Authority (DCA) and the International Finance Corporation's (IFC) Municipal Fund. However, subsequent bond issues did not have these guarantees. Since 2004, bonds worth about R2 billion (two billion) have been issued to finance a range of infrastructure developments.

The success of raising funds from local markets in the cases of Johannesburg Municipality and Senegal's water utility is not just dependent on the improved operational performance arising from the reforms and use of management contracts, but also on several other factors. These include the existence of extensive and vibrant banking and credit institutions, significantly large economies with relatively high income per capita (FinMark

Trust, 2010) and a supportive statutory framework. In South Africa, the legal/statutory regime permits local authorities to borrow. In addition, WSP (2009, p. 29) reports that municipal finance in South Africa has benefited from the government's Financial Charter:

> which classifies municipal infrastructure as a priority All banks and financial institutions have voluntarily agreed with the government on a five-year target of R23 billion for investment in municipal infrastructure. This has made it necessary for financial institutions to seek out markets in this sector and spur growth in business on competitive terms.

Improvements in financial management to secure long-term domestic market loans are helped by the presence of a competitive credit rating industry with firms such as Fitch and Moody's taking a prominent role in Southern Africa (WSP, 2009, p. 29).

Thus, the strategies and their impact are dependent on the context within which local authorities operate. The presence of competitive markets is again a major aspect and one where multi-lateral institutions and donors can act as catalysts. Both the impacts and progress resulting from donors and reforms vary. Unlike in South Africa and Senegal, reforms in Uganda's National Water and Sewage Corporation (NWSC) that have improved performance and creditworthiness have not leveraged market finance. This is not just a reflection of the weakness in the reforms within the NWSC, but also a result of the poor state of banking and credit institutions in the country. Uganda has limited banks and credit institutions compared to its neighbours, Kenya and Tanzania, and also compared to others such as Senegal, South Africa, Zimbabwe, Tunisia, Egypt and Senegal.

The limited financial infrastructure in Uganda is also a reflection of the statutory limits at play that make it difficult to borrow even where local authorities and service providers are doing well. WSP (2009) also concludes that Burkina Faso's water provider, ONEA, has made noteworthy reforms and operational successes that place it among the top African performers. But a low per capita income and the finance ministry's regulatory framework limits borrowing by state-owned enterprises. It is noted that in all these cases, the government provided guarantees for capital investment aligned or predicated on management contracts and successful performance.

Local conditions also affect the amounts of money that can be borrowed (see WSP, 2009, pp. 8–9 & pp. 33–34), but in general, borrowing for local governments and utility providers is heavily controlled (Table 4.7).

Access to loans by sub-national or local authorities has its own risks. For example, in good economic times, the value of assets that could be pledged as collateral appreciates. In crisis situations, the prices may collapse. This could lead to significant debt stress. There is no clear solution to these period crisis situations. But broadening and strengthening land-related collateral as well as continuous improvement in revenue collection is likely to be a good way to reduce risks.

112   *Beacon Mbiba*

*Table 4.7*   Borrowing from the Market for Service Provision in Africa

| Country of Service Provider | Status Regarding Borrowing from Market |
|---|---|
| ONEA, Burkina Faso | Subject to restrictions regarding borrowings for amounts exceeding CFA one billion with repayment periods exceeding one year. |
| NCWSC, Kenya | Nairobi City water and Sewage Company will need ministerial sign off prior to sourcing any substantial funding. |
| SONEDE, Tunisia | Societe Nationale d'Exploitation et de Distribution des Aaux (Tunisia) required ministerial approval on staff recruitment and sign off for any new debt. Relies heavily on government and donor funding for capex funding. |
| NWSC, Uganda | Is subject to restrictions on borrowing and relies heavily on government for capex funding. |

*Source:* Joffe et al. (2008).

## Mobilizing Donors for Market Finance in Urban Development

The significant role of donors and multi-lateral institutions has already been noted in the housing, water and sanitation sectors. The prognosis is that such donor funding has to be used creatively to support sector-wide reforms (UN-HABITAT, 2008a, pp. 148–149). The reforms enable markets to grow or help as part of a broader financial package that leverages private sector lending and promotes markets through output-based subsidies aimed at unlocking market potential or removing bottlenecks in the economy (Bovet, 1993).

However, perceived negative records of some donor interventions in Africa call for increased stakeholder participation (including consumers) in market reforms and strategies wherever market finance is used. Local honest brokers, such as expert centres, regional professional networks and university based research units (WSP, 2009, p. 11) can be useful in these processes. The United Nations Development Programme (UNDP) has acted as a broker in the land sector, while in the urban management sector, UN-HABITAT has been entrusted by various funders as both broker and project manager where local capacity is weak or where corruption is a concern. Illustrations from UN-HABITAT's recent interventions may be helpful:

- Using funding amounting to US$360,000 from the World Bank and Cities Alliance, UN-HABITAT was contracted to support the government of Mali and the National Association of Malian Municipalities to formulate a national program on slum improvement and prevention. This incorporated actions to identify and mobilize public and

# Financing Urban Development in Africa    113

private investment in slum improvements, build capacities of national and local authorities and document and disseminate the lessons and best practices.[31]

- With funds of over US$0.5 million, the Nigerian Nasarawa State sought the expertise of UN-HABITAT to help with strategic planning and management in four cities in the state (namely Lafia, Doma, Karu and Keffi) with an emphasis on capacity building.[32]

In Mali, donor funding has an in-built futurist approach to broaden opportunities for local and other financing. In the Nasarawa case, the State politicians (Governors, etc.) were aware of the capacity limitations in these regional urban centres and sought to ensure efficient and sustainable use of resources. Such use of expertise and sharing of experiences should be promoted, particularly in an African context where those institutions that have led 'turn-around' programmes could be engaged as consultants or contractors for others willing to learn.[33] Donor funding can facilitate such knowledge-based interventions.

Many African governments are keen to improve service conditions for their populations, but some remain burdened by debts. However, even in these cases, where political will and trust has been established, debt repayments can be swapped for investments in critical local government infrastructure. In Nairobi, the Italian government accepted such a 'swap' with funds targeted for redevelopment and improvement of the Korogocho slum.[34]

As summarised in Box 4.4, with South African aid to Zimbabwe, south–south aid is as crucial as north–south aid. South Africa has followed up the support for Harare infrastructure rehabilitation with a 2011 grant of R4 million to help Bulawayo City develop its water and waste infrastructure master plan (New Zimbabwe, 2011).

---

## Box 4.4 South-South Aid and Harare's Remarkable Turnaround

Zimbabwe's economic recession since 2000 and the hyperinflation in 2008 rendered government budgets and resources worthless and made established accounting or finance systems redundant. Projects like Kunzvi Dam needed to boost water supplies for Harare Metropolitan region (inclusive of Ruwa, Norton and Chitungiwiza satellite towns), estimated to cost US$370 million based on 2010 revised figures, have since been delayed. A collapsed water and sanitation infrastructure led to the cholera crisis of 2008–2009, forcing donors to take action.

The government assigned a US$17.1 million grant from South Africa to improving Harare's water and sewerage infrastructure from 2009. The resultant program focused on increasing water production, reducing water losses and collection and removal of sewage. By January 2010, 30km of replacement pipe had been laid, valves replaced and new pumps

*Continued*

## 114 Beacon Mbiba

> **Box 4.4** *Continued*
>
> Water production has now been increased by one-third, and water losses reduced. The city claims a coverage increase in Greater Harare from 50 percent to 80 percent in a six-month period. Sewage blockages have been greatly reduced. Helped by the stabilisation of currency, the city has managed a remarkable turn-around in its revenue stream. From a low of US$0.049 million, the monthly income stream achieved from water sales had already rebounded to US$4.0 million in September 2009.
>
> Rehabilitation of Harare's water infrastructure has seen the emergence, by default, of Harare Water as a separate delivery entity after the government returned to Harare City water and sewage services that had been given to ZINWA. Harare Water has generated interest from other cities, such as Bulawayo, regarding policy debates on the use of strategic business units and service delivery agreements for key local authority services.
>
> *Source:* World Bank Water and Sanitation Programme (WSP), African Development Bank (AfDB), United Nations Children's Fund (UNICEF) and World Health Organisation (WHO) (2010, p. 39) and key informant interviews, December 2010.

## RING-FENCING THE 'CASH COW': WATER ACCOUNT AND RESOURCES FOR CAPITAL DEVELOPMENT DEBATES IN ZIMBABWE

### Ring-Fencing the 'Cash Cow' Debate

To meet their legal mandates of delivering services to residents, local authorities transfer funds from accounts that generate surpluses (e.g. the rates account, water [Zimbabwe] and electricity [South Africa]) to those in need of support. Figure 4.6 shows the main sources of income for Bulawayo City where water generates between 40 and 60 per cent of the local authority's revenue.

Audited accounts for Bulawayo in Zimbabwe show that water and sewerage contributed over 40 per cent of the local authority income, accounting for less than 15 per cent of total expenditure. However, water and sewerage services generated more than 65 per cent of revenues transferred to other services. Health, education and social welfare are examples of services that do not generate much of their own income and depend on heavy subsidies from the water and rates accounts. The emerging question is whether continued transfers of large sums of revenues from water and sewerage accounts is sustainable, considering the dire need to finance maintenance work in the sector. The same argument could be extended to the rates accounts, where outdated valuation rolls and poor information systems call for investments in Geographical Information Systems (GIS) and Management Information Systems (MIS), and recruitment and retention of

*Financing Urban Development in Africa* 115

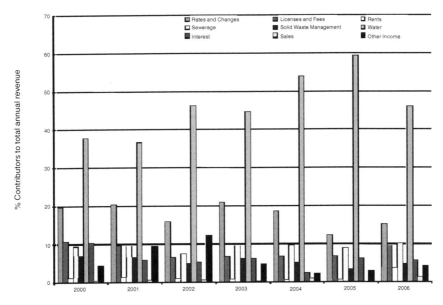

*Figure 4.6* Water as main source of revenue: Bulawayo City.

competent planners, valuers and engineers. Such investments would expand coverage and improve efficiency of the land based revenue.

In Zambia, following a decade of water management where the water account is completely ring-fenced, cross-transfer from the water account no longer exists. This has forced the other service sectors to be more efficient in using the little that they have. But there is always a limit to the total benefits given the large sums required. And in the water sector, the ring-fencing has not generated enough to support capital investments. Bulawayo City officials who have studied a similar approach in Etekwini Municipality (Durban) are of the view that ring-fencing has yielded better results largely because of the broader economic and institutional base in that city relative to cities in Zambia. At the same time, Johannesburg Water runs a successful system similar to that in Zimbabwe cities, where water revenues subsidise other services. So, which way forward?

For Bulawayo and Zimbabwean cities, the way forward may generally be something in between the following:

a) The allocation of water, sewerage and rates revenues to other services or departments should be capped at maximum, for example, 40 per cent for an agreed period, to allow some of the revenues generated in these key sectors to be used for enhanced capital investment, management and manpower improvements.

b) Capping transfers has to be time limited to encourage improved productivity, and could be revised upwards or downwards depending on

116   *Beacon Mbiba*

performance. Improved infrastructure is likely to expand and consolidate the total revenue base for these sectors with positive growth of total amounts transferred to other services, even if the percentage transfers remain capped. As with Zambia, the capping would stimulate innovations for efficient delivery of services in the other areas (health, education, welfare). Local authorities would focus government and donor grants to those sectors with limited revenue capacity.

c) Given the initial huge investment requirements, government guarantees for debt financing or special institutional arrangements like management contracts or concessions may be needed to attract private investment.

## CONCLUSIONS: REINFORCING HOLISTIC INTERVENTIONS FOR URBAN DEVELOPMENT FINANCE

UN-HABITAT (2008a, 2010) has correctly underlined that the persistent problems of urban poverty and slums are largely due to weak urban economies and finance for housing even in countries such as Mozambique, Tanzania, Malawi and Ghana where governance, accountability and national economic growth have been positive for years. This chapter has argued that instruments and programmes to raise the required urban development finance on their own will not yield sustainable results. Instead, they need to be part of broader programmes to strengthen urban economies (Tibaijuka, 2009). As captured by on-going World Bank and UN-HABITAT reports, in addressing urban economies, the broader program needs to:

- Encourage and create conditions conducive for household and private sector investments;
- Institute measures targeted at improving land information availability and access, security of tenure, contract management and dispute resolution, and entrench the gains in the rule of law and accountability as well as political stability, so as to facilitate the reduction of the costs of investments and the eventual prices of services; and
- Promote results-based management and strategic investments based on comprehensive benchmarking and continuous KPI development and monitoring.

Taking a holistic view of urban development helps to appreciate the central role of land in the process and how delays, bottlenecks and inefficiencies in this urban subsystem undermine whatever innovations may be initiated in financing of services elsewhere. The chapter underlined this link, especially as it relates to rapid physical expansion of cities such as Accra (Suleiman & Cars, 2010) and Dar es Salaam (Briggs & Mwamfupe, 2000; Kjellen, 2006). Increasing population densities outstretch capacity to provide services and

*Financing Urban Development in Africa*   117

infrastructure irrespective of the mode of the utility (see also Tremolet et al., 2010). Similar challenges have dented Lusaka WSC's commendable efforts to broaden water and sanitation coverage in the peri-urban settlements (NWASCO, 2008, p. 7).

The discussion in the last half of this chapter was pegged on utility management because it is a critical step towards creditworthiness that underpins access to market finance irrespective of whether the organisation is public or private. The initial improvements in performance have achieved 'turn around' and stability in the operations of the public utilities where PSP and commercialisation have been introduced. However, ambivalent political will (Suleiman & Cars, 2010, p. 279), limited knowhow and consumer poverty have kept public utilities vulnerable to economic shocks, and have eroded some of the gains. These structural conditions undermine 'take off' to sustainable "higher level equilibria" (Schwartz, 2009, p. 411). As asserted by Owusu (2006), in the long-term, only transparent, locally driven and politically sensitive initiatives will bring sustainable privatisation to urban Africa.

Complete lack of credible data is a conspicuous weakness of the urban development finance sector: a weakness lamented recently by Komives et al. (2005) and Tremolet et al. (2010) for water supply and electricity, and by UN-HABITAT (2008a), IAB (2010) and FinMark Trust (2010) for land information, urban economic data, housing finance and mortgages data. As revealed by UN-HABITAT (2008a, 2010) reports, the urban data unavailability and inaccessibility is most severe in Central Africa and in some countries in West Africa. Availability is better in East and Southern Africa, but accessibility remains patchy. Even in East and Southern Africa, data on land valuation and asset registers that are central to local government tax/finance are outdated, have low coverage and are not accessible. There is need for a concerted effort to promote collaborative ways to improve administrative records and the availability of and access to urban data (IAB, 2010).

The government or the public sector is a huge consumer of water and electricity. It is a major urban landlord and tenant, a major employer and also a producer of wastes in cities. The finance gap for local authorities and other providers of utility services arises partly from the government's failure, refusal or inability to pay rates, rents, utility fees and charges. Consequently, success in recovery of overdue bills and maintaining payment compliance from the government and public institutions is a major first step that would close the existing finance gaps and create conditions for market finance for utilities and local authorities. Associated with this are the issues of 'jurisdictional conflicts' and unfunded mandates where local authorities and service providers perform functions of central government and bear the costs from their own revenues without getting commensurate income or compensation from central government (UN-HABITAT, 2008a, p. 158).

With institutional cultural change, the water management experiences in Burkina Faso, Uganda, Zambia and South Africa illustrate that utilities

118    *Beacon Mbiba*

and service providers wholly owned by central or local government can operate just as efficiently as private sector operators, and can mobilise resources from local markets where legal frameworks permit and attract considerable foreign investment. Above all, they have managed to achieve turn around, register operational surpluses, restore consumer confidence and operate a 'rights based' service delivery that is affordable to or meets the needs of the poor sections of urban society.

The last section sought to highlight that even in conditions of crisis such as those in Zimbabwe, there are good lessons to be learnt, such as the role of targeted financing of critical sectors, innovations to deal with tariff arrears, raising maximum revenue from local sources and options for ring-fencing surplus revenue-generating services. Raising creditworthiness in these ring-fenced sectors has the potential to attract much needed market finance. There is need to support city level initiatives with national and regional utility support instruments, such as credit rating for local authorities, project development and a comprehensive urban indicators program.

## NOTES

1. See Map 4.1 in the fifth section of this chapter. In Uganda, National Water and Sewerage Corporation is responsible for water and sanitation.
2. In Zimbabwe, the Agriculture sector consumes 70 percent of all the water generated (GoZ, 2010a).
3. This will be discussed further in the section on 'ring fencing.'
4. Loss of revenue through corruption and waste "remains a major threat for Nairobi City" (see City of Nairobi Strategic Plan 2006–2012, p. 6).
5. Plus December 2010 interviews with city officials in Harare, Bulawayo and Gweru (Zimbabwe).
6. See MDG7 Target 10 on sustainable access to safe drinking water and sanitation; see "The Challenge of Slums: Global Report on Human Settlements 2003," Nairobi, United Nations Human Settlements Programme; and MDG Goal 11, Cities without Slums.
7. United Nations Conference on Human Settlements (HABITAT II), Istanbul, Turkey 3–14 June 1996. See UN-HABITAT, 2002.
8. See Suleiman and Cars (2010, p. 279) on how this undermines privatisation and reforms of urban water utilities in Ghana.
9. One such indicator for urban housing finance is the ratio of mortgage loans to total investment in housing (credit–to-value ratio). Currently, this is likely to be very low for most African cities. The indicator would enable inter-city comparisons and time-series monitoring of trends in the evolution of formal housing market finance.
10. Know-how and specialist skills (Harvey, 1996, p. 72) not usually found in the public sector may also be absent in the local private sector as witnessed in the water service contracts for Kampala (see section on water in this chapter).
11. Broad definitions of these models are presented in Annex 1
12. Only ten percent of the 715 reported water and sanitation PPPs were from Sub-Sahara Africa in the 1990s (see Sansom et al., 2003b, p. 18, volume 2).
13. Permission could not be obtained to use financial figures relating to projects in this section—Norton, OMPIC and New Makola II in Accra, Ghana.

Financing Urban Development in Africa   119

14. The prices and conditions were so high that most university lectures who were among the well to do middle class group at the time could not qualify.
15. Interviews with senior Harare City Officials in December 2010 indicated that the benefits of building the long-proposed Kunzwi Dam would be the same as replacing the leaking antiquated underground water pipes throughout the city. Meanwhile similar discussions in Bulawayo revealed that lack of funds for capital development has meant that the annual target to replace five kilometres of old pipes will be much higher post-2011 compared to the 2004 target.
16. For example Madina Market, north of Legon, peri-urban Accra.
17. Water lost through wastage, or lost through leakage in pipes during transmission and distribution, illegal/unauthorised connections, unauthorised use and evaporation.
18. Kampala Revenue Improvement Programme (KRIP) management contract from 1998.
19. See City of Nairobi Strategic Plan 2006–2012; Interviews with senior local government officers, Nairobi, July 2010, and Bulawayo, Gweru and Harare in December 2010.
20. See details of clear water Accra.
21. Author field observations, Accra 2002, 2005.
22. Unaccounted for water (UFW) is not just about water lost through leakages in the distribution system. It also includes water consumed but not reflected in the revenue streams due to low billing and bill collection efficiency, malpractices such as illegal connections, default payments and refusal to pay (Sansom et al., 2003b, p. 115).
23. See City of Johannesburg (2011) Johannesburg Infrastructure and Services Sector Plan 2011 pages ; 200 and 203.
24. Field notes July 2010.
25. After personnel costs, energy is the second major cost item for most water operators (see Joffe, 2009, p. 39).
26. Comprehensive data compilation and analysis for different cities is needed (for water, electricity, etc.).
27. See archives of legal cases on BASIC Services, including the famous Phiri residents or Mazibuko and Others v City of Johannesburg and Others at Centre for Applied Legal Studies (CALS), Wits Law School On-Line: http://web.wits.ac.za/Academic/CLM/Law/CALS/.
28. "Life-line" block pricing is implicitly a rights-based approach to water provision.
29. See Zambian case and the first section of this chapter.
30. A State owned entity, with 99.% government shares and 0.5% local authority shares).
31. Project "Formulation of a City without Slum Program for Mali," IMIS BAC, 2008-FCL-2030-C222–2833 UN-HABITAT Nairobi, 2008. Implemented by Regional Office for Africa and the Arab States (ROAAS), UN-HABITAT.
32. Project "Preparation of Structure Plans for Four Urban Areas in Nasarawa State, Nigeria," IMIS BAC 2008—QXB—2030-C231—2833 UN-HABITAT Nairobi, 2009. Implemented by Regional Office for Africa and the Arab States (ROAAS), UN-HABITAT.
33. Uganda's National Water and Sewage Corporation appears to be acting as consultant along these lines.
34. UN-HABITAT, Nairobi, 2008b. Implemented by Regional Office for Africa and the Arab States (ROAAS), UN-HABITAT.

## 120    Beacon Mbiba

## REFERENCES

Adams, D. (1994). *Urban planning and the development process*. London: UCL Press.

Blokland, M., Braadbaart, O., & Schwartz, K. (1999). *Private business, public owners: Government shareholdings in water companies*. The Hague: Ministry of Housing, Spatial Planning and the Environment.

Bovet, C. (1993). *Zimbabwe housing finance mobilisation study*. Key Biscayne Florida: IMCC Corporate Offices and Arlington Virginia: IMCC Washington Operations, U.S.

Briggs, J., & Mwamfupe, D. (2000). Peri-urban development in an era of structural adjustment in Africa: The city of Dar es Salaam, Tanzania. *Urban Studies, 37*(4), 797–809.

Cabannes, Y. (2004). Participatory budgeting: A significant contribution to participatory democracy. *Environment and Urbanisation, 16*(1), 2–46.

City of Johannesburg. (2010). *City of Johannesburg: Service delivery and budget implementation plan (SDBIP) 2010/2011*. Johannesburg: City of Johannesburg.

City of Johannesburg (2011) *Johannesburg Infrastructure and Service Plan 2011*. Johannesburg: City of Johannesburg.

City Council of Nairobi (2006) *City Council of Nairobi Strategic Plan 2006—2012*. Nairobi: City Council of Nairobi.

Doebele, W. A. (Ed.). (1983). *Land re-adjustment: A different approach to financing urban development*. Aldershot, UK: Lexington Books.

FinMark Trust. (2010). *2010 yearbook: Housing finance in Africa—a review of some of Africa's housing finance markets*. Parkview, Johannesburg: The Centre for Affordable Housing Finance in Africa, a division of the FinMark Trust.

Franzsen, R. C. D., & McCluskey, W. J. (2005). *Ad valorem* property taxation in Sub-Saharan Africa. *Journal of Property Tax Assessment and Administration, 2*(2), 5–14.

GoZ. (2010a). *Proceedings of the stakeholders meeting*. Harare: Ministry of Water Resources Development and Management, Republic of Zimbabwe.

GoZ. (2010b). *Zimbabwe: The 2011 national budget—Shared economy, shared development, shared transformation—Creating the fair economy*. Harare: Zimbabwe Ministry of Finance.

GoZ/USAID. (1995). *Zimbabwe shelter and urban indicator study*: Draft Final Report of Findings. Zimbabwe: Government of Zimbabwe, Ministry of Public Construction and National Housing/Zimbabwe National Coordinating Committee on Human Settlements (GoZ) and United States Agency for International Development (USAID).

Harvey, J. (1996). *Urban land economics*. London: McMillan Press Ltd.

Healey, P. (1991). Models of the development process: A review. *Journal of Property Research, 8*(3), 219–239.

IAB (2010) *Investing across borders 2010: indicators of foreign direct investment regulation in 87 economies*. Washington, DC: The World Bank.

Ingram, G. K., & Hong, Y. H. (Eds.). (2010). *Municipal revenues and land policies, proceedings of the 2009 Land Policy Conference*. Cambridge, MA: Lincoln Institute of Land Policy.

Joffe, M., Hoffman, R., & Brown, M. (2009). *African water utilities: Regional comparative utility creditworthiness assessment report*. African Water Association, Private Public Infrastructure Advisory Facility (PPIAF) and the African Development Bank: Washington, DC: The World Bank.

Kirkwood, A. D. (1997). *Standpipe maintenance in Luanda, Angola*. Paper presented at the 23rd WEDC Conference on Water and Sanitation for All:

Partnerships and Innovations. Durban, South Africa: Loughborough University, UK, Water, Engineering and Development Centre (WEDC).

Kjellen, M. (2006). *From public pipes to private hands: Water access and distribution in Dar es Salaam, Tanzania* (Unpublished PhD Thesis). Stockholm: Department of Geography, Stockholm University.

Komives, K., Foster V., Halpern J., & Wodon, Q. (2005). *Water, electricity and the poor: Who benefits from utility subsidies?* Washington, DC: World Bank.

Lambert, B. (2009). Diaspora and development? Nigerian organisations and the transnational politics of belonging. *Global Networks, 9*(2), 162–184.

Lemanski, C. (2008). Houses without community: Problems of community (in) capacity in Cape Town South Africa. *Environment and Urbanisation, 20*(2), 393–410.

Mbiba, B. (1995). *Urban agriculture in Zimbabwe: Implications for urban poverty and management.* Avebury: Aldershot, UK.

Mbiba, B., & Ndubiwa, M. (2009). Bulawayo. pages 82—140 in R. Lawrence & E. Werna (Eds.), *Labour conditions for construction: Building cities, decent work and the role of local authorities.* Oxford: Blackwell Publishing Ltd.

Mbiba, B., & Njambi, A. K. (2001). The challenge of urban and peri-urban transformations in Nairobi: Contradictions, conflicts and opportunities under globalisation. Pages 71—98 in B. Mbiba (Ed.), *Review of urban and peri-urban transformations and livelihoods in East and Southern Africa.* Urban and Peri-Urban Research Network (Peri-NET) Working Papers. London: South Bank University.

Mercer, C., Page B., & Evans, M. (2009). Unsettling connections: Transnational networks, development and African home associations. *Global Networks, 9*(2), 141–161.

Mills-Tettey, R., & Adi-Ado, K. (Eds.). (2002). *Visions of the city: Accra in the 21st century.* Accra: Woeli Publishing Services/Goethe-Institut Nationes Accra.

Mwanza, D. D. (2006). *Benchmarking of utilities for performance improvement.* Nairobi: Water and Sanitation Programme.

New Zimbabwe. (2011). South Africa extends R4M grant for Bulawayo water works. New Zimbabwe. Retrieved from http://www.newzimbabwe.com/news-4290-SAs%20R4m%20grant%20for%20Bulawayo%20water%20works/news.aspx (accessed 12th February 2014)

NWASCO. (2002). *Urban and peri-urban water supply and sanitation sector report 2001/2002, Zambia.* Lusaka, Zambia: National Water Supply and Sanitation Council (NWASCO). Retrieved from http://www.nwasco.org.zm (accessed 15th February 2014).

NWASCO. (2008). *Urban and peri-urban water supply and sanitation sector report 2007/2008, Zambia.* Lusaka, Zambia: National Water Supply and Sanitation Council (NWASCO). Retrieved from http://www.nwasco.org.zm (accessed 15th February 2014).

NWASCO. (2010). *Urban and peri-urban water supply and sanitation sector report 2009/2010, Zambia.* Lusaka, Zambia: National Water Supply and Sanitation Council (NWASCO). Retrieved from http://www.nwasco.org.zm (accessed 15th February 2014).

OMPIC. (1995). *Bluff Hill residential development design handbook.* Harare: Old Mutual Property Investment Corporation (Private) Limited.

Owusu, F. (2006). Differences in the performance of public organisations in Ghana: Implications for public sector reform policy. *Development Policy Review, 24*(6), 693–705.

Rakodi, C. (1996). Urban land policy in Zimbabwe. *Environment and Planning A, 28,* 1553–1576.

Sansom, K., Franceys, R., Njiru, C., & Morales-Reyes, J. (2003a). Contracting out water and sanitation services. *Volume 1: Guidance Notes for Service and*

## 122   Beacon Mbiba

*Management Contracts in Developing Countries.* Leicestershire, UK: Loughborough University, Water, Engineering and Development Centre (WEDC).

Sansom, K., Franceys, R., Njiru, C., & Morales-Reyes, J. (Eds.). (2003b). Contracting out water and sanitation services, Volume 2: *Case Studies and Analysis of Services and Management Contracts in Developing Countries.* Leicestershire, UK: Loughborough University, Water, Engineering and Development Centre (WEDC).

Schwartz, K. (2009). The reform of public water utilities: Successful utility reform efforts as punctuated equilibria. *Water Policy, 11,* 401–412.

Stren, R., & White, R. R. (Eds.). (1989). *African cities in crisis: Managing urban growth.* London: Westview Press.

Suleiman, L., & Cars, G. (2010). Water supply and governance in Accra: "Authentic" or "symbolic." *Water Policy, 12,* 272–298.

Thieme, T. (2010). Youth, waste and work in Mathare: Whose business and whose politics? *Environment and Urbanisation, 22*(2), 333–352.

Tibaijuka, A. K. (2009). *Building prosperity: Housing and economic development.* London: Earthscan.

Tremolet, S., Kolsky, P., & Perez, E. (2010). *Financing on-site sanitation for the poor: A six country comparative review and analysis.* Nairobi: WSP Sanitation Global Practice Team, Water and Sanitation Programme (WSP), World Bank.

UN-Habitat (1997). *The Istanbul Declaration and the Habitat Agenda.* United Nations Conference on Human Settlements (Habitat II). Nairobi: UN-Habitat.

UN-Habitat. (1998). *Financing cities for sustainable development: With special reference to East Africa.* Nairobi: United Nations Human Settlements Programme (UN-Habitat).

UN-Habitat. (2002). *The Istanbul Declaration and The Habitat Agenda, with subject index.* Nairobi: UN-Habitat.

UN-Habitat. (2008a). *The state of African cities 2008: A framework for addressing urban challenges in Africa.* Nairobi: United Nations Human Settlements Programme (UN-Habitat).

UN-Habitat. (2008b). *2008 annual report.* Nairobi: United Nations Human Settlements Programme (UN-Habitat).

UN-Habitat. (2009). *Challenges of municipal finance in Africa, with special reference to Gaborone, Botswana.* Nairobi: United Nations Human Settlements Programme (UN-Habitat).

UN-Habitat. (2010). *The state of African cities, 2010: Governance, inequality and urban land markets.* Nairobi: United Nations Human Settlements Programme (UN-Habitat)/UNEP.

World Bank. (2010). *Investing across borders.* Washington, DC: World Bank.

World Bank Water and Sanitation Programme (WSP), African Development Bank (AfDB), United Nations Children's Fund (UNICEF), and World Health Organisation (WHO). (2010). *Country status overview.* Draft report discussed with stakeholders from 8–9 April 2010. Harare, Zimbabwe: The WSP, the AfDB, UNICEF, and the WHO.

WSP. (2009). *How can reforming African water utilities tap local financial markets?* Nairobi, Kenya: World Bank.

Yahya, S. S. (2008). Financing social infrastructure and addressing poverty through wakf endowments: Experience from Kenya and Tanzania. *Environment and Urbanisation, 20*(2), 427–444.

Yeboah, C. N. (2010, 27 April). Ghana: Lending rates still at 33 percent. AllAfrica. com. Retrieved from *http://allafrica.com/stories/201004271122.html* (accessed 30th June 2010).

## ANNEX 1: UTILITY PRIVATISATION STRUCTURE: THE PUBLIC–PRIVATE CONTINUUM

*Table 4.8*  Utility Privatisation Structure: The Public-Private Continuum

| *Structure* | *Brief Description* |
|---|---|
| **Direct Public Management** | |
| Government Agency | Administrative unit of government. Includes the 'archetypal' municipal waterworks (local) as well as state or national public utilities (regional or supra-local). May be increasingly commercialized in their operations e.g. through performance–based rewards to agency officials, revenue collection and metering. |
| Parastatal | Water boards, corporations, authorities or trusts governed by public laws. Responsibilities and powers specified by special law. Supposed to be autonomous but face varying degrees of government involvement in daily business. |
| **Indirect Public Management** | |
| Publicly owned Corporation | Owned by the public, but act independently. Governed by corporate law. Intended to be entrepreneurial/commercial. Includes public water PLCs. |
| **Delegated Private Management** | |
| Service Contract | A contract for the execution of specified services, by a private entity. |
| Management Contract | The government pays the private operator to manage facilities, yet retains much of the operating risks. |
| Lease Contract/Affermage | A private operator pays fees to the government for the right to manage the facility and takes some of the operating risks. |
| Concession | A full concession implies that a private company runs a water undertaking for a given (usually long) period during which it also assumes significant investment and operational risks. Partial concessions include various forms of Build-Operate-Transfer arrangements. |
| **Direct Private Management** | |
| Divestiture or 'partial privatisation' | Private (government regulated) joint stock companies. The government transfers part of the equity in the state-owned company to private entities (operations and institutional investors). The private stake may or may not imply private management of the facility. |
| Divestiture or 'full privatisation' | Private (government regulated) utility. All assets privately owned. |
| NWSC, Uganda | Is subject to restrictions on borrowing and relies heavily on government for capex funding. |

*Source:* Adopted from Kjellen (2006); WSP (2009); Tremolet et al. (2010).

Kjellen, M. (2006). *From public pipes to private hands: Water access and distribution in Dar es Salaam, Tanzania.* Unpublished PhD Thesis, Department of Geography, Stockholm University.

Tremolet, S., Kolsky, P., & Perez, E. (2010). Financing on-site sanitation for the poor: A six country comparative review and analysis. Nairobi, Kenya: WSP Sanitation Global Practice Team, Water and Sanitation Programme (WSP), The World Bank.

WSP. (2009). *How can reforming African water utilities tap local financial markets? Insights and recommendations from a practitioners' workshop in Pretoria, South Africa, July 2007 (revised in 2009).* Nairobi, Kenya: Water and Sanitation Programme-Africa, The World Bank.

# 5 Upgrading Informal Settlements in African Cities

*Solomon Mulugeta*

## BACKGROUND

Housing is one of the basic needs of human beings, just like food, water and clothing. As such, housing is not a privilege but a right. In fact, the right to housing is one of the integral elements of the economic, social and cultural rights of human beings as recognised by the member states of the United Nations. In connection with this, Article 25 (1) of the Universal Declaration of Human Rights (UDHR), which was adopted in 1948, stipulates the following[1]:

> Everyone has the right to a standard of living adequate for health and wellbeing of himself and his family, including food, clothing, housing and medical care, and necessary social services and the right to security in the event of unemployment, sickness, disability, widowhood, old age, or other lack of livelihood in circumstances beyond his control.

This provision of UDHR attests to the fact that the nations of the world recognised housing rights as a component of the right to an adequate standard of living as early as 1948. However, due in part to decades of either inadequate or inappropriate actions by most signatories of this declaration, more than 1 billion people around the world are presently inadequately housed. The principal forms of settlements that presently provide largely makeshift shelters to nearly every inadequately housed person around the world are informal settlements that are commonly known as slums and squatter settlements. What is more, about 100 million of those who are inadequately housed are fully homeless, without any form of roof over their heads.

The urban populations of the world that are presently living in slums and squatter settlements are almost exclusively citizens of developing countries. For example, out of a total of 923 million people residing in informal settlements around the world in 2001, approximately 98 per cent were living in the developing world. During the same year, about 72 per cent of Sub-Saharan Africa's urban population were living in informal settlements. Comparatively, about 43.1 per cent of the urban populations of the

Asia-Pacific region and 32 per cent of those of Latin America were living in similar settlements, whereas only 9.6 per cent of the urban populations of countries in transition economies and five per cent of those with advanced economies were living in such settlements during the same period (Tannerfeldt & Ljung, 2008; UN-Habitat, 2005a).

The principal aim of this chapter is to explore the nature, roots, overall characteristics and trends of informal settlements in the developing world and the actions taken by various stakeholders to mitigate the problems they pose to orderly urban life. More specifically the study attempts to provide a modest characterisation of informal settlements and the dangers they pose to the quality of urban life in Africa. The relationships between informal settlements and rural settlements and the benefits as well as the modalities of upgrading these settlements will also be explored. In order to achieve these objectives, the chapter is divided into five sections. The first section provides general background and addresses the issue of how informal settlements are defined. In the second section, a characterisation of the quality of life in informal settlements is presented with a particular emphasis on the case of the cities of Sub-Saharan Africa. The third section presents the root causes of the proliferation of slums and squatter settlements in Africa, while in the fourth section, the need for and the modalities of upgrading such settlements are discussed. Concluding remarks are presented in the fifth section.

## Defining Informal Settlements

The terms "informal settlements," "slums," "squatter settlements," "spontaneous settlements," "shanty towns" and "shacks" are used interchangeably by many scholars. It strongly appears that it is the more or less similar physical characteristics and socio-economic conditions of the inhabitants of these settlements that have led many writers to use these terms interchangeably. In fact, almost all of these settlements tend to be characterised by predominantly shabby and densely packed dwellings located in poorly serviced and squalid residential environments. In most cases, their inhabitants tend to be people belonging to the lowest income stratum and are as such living in highly overcrowded and extremely unsanitary conditions.

The interchangeable use of the terms has undoubtedly led to misconceptions with regard to what makes some of these settlements either similar or different. As Matovu (2000) argues, these misconceptions have considerable policy implications. In connection with this, Matovu adds one more term, "urban low income settlements," and states the following:

> The perceived definition of these terms has a bearing on government policies regarding such settlements. The nature of government response to these settlements, whether tolerant or aggressive, is determined by its perception of these settlements.

126 *Solomon Mulugeta*

The policy implications referred to by Matovu are particularly relevant to the misperceptions that concern the terms "slums" and "squatter settlements." The term "slum" has been widely used to describe both inner and peripheral squatter settlements nearly as much as it has been traditionally invoked to describe any poorly built or rundown residential areas of a city. A "squatter settlement" actually refers to illegal occupancy of land regardless of the quality of its built environment or the condition of most of the housing units of which it is made.

Illegal occupancy of urban land ranges from random actions of individuals or groups over a prolonged period of time to a relatively large scale, highly organised and swift invasion of vacant urban land as was the case when about 20,000 people invaded 211 hectares of abandoned private land in two peripheral districts of Buenos Aires in 1981 (Hardoy & Satterthwaite, 1995). In most cases, those who invade either public or private land tend to exploit existing gaps in the policy or practice of urban land administration to erect makeshift residential structures. The construction of such shelters usually takes place at night under the cover of darkness and with the support of relatives or friends.

In contrast, a settlement that was once affluent or legally occupied may develop into a slum due to overcrowding, inadequate servicing or simply as a result of prolonged neglect and disrepair. What is more, some slums that are integral parts of major cities of Africa today were once outlying rural communities or villages before the cities expanded and subsumed them. This means that while squatter settlements tend to be overwhelmingly slums, all slums are not necessarily squatter settlements.

Although it is said that "everyone knows a slum when he sees one" (Tannerfeldt & Ljung, 2008), there isn't as such a universal agreement on what constitutes a slum. As Matovu (2000) rightly argues, it is either "country or city specific because what may be good enough in one place is problematic and offensive in another." Irrespective of this reality, for the purpose of this study, the operational definition provided by UN-Habitat (2005a) has been adopted. According to this operational definition, a slum household is one that lives in a dwelling that lacks one or more of the following:

1. Sufficient amount of water for family use, at an affordable price, available to household members without being subject to extreme effort, especially to women and children.
2. Improved sanitation either in the form of private or public toilet shared with a reasonable number of people.
3. Security of tenure as confirmed through:
   a) evidence of documentation that can be used as proof of secure tenure status; and,
   b) either de facto or perceived protection from forced evictions.
4. Structural quality and durability to protect its inhabitants from the elements of climatic conditions such as rain, heat, cold, and humidity.

## Upgrading Informal Settlements in African Cities    127

4. Sufficient living area for the household where not more than two people share a room.

The definition of a slum household that is shown above adequately describes the slums that are component parts of the built-up areas of most of the major cities of Sub-Saharan Africa. In the recent past, scholars have increasingly preferred to use the term "informal settlements" to refer to both types of settlements, apparently to play down the social and political implications of the pejorative undertones that the terms "squatter" and "slum" carry.

The term "squatter settlement" almost invariably evokes poverty, squalor, and illegality. Similarly the various terms that are used across the continents to refer to the same type of settlement, including the more popular ones such as "favela," "barrios," "shanty town," "bustee," "skid row" and "ghetto," also carry serious negative connotations. The term "slum" is actually no less pejorative than these, as it clearly denotes rundown and congested residential areas that are characterised by high incidence of crime, including widespread prostitution and frequent homicide.

Not surprisingly, both squatter and slum communities tend to be opposed to the common use of these terms because their negative connotations may ultimately lead to the singling out of their neighbourhoods as problem areas or cancers that should be removed. Even though the term "informal settlements" doesn't fully do away with the negative connotations, the fact remains that for now, scholars do not have a more politically correct or tolerable term that can describe either type of settlement. Based on this understanding, the term "informal settlements" is used to refer to both slums and squatter settlements in this study.

## CHARACTERISTICS OF INFORMAL SETTLEMENTS

Informal settlements around the world display a number of inherent traits that are fairly similar. They are predominantly inhabited by the urban poor, the majority of whom lack the qualifications that could earn them well-paying and secure jobs in the formal economy. The incomes they earn from the informal activities they engage in to survive are typically very low and intermittent. They cannot therefore find affordable rental accommodations in the formal housing sector.

Squatter settlements usually spring up when a good proportion of such needy individuals build makeshift shelters in an incremental way by illegally occupying vacant urban land. An exceptional situation exists in Addis Ababa, Ethiopia, where close to two decades of brutal Marxist rule has so severely disrupted the functioning of the urban housing market that many middle-income households had to resort to squatting, especially in the 1970s and 1980s, in order to put roofs over their heads.

128 *Solomon Mulugeta*

A substantial proportion of squatter houses around the world therefore tend to be owner occupied[2]. However, there are also "slum landlords" or "slumlords" as they are colloquially referred to. These are individuals who purposely build shacks in response to the shelter needs of people who cannot afford to pay the monthly rents of formal sector accommodations. A good number of these "slumlords" are absentee landlords. They are typically either highly placed government officials or simply local merchants.

The other common feature among informal settlements is that they are usually located at the peripheral areas of major cities. More commonly, they tend to appear within 10 kilometres of the central business district (CBD), often as an appendage to the main built-up area. In some cases, they emerge in more distant locations with a clear separation from the city. This, for instance, is the case in Epworth, Harare, where an informal settlement accommodating an estimated 250,000 people developed outside the city, about 12 kilometres from the CBD.

These settlements are located on the peripheries of the cities principally as a result of poor governance and inappropriate or outdated legal and institutional frameworks, which drive the price of urban land far beyond the reach of even the moderate and middle income households.

The likelihood of land invasion by squatters, however, is much greater in countries where all urban land is nationalised than where it is freely bought and sold. For instance, squatting was almost impossible in Addis Ababa before the July 1975 nationalisation of all urban land. Until then, nearly all the private land owners were vigilant enough to keep out squatters from their properties. In more or less similar fashion, various public and religious institutions also put in place mechanisms for deterring the invasion of their properties by squatters.

The nationalisation of all urban land inadvertently did away with mechanisms to protect vacant urban land from illegal occupation. It opened a wide opportunity for squatters to occupy vacant spaces around the city. Thus, due to the combined effect of the abolition of private ownership of land and the acute housing shortage that followed the nationalisation of all rental accommodations, the estimated population of Addis Ababa that lived in squatter settlements soared from what was almost non-existent before 1975 to about 15 per cent by the mid-1990s[3].

When informal settlements sprout in the inner city locations, they usually locate themselves in marginal areas that were either reserved for later use or simply left out of development action due to reasons such as non-suitability for housing or other forms of development. Thus, such areas usually happen to be vacant lands bordering railway tracks, steep slopes that have the risks of landslides, valley bottoms, former quarry sites or plains that have serious problems of either water logging or flooding. In some cases, inner city slums may occupy portions of prime urban land for mainly historical reasons. In some exceptional circumstances, squatters may successfully invade and stay in more suitable parts of the inner city.

Characteristically, land invasion or squatting tends to be intensified during political crises, when local governments are not focused enough to exercise effective control over developments that take place in certain peripheral localities within their jurisdictions. The law enforcement ability of municipal authorities can be temporarily overwhelmed during the periods of confusion or political uncertainty that usually follow violent changes of government or widespread public unrest. This opens up opportunities for squatters to invade vacant urban land. Irrespective of the conditions under which squatters operate, the haste that characteristically dictates the manner by which they subdivide vacant land and erect dwellings usually results in a haphazard packing of a large number of predominantly unfinished makeshift shelters into a very narrow area.

Even though informal settlements tend to display similar characteristics in origin, location and overall content, the severity of some of the key housing and social problems faced by their inhabitants may vary considerably, depending largely on the geographical, historical and socioeconomic backgrounds of the wider society to which they belong. For example, the proportion of people living in such settlements and the degree of overcrowding that they display varies considerably even between developing nations. In India, 55 per cent of Mumbai's population lives in informal settlements, which cover only six per cent of the city's land area[4]. In Uganda, 40 per cent of Kampala's population lives in informal settlements that cover 20 per cent of the land. According to UN-Habitat (2005a), "there are 40 per cent more slum dwellers in African cities than in an average city worldwide."

There is sometimes so much difference in the quality of life in informal settlements that the appearance of a residential neighbourhood that is dubbed substandard in a predominantly affluent society may easily be seen as an economically better off community if it were located in a setting where the majority of the population were poor. Due mainly to this reason, there may be very little resemblance in terms of layout and build between the informal settlements of, for example, Turkey and India, Brazil and Kenya, or even Tunisia and Zimbabwe. Largely owing to the same reasons, the nature and severity of the problems of daily life faced by people living in such communities, and the threats that their existence poses to orderly living in the cities of which they are a part, also varies from place to place.

## Some Aspects of the Quality of Life in the Informal Settlements of Sub-Saharan Africa

Due to the low socioeconomic status of their inhabitants and the manner in which they are created, urban informal settlements in Sub-Saharan Africa characteristically display woefully poor housing conditions in terms of overall habitability, access to basic services and tenure security. The dwellings are constructed using materials that range from crude plastic sheeting, cardboards or scrap metal, to various types of largely substandard cinder

## 130   *Solomon Mulugeta*

blocks, stones or bricks. Nonetheless, in many parts of the continent, most of these dwelling units tend to be predominantly attached structures that are made of wattle and daub. They have no proper foundations and ceilings. They also tend to have dirt floors. On top of that, it is not uncommon for the roofs of these dwelling units to leak rainwater due either to poor construction or lack of proper repair.

Another critical factor that characterises the majority of dwelling units in the informal settlements of urban Africa is the fact that they tend to be very small structures with one or two rooms at the most. For example, in the slums of Kampala, 54 per cent of the households live in single room houses known as "muzigo" (UN-Habitat, 2007). In most cases, separate kitchens and toilets are a luxury for the average household living in such settlements. Thus, the already limited space of the living room naturally becomes a multi-purpose room for the members of the household.

Moreover, room densities in such dwelling units could easily be several times larger than the maximum of two persons per room as the acceptable standard for healthy living by UN-Habitat. To make matters worse, in situations where one or another member of the household is running a home-based informal business enterprise to augment the characteristically meagre and intermittent family income, the living room also serves as a commercial establishment. If the business is about selling traditional drinks, children and even the elderly may be forced to spend much of the day and early evening hours uncomfortably outside the house in the usually very narrow, crowded, trash-littered, dusty or muddy, foul smelling alleyways.

Regarding basic services in informal settlements in urban Africa, only a fraction of the housing units, if any, have connection to water mains and power grids. In fact, the majority of the squatter families in the continent have to buy water from private vendors at prices that are much higher than the amount charged for supplies by the public sector. The proportion of the urban population of Africa that has no access to safe water is between 35 to 50 per cent. Thus, it is no surprise that the overwhelming majority of the slum or squatter households of the continent have no direct access to potable water. In most cases informal settlement households access electricity through illegal connections to the nearby power grid. The amount of electricity that flows to individual houses under such illegal arrangements is often so low that it cannot even provide adequate lighting, let alone be used for other crucial household needs such as cooking or ironing of cloths.

Regarding housing tenure, inner city informal settlements tend to have a markedly high proportion of rental accommodation. This is the case, for instance, in some of the rundown areas of inner Addis Ababa, where rental accommodation comprises up to three-quarters of the housing units. Peripheral informal settlements, on the other hand, usually consist of a high proportion of self-built or owner occupied units. Nonetheless, their illegal status clearly implies that they may be subject to demolition at any time, certainly without any compensation and often without adequate prior warning.

## Upgrading Informal Settlements in African Cities   131

While households living in these types of settlements account for a substantial proportion of the city's population, the majority live under constant threat of forced evictions as municipal governments are unwilling to give them title deeds. Due mainly to this, almost all of them are reluctant to significantly improve the qualities of their dwelling units even when their household income increases. Although evictions often take place when the lands occupied need to be reclaimed for some public use, it is not uncommon for municipal authorities to raze down squatter homes either to prove that they are in control or simply to discourage further development of such settlements. In countries where the public sector owns either some portions or the totality of urban land and rental housing, forced evictions that occur in the informal housing sector tend to affect both homeowners and tenants in a similar fashion.

As mentioned earlier, most of the dwelling units in informal settlements tend to be haphazardly packed into very narrow areas. Thus, the population densities in such areas often rise to thousands of persons per hectare, especially in the older and well-rooted communities. This, for instance, is the case in Kibera slum in Nairobi. Here, more than half a million people dwell in a highly crowded manner in an informal settlement that covers only 235 hectares[5]. Even though overcrowding is a common feature of informal settlements in Sub-Saharan Africa, the kind of congestion in Kibera is exceptional.

In most cases, the growth rates of the populations of informal settlements tend to be markedly higher than the average for the city they are a part of, due mainly to both high rates of natural increase and in-migration. In addition to receiving migrants from nearby and distant localities, such settlements often gain a considerably large number of new settlers from the inner quarters of the very city of which they are a part.

The dependency ratios of these settlements are usually very high, mainly because about half of the population are children under 15. The prevalence of poverty is invariably high, with no less than half of the inhabitants living below the absolute poverty line. Not surprisingly, their rates of unemployment could easily exceed the 33 per cent mark. In the worst cases, well over half the working-age populations in these settlements may be unemployed, as was the case in some parts of the Ethekwini Municipality of Durban, South Africa. About 57 per cent of the labour force was without employment during the first half of the current decade[6].

## Threats to Orderly Living

The high population densities in informal settlements create poor conditions for healthy living. Not only are the houses in informal settlements too small, but they may also be shared by two or more households in the most difficult circumstances. Life in such congested spaces is difficult for raising children. Playgrounds are limited or non-existent. School-going children cannot do their homework at night because of both lack of adequate space

## 132 *Solomon Mulugeta*

and proper lighting. The girl child is further disadvantaged. She is expected to help her mother in looking after her younger siblings. She fetches water from distant vendors or springs on a daily basis. It is therefore evident how daunting it is for a child born and raised in an informal settlement in urban Africa to succeed in school and manage to find gainful employment in the highly competitive job market.

Further, the widespread absence of proper toilets, the constant presence of open sewers and the heaps of uncollected garbage, together with the characteristic overcrowding of informal settlements expose their inhabitants to health threats. This includes tuberculosis, which, in association with AIDS, has increasingly become a major cause of death in the informal settlements of many cities of Africa.

Children and women bear the brunt of the discomfort in an informal settlement, as they remain confined to the house for much longer than adult males. The women especially suffer significantly, not only because they have to take care of both the healthy and the sick children, but also because they have to cook for the household. Beyond this, it is almost invariably the women who are required to run home-based businesses while at the same time managing the household chores in such a cramped environment.

Because the living room of the average slum or squatter dwelling also serves as a kitchen, both women and children are continuously exposed to the smoke from the open hearth that is familiar in such dwellings. The health risk of children living in such settlements is particularly accentuated by the fact that the meagre incomes earned by the average slum households are not even sufficient enough to ensure food security for the entire household. Largely owing to this, the slums of urban Africa tend to have proportionally twice as many malnourished children as are found in their non-slum areas. For instance, the proportion of malnourished children under the age of five is above 20 per cent in the slums of Kenya, Malawi, Mozambique and Uganda, whereas the comparative figure for children in the non-slum areas of these countries is markedly under 10 per cent.

The haphazard construction of too many dwelling units in narrow areas also creates a considerable threat to orderly living in both the informal settlements and other parts of the city in several ways. For instance, the manner in which houses are built creates a highly chaotic land use pattern that cannot be corrected without causing a massive and costly dislocation of thousands of households. Such dislocations, if and when they happen, take place without advance preparation of commensurate and affordable accommodation for the evictees, and result in worse slums elsewhere in the city. In the unlikely situation that new houses are built in advance for evictees, the new dwellings are usually located far from the city centres, which are usually the main areas of employment for the urban poor.

The characteristically chaotic land use pattern makes servicing informal settlements extremely difficult. It is challenging, if not impossible, to build roads or to lay power grids and water mains in the major parts of such settlements even when the political will and the resources required to do so exist. As a result, these settlements lack even the most basic infrastructure, including access roads, street lights, water supply and drainage.

Due largely to this problem, it is often very difficult or impossible to provide critically important emergency services to the inhabitants of these settlements. For instance, women in labour may die in the process of childbirth simply because they cannot access ambulance services. A fire that accidentally breaks out in one or another corner of the settlement may easily run out of control and gut hundreds of dwellings that cannot be accessed by fire engines.

The high unemployment and poverty that characterise informal settlements also pose a substantial threat to the orderly way of life in both the slum and non-slum areas of urban Africa. As already indicated, the rates of unemployment could easily rise to above 50 per cent in some parts of such settlements. Among the principal reasons behind this are the peripheral locations of most of these settlements, the predominantly poor academic qualifications of their residents and above all, the poor performance of the various economic sectors of the countries concerned.

The widespread unemployment, the woefully unsanitary, overcrowded and non-dignifying residential environment, together with the characteristically narrow, winding, unlit and rarely policed roads and alleyways of these settlements encourage the proliferation of various types of criminal actions ranging from simple pick-pocketing to more sophisticated drug dealing and high rates of homicide that can easily spill over to the rest of the city. Under such circumstances, it is not surprising if these settlements serve as centres of open prostitution and as areas where certain ill-prepared, cheap and health threatening homebrewed liquors are bought and sold without any supervision by law enforcement officers. What is more, it is not unlikely for such settlements to serve as hiding places for members of organised crime.

## MAJOR FACTORS BEHIND THE PROLIFERATION OF INFORMAL SETTLEMENTS

Many factors contribute to the proliferation of urban informal settlements in Africa and the rest of the developing world. In Sub-Saharan Africa, they include highly accelerated rates of urban population growth, high incidence of rural and urban poverty, inappropriate policies, archaic legal and institutional frameworks, dysfunctional land markets, poorly developed financial markets and lack of good governance and political will. A brief description of the ways in which these factors have influenced the state of affairs in African cities in this regard is presented below.

## Highly Accelerated Urban Growth Rates

During the second half of the 20th Century, Africa witnessed an urban growth rate approximately twice that of the global annual average. Although the continent's annual average urban growth rate has dropped

134  *Solomon Mulugeta*

from a high of about 4.2 per cent in the early and mid-1990s to a low of about 3.3 per cent in 2008 as shown in Table 5.1, it is still about 1.7 times as high as the comparative figure for the world. If the continent continues to grow at this rate, its total urban population, which was about 372 million in 2007, will rise to about 568 million by 2020. In comparison, Europe's projected urban population for the same year will be 540 million (Tanner-feldt & Ljung, 2008).

The accelerated urban growth rate of Africa is consistent with the pattern of urban growth observed in nearly all of the least urbanised regions of the world. However, the speed of urbanisation must be distinguished from the level of urbanisation. In 2007, only about 38.6 per cent of Africa's 964 million inhabitants lived in urban places, meaning that the continent was approximately half as urbanised as the developed world. But following global patterns, the urban populations of the least urbanised regions of Africa, especially those of Eastern and Central Africa, are currently growing at rates that are well above four per cent per annum.

The accelerated urban growth rate of Africa is a product of the comparatively high rates of natural increase and net rural-to-urban migration. While high rates of natural increase continue to fuel the growth of the population of nearly all of the urban places in Sub-Saharan Africa, it strongly appears that it is the largest cities of the continent that both attract and absorb the majority of domestic migration, be it of rural or urban origin. This is evident from the fact that the number of the largest cities of the region with population sizes of one million or more rose from only six in 1975 to 22 in 2003. During this period the population size of Lagos, the regions' largest city, soared from what was just under 2 million in 1975 to the shocking size of 10.1 million in 2003 (UN-Habitat, 2005a) [7].

Much has been written over the last several decades to indicate that a high proportion of the high rates of domestic migration to cities in Africa was almost exclusively induced by rural poverty. Nonetheless, it now appears that rapid economic growth, if and when it occurs, also tends to have either the same or even stronger effect on the rate of rural-to-urban migration in the continent (Drakakis-Smith, 2000).

Irrespective of the nature of the factors that induce rapid urban migration in Africa, the tens of thousands of young rural men and women that arrive in the major cities every year are simply too ill qualified to find even low paying formal sector jobs at their destinations. Thus, they join the informal sector in order to win their daily bread and survive in the cities. Nothing indicates this better than the fact that the informal sector presently provides jobs for about 50 to 70 per cent of the urban labour force in most African cities.

As incomes earned from informal sector jobs are by their nature very low and intermittent, most migrants naturally seek shelters in the informal settlements where they can either erect their own makeshift shelters or simply become tenants of slum landlords. Due mainly to this reason, Africa's

*Table 5.1*  Average Annual Urban Growth Rates by Major Areas and Regions, 1960–2025 (%)

| Index | Major area, region and country | 1950–1970 | 1970–1990 | 1990–2000 | 2000–2010 | 2010–2020 | 2020–2025 |
|---|---|---|---|---|---|---|---|
| 1 | **World** | 2.98 | 2.61 | 2.26 | 2.19 | 1.87 | 1.58 |
| 2 | More developed regions | 2.09 | 1.05 | 0.64 | 0.83 | 0.62 | 0.48 |
| 3 | Less developed regions | 4.04 | 3.79 | 3.07 | 2.74 | 2.29 | 1.91 |
| 4 | Least developed countries | 5.14 | 4.83 | 4.07 | 3.76 | 3.69 | 3.51 |
| 5 | Less developed regions, excluding least developed countries | 3.98 | 3.71 | 2.99 | 2.65 | 2.14 | 1.72 |
| 6 | Less developed regions, excluding China | 4.08 | 3.78 | 2.81 | 2.45 | 2.25 | 2.07 |
| 7 | **Sub-Saharan Africa** | 5.10 | 4.59 | 3.92 | 3.69 | 3.57 | 3.40 |
| 8 | **Africa** | 4.82 | 4.27 | 3.49 | 3.29 | 3.20 | 3.05 |
| 9 | **Eastern Africa** | 5.71 | 5.56 | 4.14 | 3.83 | 4.13 | 4.03 |
| 30 | **Middle Africa** | 5.10 | 4.15 | 4.04 | 4.00 | 3.62 | 3.28 |
| 40 | **Northern Africa** | 4.36 | 3.63 | 2.49 | 2.20 | 2.01 | 1.81 |
| 48 | **Southern Africa** | 3.19 | 3.07 | 2.97 | 2.00 | 1.28 | 1.15 |
| 54 | **Western Africa** | 6.02 | 4.87 | 4.05 | 3.95 | 3.74 | 3.47 |

*Source:* United Nations, Department of Economic and Social Affairs. (2011). *Population division: World urbanization prospects, 2011 revision*. New York: United Nations office.

## 136  *Solomon Mulugeta*

slum and squatter population has been growing at about 4.5 per cent per annum in recent years. This figure is two percentage points higher than the rate of natural increase of the total urban population (2.7 per cent). As UN-Habitat put it,

> Based on these estimates, if no effective pro-poor policies are undertaken, urban slum populations are likely to double, on average, every 15 years, while the total population doubles every 26 years. In 2015, the urban slum population of Africa should reach 332 million. (UN-Habitat 2005a)

In addition to what is stated above, two other factors of population dynamics contribute greatly to the rapid growth of the slum population of urban Africa. The first is the fact that migrants of rural origin who settle in the slums of African cities are predominantly young people, due mainly to selective migration. Secondly, the rates of contraceptive use by married women of childbearing age in African cities are low[8], while those of particularly younger women, especially those aged 15–19 years, appear to be even lower. In general, the rate of contraceptive use tends to rise with the age of married women of childbearing age.

On average, about 23.9 per cent of married women aged 15–49 used contraceptives in Sub-Saharan Africa between the years 2000 and 2005. The comparative figure plummeted to 14.1 per cent for women aged 15–19. The corresponding figures for those in the 20–24 and 25–29 age categories were 21.8 and 24.8 per cent respectively.

## Deepening Urban Poverty

The rapid growth of the slum populations in Africa is also due the fact that much of the accelerated urban growth rates have not been accompanied by commensurate expansion of the economies of many countries in the continent. In fact, what has become increasingly clear in the recent past is

*Table 5.2*  Distribution of African Countries by Real GDP Growth Rates, 1990–2011

|                 | 1990–1999 | 2000–2009 | 2010 | 2011 |
|-----------------|-----------|-----------|------|------|
| Negative        | 5         | 1         | 1    | 3    |
| 0–3 %           | 24        | 11        | 9    | 9    |
| Above 3% to 5%  | 15        | 22        | 15   | 18   |
| Above 5%        | 7         | 18        | 27   | 22   |
| Not Available   | 2         | 1         | 1    | 2    |
| Total           | 53        | 54        | 53   | 54   |

*preliminary estimates

## Upgrading Informal Settlements in African Cities    137

that the economies of many Sub-Saharan African nations have been either stagnating or moving forward at a snail's pace, especially during the last two decades. Some economies even contracted.

As shown in Table 5.2, only seven African nations had real GDP growth rates of more than five per cent during the 1990–1999 decade, whereas the comparative figures for 24 countries was between zero and three during the same period. The number of countries whose economies were contracting during this period was five. All of this was happening in a continent that was, as mentioned above, displaying aggregate urban growth rates of more than four per cent during the greater part of that decade[9]. Not surprisingly, scholars have dubbed this phenomenon "urbanisation without growth."

Table 5.2 also shows that the real GDP growth rates of about 34 per cent of the countries in Africa were above five per cent per annum between 2000 and 2009. However, an examination of the distribution of the same countries by real per capita GDP growth rates shows a considerably different picture. In fact, only 7 of the countries had real per capita GDP growth rates of more than five per cent in 2010. The comparative figures ranged between 0 and 1.5 per cent for 10 countries, whereas those of 6 countries were actually negative (African Development Bank, 2010). Thus, the fact remains that while the urban populations of Africa were persistently growing by leaps and bounds, the performance of their national economies has for the most part been poor.

One of the main consequences of the mismatch between the demographic and economic growth rates of many countries of Sub-Saharan Africa in the recent past has been persistently high rates of inflation, deepening poverty, worrisome polarisation of incomes, fast-growing rates of unemployment and homelessness in their major cities.

In fact, as the latest available data indicates, the proportion of both the rural and urban populations of African nations living below the poverty line is alarmingly high. At the national level, more than 40 per cent of the populations of most of these countries are still living below the poverty line. The incidence of poverty passes even the 70 per cent mark in some cases, such as experienced in the Democratic Republic of Congo (DRC) in 2006, when 71.3 per cent of the total population was found to be living below the poverty line. Sierra Leone closely follows DRC in this case with a figure of 70 per cent in 2003.

Even though rural areas tend to have higher incidences of poverty than urban areas as shown in Table 5.3, more than half of the urban population in several countries is already in a poverty trap.

In order to appreciate the impact of both fast-growing populations and the high incidence of poverty on the quality of urban housing, the figures given in Table 5.3 need to be interpreted within the context of the types of houses that those in a poverty trap can afford to build. The woefully high incidence of urban poverty that currently plagues African cities is very much tied to the fact that as stated above, about 50 to 70 per cent of

138   *Solomon Mulugeta*

*Table 5.3*   Population Living Below Poverty Line in Selected Countries of Africa

| Country | Survey year | Rural | Urban | National |
|---|---|---|---|---|
| | **Population Below National Poverty Line (%)** | | | |
| Algeria | 1998 | 16.6 | 7.3 | 12.2 |
| Angola | 2001 | 94.3 | 62.3 | 68.0 |
| Benin | 2003 | 46.0 | 29.0 | 39.0 |
| Botswana | 1993 | 44.8 | 19.4 | 32.9 |
| Burkina Faso | 2003 | 52.3 | 19.9 | 46.4 |
| Burundi | 2006 | 68.9 | 34.0 | 66.9 |
| Cameroon | 2007 | 55.0 | 12.2 | 39.9 |
| Cape Verde | 2007 | 44.3 | 13.2 | 26.6 |
| Chad | 2003 | 58.6 | 24.6 | 55.0 |
| Central Afr. Rep. | 2008 | 69.4 | 49.6 | 62.0 |
| Comoros | 2004 | 48.7 | 34.5 | 44.8 |
| Congo | 2005 | 57.7 | 55.4 | 50.1 |
| Congo Dem. Rep. | 2006 | 75.7 | 61.5 | 71.3 |
| Cote d'Ivoire | 2008 | 54.2 | 29.4 | 42.7 |
| Egypt | 2008 | 30.0 | 10.6 | 22.0 |
| Eritrea | 1993–1994 | | 62.0 | 53.0 |
| Equatorial Guinea | 2006 | 79.9 | 31.5 | 76.8 |
| Ethiopia | 2005 | 39.3 | 35.1 | 38.9 |
| Gabon | 2005 | 44.6 | 29.8 | 32.7 |
| Ghana | 2006 | 39.2 | 10.8 | 28.5 |
| Guinea-Bissau | 2002 | 69.1 | 51.6 | 64.7 |
| Kenya | 2005–2006 | 49.1 | 33.7 | 45.9 |
| Liberia | 2007 | 67.7 | 55.1 | 63.8 |
| Madagascar | 2005 | 73.5 | 52.0 | 68.7 |
| Malawi | 2006 | 47.0 | 25.0 | 45.0 |
| Mauritania | 2008 | 59.4 | 20.8 | 32.0 |
| Morocco | 2007 | 14.5 | 4.8 | 9.0 |
| Mozambique | 2008 | 56.9 | 49.6 | 54.7 |
| Senegal | 2005 | 61.9 | 35.1 | 50.8 |
| South Sudan | 2009 | 55.4 | 24.4 | 50.6 |
| Sudan | 2009 | 57.6 | 26.5 | 46.5 |
| Rwanda | 2011 | 48.7 | 22.1 | 44.9 |
| Uganda | 2009 | 27.2 | 9.1 | 24.5 |
| Zambia | 2006 | 76.8 | 26.7 | 59.3 |
| Zimbabwe | 2003 | 82.4 | 42.3 | 72.0 |

*Source:* African Development Bank. (2008). *Gender, poverty and environmental indicators on African countries*; African Economic Outlook. (2012).

the urban labour forces in Sub-Saharan Africa are earning their incomes from informal sector employment. A further critical factor is that due to a relentlessly high inflation rate, the majority of these households spend anywhere between two-thirds and three-quarters of their earnings on food alone in order to survive in a city environment[10]. It is therefore unthinkable for most of them to save any money, let alone to consider living in houses that meet the minimum standards. Furthermore, they cannot contemplate accessing mortgages, because they have neither regular income nor anything to represent collateral to qualify for loans in the formal money market. Micro-finance services lack the capacity to provide medium-term loans for housing construction. Even in situations where such services appear to be somewhat expanded, their use is largely confined to the stimulation of small enterprises.

## Inappropriate Policies and Weak Institutional Capacity

A critical factor behind the mushrooming of informal settlements in Africa is that urban development is largely an unmanaged process in the continent. This lack of management largely stems from the inappropriate national urban policy frameworks on the one hand, and the weak institutional capacity of both national and local governments on the other. At the national level, most Sub-Saharan African countries simply lack a comprehensive urban development strategy. Due in part to this reason, these countries lack clear national policy guidelines for dealing with existing informal settlements and for implementing measures required to prevent the formation of new slums and squatter settlements.

The major policy decisions that directly or indirectly affect the process of urban development in many African countries are made in a highly fragmented manner by sector ministries. As Cities Alliance (2006) puts it, "cities are often as much affected by implicit urban policies (such as energy pricing or housing finance rates) as by explicit policies (such as by establishment of metropolitan structures and specific investments in the urban area)". In the absence of national urban development strategies, these implicit or explicit urban policies will have the upper hand in dictating the path of development that urban centres are forced to follow. Further, both the implicit and explicit polices that govern urban development are often either outdated or simply copies of policies developed for industrially advanced economies. Thus, the legal and regulatory frameworks that govern urban management in many countries of the region usually prove either inapplicable or unfit for guiding urban development in the preferred direction.

Local governments, irrespective of the nature of the directives they receive from higher government bodies, tend to be too weak to effectively control and guide urban growth and development. Their weaknesses largely stem from their inability to shoulder broad responsibilities, due mainly to their lack of autonomy. As Tannerfeldt and Ljung (2008) rightly argue, urban development happens principally "as a result of local efforts and

140 *Solomon Mulugeta*

local resources." They particularly stress that "slum upgrading and safety should normally" be "a direct responsibility of local government with support from central government." Cities Alliance (2006) also underlines this fact when it states the following:

> Local government is especially relevant in city development. It is closer to the main stakeholders, it can become the knowledge hub for urban innovation, and it plays an important role in delivery (directly or indirectly through subcontracting, concessions, and the like) of facilities and services that are the responsibility of local government or the equivalent publicly accountable bodies. (Cities Alliance, 2006)

Local governments have to exercise a sufficient degree of self-rule in order to make a positive and lasting impact on the urban development process. However, it strongly appears that only a few municipal governments in Africa, if any, enjoy the kind of autonomy that enables them to bring about such a lasting impact. The principal factor behind this is the over-centralisation of power by central governments, which limits the political and legal mandates of most municipal authorities in the continent. The powers of most local governments is in fact so much constrained that they have very little or no influence over the opinions or actions of the various national authorities or agencies that are responsible for the production and delivery of critically important public services.

The activities of these national authorities usually take place in a fragmented manner as each agency tends to be responsible for the provision of only a single key public service, such as electricity, water supply, fixed line telephone and major roads. Even though municipal governments are as a rule responsible for the provision of bundles of several other key services such as fire protection, solid waste collection and disposal and the management of urban roads and public parks, they tend to be technically and financially much less equipped than most of the major service-providing national agencies.

This fragmented approach to the production and delivery of urban services inflicts many and often mutually reinforcing damages on the wider urban environment. For instance, the multiplicity of national agencies that are responsible for the provision of several key urban services by itself seriously complicates the urban management process as each organisation tends to plan and execute its activities independently.

Because inter-agency relationships are often seriously constrained by the sheer absence of mechanisms for coordinating their activities, it is not uncommon for the efforts of one governmental institution to be significantly frustrated by either the action or inaction of another public organisation. This is particularly the case in a city like Addis Ababa, where certain key public services are provided to informal settlements often without the consent of municipal authorities. Such developments, as a rule, tend to

## Upgrading Informal Settlements in African Cities 141

encourage the rapid expansion of informal settlements because squatters naturally take the connection of their residential sites to key infrastructure, such as access roads, power grids and water mains, as a strong sign of the recognition of their settlements by municipal authorities.

Furthermore, when one of the national agencies and a given local government encounter one another in discharging their respective responsibilities, the former tends to dominate. For instance, where inappropriately located telephone poles have to be removed in order to upgrade an existing street, municipal authorities are generally required to wait for both the decisions and actions of the national telecommunications authority concerning the status of those telephone poles.

The waiting time for the appropriate decision or action by that particular governmental entity may sometimes last for months or even a year or more, thereby exposing municipal authorities to increased costs in terms of both labour and material in a country where double digit inflation rates are most probably more of the norm than the exception. Beyond this, municipal authorities may be required to pay compensation to the national telecommunications authority for all the costs that the latter incurs in the process of the removal and replacement of the unwanted telephone poles at rates that it determines unilaterally. As municipal authorities tend to operate on low budgets, the long waiting time in combination with the unfair rates of compensation and the almost inevitable effects of the chronic corruption that usually mars the operations of urban local governments finally compromise the quality of the upgraded street that emerges at the end of the project period. It is thus clear that the upkeep of such a poorly built street will continue to drain municipal coffers for many years to come.

The functions of most municipal governments in Africa are seriously compromised by either the absence or inadequacy of political commitment and the sheer lack of professionalism. These problems are usually an outcome of two common organisational shortcomings. First, there is an absence of clear separation of powers between state and municipal functions.

This often results in the mixing up of political and professional activities. The problem is particularly serious when municipal leaders happen to be political appointees rather than elected mayors and councillors. In such situations, municipal authorities not surprisingly tend to be more loyal to national governments than to the citizenry. Even when municipal leaders happen to be elected officials, it is not uncommon for many of them to set aside their leadership roles and meddle with the day-to-day operations of both middle and lower level professionals.

Such interference not only results in the violation of professional and ethical standards, but also instils a sense of fear and insecurity among professionals. Many have to make the hard choice between pleasing their corrupt bosses and upholding the rule of law at the cost of either their jobs or personal freedom and well-being. In such a working environment where the greed of municipal leaders leaves no room for professional ethics,

## 142 *Solomon Mulugeta*

zoning ordinances are frequently violated by the discretionary actions of the bosses.

High sounding urban development programmes, such as sites and services or slum and squatter upgrading projects, are nothing more than lip service given to those in need in order to secure their votes during elections. Urban development programmes can never be effectively implemented in the absence of a genuine political commitment of those in authority.

Secondly, local governments tend to be markedly ill-staffed as their salary scales can neither attract nor retain highly qualified professionals[11]. The low salary scales of the personnel of most African municipal governments are a significant cause of chronic corruption that renders city governments woefully ineffective when it comes to the design and implementation of pro-poor urban development programmes.

### The Rural Connection

As indicated, one of the major factors behind the mushrooming of urban informal settlements is the high rates of net in-migration. The majority of the migrants are usually young people from nearby and distant rural areas. The quality of life that such migrants experience once they have entered the city is dictated by the meagre income that they earn from engagement in informal activities. Given their income, it is only in the outer informal settlements that they can find affordable accommodation, either as tenants of slumlords or as occupiers of self-built shacks. Once they have settled in those areas, they encourage potential migrants to leave rural areas and join them.

Because rural-to-urban migrants happen to be predominantly young people of child bearing age, their fertility rate remains high long after they have entered the city. Many scholars argue that this contributes strongly to the rapid growth of city populations, thus overstretching the ability of urban centres to cope with the daunting pressures of "overpopulation." Largely based on this understanding, researchers and policymakers long viewed rural-to-urban migration as a serious problem that deserved remedial policy action. Consequently, many thought for decades that the best way to minimise the perceived problem of overpopulation was the introduction of effective rural development programmes that could eventually encourage potential migrants to stay either in the rural areas or in the nearby small towns. Apparently led by such thinking, the former Marxist regimes of Sub-Saharan Africa, such as those of Ethiopia and Tanzania, even resorted to the introduction of pass laws that either directly or indirectly restricted the flow of people from rural areas to the major cities of Addis Ababa and Dar es Salaam.

In more recent times, the once widely held policy of keeping rural-to-urban migration in check has increasingly lost currency due to new attitudes that urban slums have certain positive impacts, both environmentally and socially. Many scholars now contend that the environmental impact of high density of informal settlements is considerably smaller than that of dispersed rural communities. As the fertility rates of new slum dwellers have been found to be considerably lower than originally thought, there is no longer meaningful justification for the fear of overpopulation.

Furthermore, scholars argue that the risk of overpopulation is indeed far stronger in labour-intensive subsistence agricultural activities. Urban migration reduces this risk significantly by freeing up more cultivable land, thereby leading to less damage to the physical environment on the one hand, and to a more efficient modern agricultural system on the other. Moreover, many now argue that it is unwise to try to stop rural-to-urban migration. In fact, all things considered, it is the person who has migrated to the city that has far greater opportunities to disentangle herself or himself from the grips of poverty in a matter of a few years compared to the one who has chosen to stay in a rural area as a subsistence farmer.

The other positive view of life in urban informal settlements holds that as the experiences of many countries show, it is only when a substantial proportion of the rural population has moved to the cities that a meaningful and mutually reinforcing economic growth takes place in both urban and rural areas. Most researchers think that irrespective of how or where the migrant lives in the urban environment, it is only after the proportion of the urban population of a country reaches or exceeds the 40 or 45 per cent mark that this symbiotic urban–rural relationship begins to make significant positive impacts on the quality of life in both areas. This thinking thus supports increased rural–urban migration even if it means the swelling of the population of the informal settlements in the short run.

## UPGRADING INFORMAL SETTLEMENTS

Even though the emergence of informal settlements in the developing world dates back to the colonial period, government responses to the problem started mainly in the early post-independence decades of the 1960s and 1970s. More than anything else, it was the sudden and large-scale influx of rural populations into the major cities of such countries due to the abrupt end of the colonial policies that used to keep such migrants at bay that prompted most governments to seek solutions for the informal settlement problem in those days. Initially, most governments tried to address the problem by allocating budgets for the direct construction of what were then deemed to be largely low-cost dwellings. With the rather naive anticipation that the best solution for the problem of informal settlements was to replace them with more acceptable purpose-built apartments and core houses, many of them also introduced programmes for the clearance of informal settlements and redevelopment of the areas concerned. This led to massive evictions of slum and squatter households in many parts of the world.

144   *Solomon Mulugeta*

Policymakers attempted to do away with the problem of informal settlements by relocating slum households primarily in areas outside the city. This idea lost currency as it meant moving urban low-income households to locations that were too far away from the city centre, which served as their main source of employment. An attempt to correct this problem later led to the development of a policy that required temporarily relocating slum residents until new houses were built for them on their original sites.

However, it did not take long before the policymakers realised that the new apartment dwellings were unaffordable for the majority of the people who were expected to benefit. Moreover, the high rise buildings could not provide adequate ground-level space for the neediest households to augment their incomes by running home-based businesses as they would do before the onset of the slum clearance programme. In addition, policymakers became increasingly aware that the eradication of informal settlements simply helped exacerbate the urban housing shortage by reducing the housing stock.

The increased awareness of the detrimental impacts of slum clearance programmes on urban housing provision did not bring the practice of evicting slum and squatter households to a complete halt. The sporadic bulldozing of slum and squatter settlements continues to take place in many countries. Nonetheless, a positive outcome of the increased awareness of the negative consequences of eradicating informal settlements was that it made scholars and policymakers to rethink their decisions.

Rather than attempt to handle slum and squatter settlements as a general concern, focus shifted on addressing the housing plight of the urban poor in particular. Among the notable works that the rethinking of the issues produced at the height of this period was the seminal work of J. F. C. Turner, which was published in the closing years of the 1960s, just in time to popularise the concept of aided self-help housing.

The central idea of Turner's thinking was that urban low-income households needed a measure of government support in order to access decent housing. By the early 1970s, many policymakers and scholars around the world were not only aware of the solutions suggested by Turner, but they were also willing to put them to test. It was this change of mind that led to the recognition of the informal sector and consequently to the realisation of the need for upgrading informal settlements (Tibaijuka, 2009).

Another important landmark of the early 1970s was that it was during this period that the United Nations and the World Bank recognised "housing investment as an integral part of economic development." Similarly, the mid-1970s had other milestones of great significance in the evolution of the responses of the international community to the housing plight of the urban poor of the developing world. For instance, the United Nations Habitat and Human Settlements Foundation was established in 1974. According to Tibaijuka (2009), this new arm of the UN was mandated by the General Assembly to "serve as an international financial institution with authority to lend to member states [and] mobilise resources for their shelter and infrastructure programmes." In 1977, this organisation was merged with the UN Department of Housing, Building and Planning to create the United Nations Centre for Human Settlements (UNCHS) or UN-Habitat.

The increased recognition that Turner's ideas gained and the growing interest that the UN showed in addressing the issue of informal settlements in the developing world considerably influenced the urban development strategies that many developing countries followed from the 1970s on. In particular, the enthusiasm that many UN member states showed towards improving the conditions of their urban housing stock eventually led to World Bank support for programmes aiming at meeting the housing needs of the urban poor.

Even though the World Bank was not formally committed to funding urban housing programmes until the publication of its Housing Sector Policy in 1975, it began to provide support for informal settlement upgrading projects in Latin America prior to making its new policy known to the wider public (Tibaijuka, 2009). The sites and services schemes that gained popularity in Sub-Saharan Africa and in other parts of the developing world by the early 1970s were also rooted in the interest shown by the World Bank to support such projects.

The popularity of the sites and services or the self-help housing schemes, however, did not last long due to a combination of constraining factors ranging from the paucity of funds for housing construction to the lack of effective and sustained political commitment. Of all the factors that limited the success of these programmes, perhaps the most discouraging was the slow and silent evictions that a good proportion of the beneficiaries succumbed to as their dwellings were sooner or later bought out by wealthier households.

Because the majority of the beneficiaries were simply very poor households who had various other unmet social and economic needs, they could not resist the attractive prices that the wealthier households offered for the new dwellings that they occupied through aided self-help or sites and services programmes. Due in part to these and several other related operational shortcomings, the low-income housing policies of the 1970s failed to make a dent in the growing problem of the formation of informal settlements in the developing world.

As the earliest planned interventions in the urban housing sector failed to thwart the persistence and accelerated growth of large informal settlements, interest in the *in-situ* upgrading of such settlements started to gain currency in many developing countries. Thus, by the mid-1980s, slum and squatter upgrading programmes were firmly rooted as the most preferred policy response to the housing plight of the people dwelling in the informal settlements of many countries of Sub-Saharan Africa and the rest of the developing world. Nonetheless, it is important to bear in mind here that in many countries, informal settlement upgrading programmes have been implemented side-by-side with the periodic execution of elements of the

146    *Solomon Mulugeta*

older urban housing policies, such as the direct construction of ostensibly low-cost dwellings by governments and the relocation of some slum and squatter households.

The eviction of slum and squatter households usually happens when such settlements occupy lands declared to be of critical importance for other public use. This was, for instance, the case when 800,000 people were forcibly removed from their homes in Seoul, South Korea, to improve the image of the city for the Olympic Games in the late 1980s. As recently as 2001 and 2002, about 1.8 million people were evicted from their homes whilst about "3.9 million were under immediate threat of eviction in Asia" (The Asian Coalition for Housing Rights, October 2003). In some cases, slum dwellers are evicted when their settlements happen to be located in areas that are threatened by high risks of environmental disaster, such as flooding or landslides.

## The Benefits of Upgrading Informal Settlements

Upgrading informal settlements is an urban development programme that involves the provision of integrated services, which are intended to significantly improve the welfare of households living in slum and squatter settlements. As such, it invests in citizens with the prime objective of thwarting the deteriorating trends that are observable in such settlements. It also strives to prevent the formation of new slums. Its principal components include improvements in the quality of infrastructure and housing, and the formalisation and titling of property to ensure tenure security and to stimulate investment.

Improvements in the quality of infrastructure in such settlements typically involve the provision of access roads, lighting, potable water, sanitary facilities, waste collection services, schools, health facilities and community centres. Even though the general expectation is that improvements in the quality of the physical housing takes place incrementally following the regularisation of property, direct assistance may be provided to the neediest households depending largely on the gravity of the problem and the availability of funds. Irrespective of these facts, a programme for the upgrading of informal settlements does not necessarily view all slum and squatter dwellings as immune from demolition. In fact, under certain compelling situations, some dwelling units may have to be demolished to give way for improvements in neighbourhood infrastructure or simply to move households in cases where their dwellings are located in areas that have very high risks of environmental disaster.

While an informal settlements upgrading programme is typically spearheaded by national governments or municipal authorities, its success depends largely on the active participation of the key stakeholders, including the target populations, community groups, NGOs and the private sector. Successful informal settlements upgrading programmes benefit both the residents of such settlements and the non-slum population of the city by significantly lessening the threats that the existence of such settlements poses to orderly living. According to Cities Alliance[12], upgrading of informal settlements particularly benefits a city in the following ways:

- Fostering inclusion: Slum upgrading addresses serious problems affecting slum residents, including illegality, exclusion, precariousness and barriers to services, credit, land, and social protection for vulnerable populations, such as women and children.
- Promoting economic development: Upgrading releases the vast untapped resources of slum dwellers who have skills and a huge desire to be a more productive part of the economy, but are held back by their status and marginality.
- Addressing overall city issues: It deals with city issues by containing environmental degradation, improving sanitation, lowering violence and attracting investment.
- Improving quality of life: It elevates the quality of life of the upgraded communities and the city as a whole, providing more citizenship, political voice, representation, improved living conditions, increased safety and security.
- Providing shelter for the poor: It is the most effective way to provide shelter to the urban poor at a very large scale and at the lowest cost.

These observations indicate that informal settlements upgrading programmes uphold the fundamental rights of people to decent housing and dignified living as stipulated in Article 25 (1) of the Universal Declaration of Human Rights. What is more, Cities Alliance stresses that slum upgrading is affordable, flexible and viable. As regards affordability, they contend that slum upgrading "costs less and is more effective than relocation to public housing." With regard to flexibility, Cities Alliance maintains that informal settlements upgrading "can be done incrementally by the city and by the residents at a pace that is technically and financially possible for both." They believe that the viability of the programme comes mainly from the fact that "the poor can and are willing to pay for improved services and homes." [13]

The benefits of upgrading informal settlements as discussed above can be satisfactorily achieved only when the policy environment ensures the active participation of all the key stakeholders in the conception, design and implementation of slum and squatter improvement programmes. Among the leading actors in this regard are the residents of the informal settlements, for which the upgrading programmes are intended.

Of no less significance is the degree to which local governments are empowered to assume broader responsibilities and to access the resources required to effectively oversee the planning and execution of informal settlements upgrading programmes. Up to this point, however, most national governments have either by design or by default chosen to operate in a

## 148 *Solomon Mulugeta*

policy environment that did not give much credence to the need for empowering either the citizens or local governments. Partly owing to this, most informal settlements upgrading programmes around the world have had only limited successes regardless of the substantial resources that were allocated to them over several decades.

## Recent Approaches to the Upgrading of Informal Settlements

While it now appears that there is a worldwide consensus on the major benefits of upgrading informal settlements, the modalities and the short-term outcomes of such urban development programmes may vary significantly from one country to the next. In general, some informal settlement upgrading programmes strive to be community-led and reasonably comprehensive in their approaches to the highly challenging issues of improving the lives of slum and squatter dwellers. Others tend to be much less citizen driven and focus only on the improvement of one or two aspects of the complex and multifaceted problems of such settlements.

For instance, recent slum and squatter upgrading strategies pursued in Durban, South Africa and in Kampala, Uganda set out to be primarily people driven, focused on particular target areas and addressing wider community issues ranging from improving neighbourhood infrastructure to land titling. Comparatively, even though the informal settlements upgrading programmes of Addis Ababa were participatory to some extent, they focused largely on addressing the citywide problem of improving neighbourhood infrastructure in general and upgrading access roads in particular.

More often than not, variations in the modalities of informal settlements upgrading programmes stem from differences in the historical background and socioeconomic realties of the countries concerned, as well as the degree of citizen participation. They also vary in the contents of the package of services provided to the target communities.

In several countries in Sub-Saharan Africa, it is either the scarcity of funds or operational constraints brought about by the outdated or dysfunctional legal and institutional frameworks that have been the major factors behind the unsatisfactory outcomes of many slum and squatter upgrading programmes. Above all, in countries where both the beneficiary populations and the local governments are not sufficiently empowered, it is simply impossible to conceive, design and implement inclusive, holistic, effective and viable informal settlements upgrading programmes.

Due mainly to the inadequate rates of citizen participation in the formulation and implementation of informal settlements upgrading policies, and owing to the absence of democratic local governments in many countries, many informal settlements upgrading programmes worldwide have fallen short of attaining their declared goals in the last few decades. Even though Internet sources display an impressive list of examples of best practice in the upgrading of such settlements, it turns out that there are far more stories of

_Upgrading Informal Settlements in African Cities_  149

frustrated aspirations, total failures and even adverse outcomes than success stories in slum and squatter upgrading programmes to date.

Thus, as stated earlier, not only are many large slums showing very little or no improvement, the sporadic eviction of households living in such settlements is also continuing to take place in many parts of Africa and the rest of the developing world. This, however, does not mean that humanity has failed to find solutions for the problem of informal housing. As shown below, the most plausible solution to this problem appears to be the community-led informal settlements upgrading programme. However, prior to discussing the relevance of community-led informal settlement upgrading problems, a cursory glance at the relationship between the MDGs and informal settlements upgrading programmes is in order.

## MDGs and Informal Settlements Upgrading

As already discussed, the poor performance of the economies of many countries in Sub-Saharan Africa, the deepening poverty and the increasing polarisation of incomes are to a large extent responsible for the proliferation of informal settlements. Based on the awareness that the continuation of business as usual would not reverse the deteriorating trends of the living conditions of the people of the developing world, the member states of the UN convened a summit in New York in September 2000 and agreed to significantly scale up poverty reduction programmes. The major outcome of the summit was the Millennium Declaration, which committed the member states to put in place all the measures required to significantly improve the living standards of the people of the developing world by 2015.

The Millennium Declaration spelt out the following eight Millennium Development Goals (MDGs):

1. Eradicate extreme poverty and hunger;
2. Achieve universal primary education;
3. Promote gender equality and empowerment of women;
4. Reduce child mortality;
5. Improve maternal health;
6. Combat HIV and AIDS, malaria and other diseases;
7. Ensure environmental sustainability; and
8. Develop global partnership for development.

Because all of the MDGs are interrelated, the successful implementation of any one of them would considerably contribute towards the achievement of most of the others. As such, each has its own specific targets.

The MDG that specifically aims at improving the living conditions of the people living in informal settlements is Goal 7, Target 11, which intends to achieve "a significant improvement in the lives of at least 100 million slum

150 *Solomon Mulugeta*

dwellers" by 2015. This is an extremely ambitious project, the successful implementation of which will cost billions of dollars in nearly every country that tries to achieve the MDGs. Due mainly to this reason, the successful achievement of Goal 7, Target 11 is as much dependent on efforts made by the industrially advanced nations to make good on the promises they made in Goal 8, as it relies on the necessary measures that the developing nations have to put in place in order to democratise and to attain peace, security and development.

However, as the experience of many African countries shows, the likelihood of them achieving Goal 7, Target 11 of the MDGs by the specified date is low for three main reasons. First, the economies of many countries of the region are not growing strongly enough to suggest that they are well poised to achieve the MDGs. In fact, only a handful of countries of Sub-Saharan Africa have so far managed to consistently register real GDP growth rates of about six per cent or more, a figure that is generally taken as a good indicator of their likelihood to achieve a good number of the MDGs. Christine Kessides confirms this when she states the following:

> It is estimated that, assuming continued population growth of two per cent per year, cutting poverty rates from 47 per cent in 2001 to 22 per cent in 2015 in line with the Millennium Development Goals would require that the real GDP of African countries grow by at least six per cent per year, or slightly less if inequality improves (Iradian, 2005). Only four countries—Botswana, Mauritius, Mozambique, and Uganda—sustained growth rates close to this target in the past decade, thanks to strong industry and services. (Kessides, 2006)

Secondly, the generous financial assistance and better terms of trade promised by the industrially advanced countries have not materialised to date. In fact, until mid-2007, it was only two industrially advanced nations, namely Sweden and the Netherlands, that had complied with their promises of providing up to 0.7 of their GNP to the developing world in support of the implementation of the MDGs. Thirdly, most countries of the region simply lack the political culture and the legal and institutional framework that are required to scale up poverty reduction programmes at rates that can help them to achieve the MDGs. Thus, it strongly appears that little progress is being made in most countries in Sub-Saharan Africa by way of achieving Goal 7, Target 11 of the MDGs.

## Community-Led Informal Settlements Upgrading Programmes

Community-led informal settlements upgrading programmes are neither a product of academic research nor the creation of policymakers. They are the product of the organised responses that slum and squatter households around the world give to the largely non-inclusive urban housing policies of their respective countries and to the perpetual threats of eviction with which they have been living.

In fact, it was largely after such households lost faith in the will and abilities of their governments to reverse the deteriorating trends of their residential environments that they resorted to various forms of organised struggles to influence the outcomes of policies affecting informal settlements. Initially, their responses started by spontaneously putting up stiff but largely unsuccessful resistance to evictions. Later, many of them set up slum dwellers' associations in order to challenge policies that adversely affected their well-being. After a little while, these associations coalesced into national federations of slum dwellers.

A good example is the Indian Alliance or the network of slum communities in India, which set up the National Slum Dweller's Federation (NSDF) in 1974. The NSDF was particularly encouraged by the professional assistance it received from an NGO known as Society for the Promotion of Area Resource Centres (SPARC), and the emergence in 1986 of Mahila Milan, a network of women's associations that enabled women pavement dwellers to begin work on housing with SPARC (CLIFF, 2003).

Presently, there are a fairly large number of similar slum dwellers' associations in Africa, Asia and Latin America. As voices of slum and squatter dwellers, many of these grassroots associations have managed to make municipal authorities to listen to the urban poor, especially in those countries where the degree of suppression of political dissent is severe. A good example is the federation of all slums and informal open-air markets in Kenya. It has assisted residents of Kibera who are living and trading along the railway line to prevent the demolition of their houses and businesses by effectively negotiating with the Kenya Railway[14].

The presence and growing influence of networks of slum dwellers' associations around the world has, in particular, elevated issues concerning informal settlements upgrading and the constant threats of eviction under which slum and squatter households live. With the clear intent of building on the encouraging foundations laid by slum dwellers' associations, several international organisations that aim to nurture the global network of slum dwellers' associations and streamline the informal settlements upgrading efforts of national and local governments, NGOs and other relevant stakeholders have emerged as reliable partners of these associations during the last three decades. For example, the UK charity-based organisation, Homeless International, has been working "as an ally of Shack/Slum Dwellers International, the international network of slum dwellers federations," in addition to continued cooperation with its member federations for over two decades now. The Community-Led Infrastructure Finance Facility (CLIFF) has been engaged in the promotion of community-based informal settlements upgrading programmes around the world, at least as of 2002. CLIFF's activities are not limited to providing support in the areas of finance. As its August 2003 Annual Report shows,

## 152  *Solomon Mulugeta*

> [it] offers the opportunity for a diverse range of organisations to combine not only funding, but also insights and knowledge that emerge when organisational resources, including those of the poor, are combined in a manner that crosses long-standing institutional boundaries.

When it comes to funding, global donors, such as the UK's Department for International Development (DFID) and the Swedish International Development Cooperation Agency (Sida) have been funding community-led informal settlements upgrading programmes. While the funds set aside by these donors are principally channelled through the World Bank, it is Cities Alliance, an organisation which was jointly established by the World Bank and UN-Habitat in 1999, that administers the project on behalf of DFID and Sida.

Partly owing to the growing recognition and international assistance that they have managed to attract, community-based informal settlements upgrading programmes are registering impressive outcomes in improving the lives of slum and squatter households in many parts of the developing world, including Sub-Saharan Africa. They demonstrate impressive ability to mobilise savings and to manage the meagre resources they have collected from slum and squatter households. This has given them respect and widespread acceptance by national and local governments, as well as by the donor community.

A very good example in this case is the Kisumu Slum-Dwellers Association (KSDA) in Kenya. In a cooperative framework, it succeeded in mobilising its members to contribute shares for use as collateral to access credit for housing improvement. The association did so by committing to repay the loan from the rent that would be collected from the new dwellings that they intended to build.

Also equally exemplary was a saving initiative launched by the Kisumu Muungano wa Wanavijiji, under the umbrella of the Federation of Slum dwellers in Kenya. The initiative started in 2003 and established five daily savings groups. Money saved in this way was loaned to members for purposes of improving household welfare. Beyond daily savings and lending, the activities of the association included HIV awareness schemes and counselling services for youth and children (UN-Habitat, 2005b). Certainly, the experience of the Kisumu Slum Dwellers Association and several other similar grassroots associations around the world proves beyond doubt that, as stated by Cities Alliance, the poor can and are willing to pay for improved housing and services.


## CONCLUDING REMARKS

According to the Universal Declaration of Human Rights, every person has a right to adequate housing. However, approximately one-third of the

## Upgrading Informal Settlements in African Cities   153

urban population of the world is presently living in informal settlements in overcrowded and unsanitary conditions. About 98 per cent of the world's urban populations that live in urban informal settlements are citizens of the developing world. With 72 per cent of its urban population living in informal settlements, Sub-Saharan Africa is presently unparalleled by any other region of the developing world in the magnitude of the challenges that it faces as it deals with such settlements.

This report has presented the salient features of informal settlements, the quality of life in such surroundings, the main threats that their existence poses to orderly ways of living and the main factors that contribute to their proliferation, with specific reference to the case of Sub-Saharan Africa. It has also highlighted their rural connections and presented a concise survey of worldwide policy responses to the problem of informal settlements. Particular emphasis has been put on the modalities and outcomes of such responses by providing fitting examples where possible.

In general, the main findings of the study have shown that informal settlements continue to pose serious challenges to both policymakers and scholars, in spite of all that has been done in the recent past in an attempt to reverse the downward trends that they continue to exhibit, especially in Sub-Saharan Africa. Even though the Millennium Declaration has unequivocally called for a concerted worldwide action to significantly scale up poverty reduction programmes with the vision to significantly improve the lives of at least 100 million slum dwellers by 2015, the facts on the ground show that most countries in Sub-Saharan Africa are simply not well poised to achieve Goal 7, Target 11 of the MDGs.

Irrespective of these facts, there is now a growing worldwide consensus that it is in the best interest of cities to upgrade their informal settlements and put in place measures that significantly deter the formation of new slum and squatter settlements. However, there is still no universal agreement on the modality of informal settlements upgrading that yields the best results. Nevertheless, based on examples of best practices around the world, there seems to be very little or no disagreement among policymakers and scholars that community-led informal settlements upgrading programmes are far preferable to most other approaches. The advantage of this approach does not rest only on its inclusive, holistic and flexible attributes, but also in its inherent capacity to instil a sense of programme ownership among the beneficiaries. Because the poor are both capable and willing to pay for improved homes and services, such a sense of ownership goes far in ensuring the viability of programmes for upgrading informal settlements.

Last but not least, this study has argued that the presence of a supportive policy environment is of paramount importance for community-led informal upgrading programmes to succeed. Such a policy environment must be pursued on two fronts. First, the creation of such a policy environment requires a comprehensive overhaul of national policies and regulations that affect the outcome of urban development programmes. As such, it must effectively

## 154   Solomon Mulugeta

identify existing gaps in policy and regulations, and take the necessary remedial measures. Above all, such a reform should focus on empowering local governments so that they are able to handle broader responsibilities. Secondly, the revision of the national legal and institutional framework has to recognise the poor as rightful urban residents. Such recognition has to be buttressed by clear regulations and procedures that protect their rights. These pro-poor regulations and procedures should put down guidelines for property regularisation. They should adjust regulatory standards to what the poor can afford, improve their access to credit, and encourage the private sector to support efforts for upgrading informal settlements. Above all, they should create an environment that would encourage the urban poor to exploit their problem-solving potentials to the fullest.

## NOTES

1. http://www.un.org/Overview/rights.html Accessed September 2005.
2. www.unhabitat.org/pmss/getElectronicVersion.aspx?nr=2332&...Accessed October 2010.
3. Almost all of the inner city slums of Addis Ababa are quasi legal in origin as they were built by lawful property owners who responded to the housing needs of the city's predominantly low income population by erecting mostly substandard rental accommodations.
4. http://en.wikipedia.org/wiki/Slum#Characteristics. Accessed i April, 2010
5. Some sources report that no less than 700,000 persons live in Kibera while some others state that 1 out of every 5 residents of Nairobi live in this informal settlement.
6. http://www.unhabitat.org/pmss/getElectronicVersion.asp?nr=2336&alt=1. Accessed October 2010
7. There are some conflicting figures on the actual size of Lagos. For instance, a statistical report published by the African Development bank indicates that the city's population was 9.47 million in 2007.
8. More than 70% of married women aged 15–49 did not use contraceptives in 33 African countries between the years 2000 and 2005 (African Development Bank, 2008b).
9. During the earlier part of the 1990s the average aggregate real GDP growth rate of Africa was 1.3%, and it did not exceed 2.6% during the second half the decade.
10. In recent decades, many countries of Sub-Sahara have been witnessing double digit inflation in general and a an alarmingly fast rise of food prices in particular due to such factors as increasing westernization or industrialization of urban food systems, devaluation of local currencies and loss of agricultural subsidies. For instance, the price in of basic food stuffs in Zimbabwe rose by 70 percent in just three months in 1997/8 following the devaluation of Zimbabwean dollar (Drakakis-Smith, 2000). Even though average inflation for the continent remained under 10% during the greater part of the post 2000 period, countries such as Angola, Eritrea, Ethiopia, Guinea, Sao Tome and Principe and Zambia were experiencing double digit inflation as late as 2007 (African Development Bank, 2008a).
11. This is, for instance, the case in Ethiopia where the majority of municipal personnel tend to be underpaid (UN-HABITAT; 2007a).

12. www.citiesalliance.org/ca/slum-upgrading#Policyframework Accessed April, 2010
13. www.citiesalliance.org/ca/slum-upgrading#Policyframework Accessed April, 2010
14. http://practicalaction.org/docs/wuf04_kenya_best_practic.pdf Accessed April, 2010.

## REFERENCES

African Development Bank. (2010). *African economic outlook 2011.* Tunis: The African Development Bank Group.

African Development Bank. (2008). *Selected statistics on African countries 2008.* Tunis: The African Development Bank Group.

Asian Coalition for Housing Rights. (2003, October). *Housing by People in Asia: Newsletter of the Asian Coalition for Housing Rights, 15.* Bangkok, Thailand: Asian Coalition for Housing Rights.

Cities Alliance. (2006). *Guide to city development strategies: Improving urban performance.* Washington, DC: The Cities Alliance.

Cities Alliance. (2008). *Annual report.* Washington, DC: The Cities Alliance.

Cities Alliance (2010). What is slum upgrading. Retrieved from www.citiesalliance. org/ca/slum-upgrading#Policyframework Accessed April, 2010

CLIFF. (2003). *Annual report: Community-led infrastructure finance facility to August 2003.* Retrieved from http://www.homeless-international.org/Files/ HOM/PDF/A/A/B/cliffar_2003_24059_1.pdf (accessed 13 February 2014)

Drakakis-Smith, D. (2000). *Third world cities.* London: Routledge.

Hardoy, J. E., & Satterthwaite, D. (1995). *Squatter citizen: Life in the urban third world.* London: Earthscan.

Iradian, G. (2005). Inequality, poverty, and growth: Cross-country evidence (IMF Working Paper WP/05/28). Washington, DC: International Monetary Fund, Middle East and Central Asia Department.

Kessides, C. (2006). *The urban transition in Sub-Saharan Africa: Implications for economic growth and poverty reduction.* Washington, DC: The Cities Alliance.

Matovu, G. (2000). *Upgrading urban low-income settlements in Africa: Constraints, potentials and policy options.* Unpublished paper presented to Regional Roundtable on Upgrading Low-Income Settlements, Johannesburg, South Africa.

Tannerfeldt, G., & Ljung, P. (2008). *More urban less poor: An introduction to urban development and management.* London: Earthscan.

Tibaijuka, A. K. (2009). *Building prosperity: Housing and economic development.* London: Earthscan.

UN-Habitat. (2005a). *Urbanisation challenges in Sub-Saharan Africa.* Nairobi: UN-Habitat.

UN-Habitat. (2005b). *Situation analysis of informal settlements in Kisumu.* Nairobi: UN-Habitat.

UN-Habitat. (2007). *Situation analysis of informal settlements in Kampala: Kivulu (Kaguugube) and Kinawataka (Mbuyu 1) Parishes.* Nairobi: UN-Habitat.

# 6 The Way Forward

*Nadège Désirée Yaméogo, Abebe Shimeles,*
*Steve Kayizzi-Mugerwa and Mthuli Ncube*

## BACKGROUND AND URBAN DEVELOPMENT CHALLENGES

Unlike in other regions around the world, Africa's fast-growing cities have failed to serve as engines of economic growth. Instead, the continent is characterised by an increasing urban poverty. This is despite the fact that it has experienced the highest urban growth in the world, with 17 of its cities being among the world's 100 fastest growing.

As mentioned in Chapter 2, African cities are yet to fulfil their potential to generate economic growth and alleviate poverty. These cities have remained largely primary commodity producers, and have exhibited less economic dynamics than those in other developing regions. The continent's economic growth has not been associated with any observable change in the structure of its countries' economic activities. Therefore, over the past decades, the continent has faced enormous urbanisation[1] challenges characterised by slum proliferation, weak and inappropriate infrastructure, growing insecurity, marginal role of governments, weak capacities of municipal authorities, and environmental and climate change issues.

As stated in the previous chapters, inappropriate policies, weak institutional capacity and lack of investment have contributed to the mushrooming of informal settlements in African cities. Most of them lack a comprehensive urban development strategy. As a result, the rapid urban growth has outpaced the municipal or government capacities to build essential infrastructure to cope with its development.

Rural–urban migration and the expansion of urban boundaries are one of the main reasons for such a high rate of urban growth in the continent. As mentioned in Chapter 5, the major factors that have contributed to the proliferation of informal settlements include accelerated rates of urban population growth, high incidences of rural–urban poverty, inappropriate policies and regulatory frameworks and poor financial resources. Furthermore, non-spatial factors such as fiscal, industrial, defence, agricultural and immigration policies have significant implications on the rates, form, nature and extent of urban growth. In other words, government policies have major impacts on the outcomes of the urbanisation process.

The proliferation of slums indicates the inappropriateness and ineffectiveness of housing policy. To a certain extent, this imposes important constraints on government policies regarding income tax collection and redistribution. Governments have poor knowledge of the prevailing state of slum dwellers, and are unable to control their future development. Therefore, they have very limited fiscal capacity to provide urban infrastructure and social facilities. With a very limited carrying capacity of facilities and infrastructure in urban areas, the quality of services in cities and towns has declined. In some cases, it has simply collapsed under the incessant pressure. The unprecedented surge in urbanisation has generated serious challenges for governments in the areas of planning, infrastructure, employment, social services, security and environment. The lack of adequate infrastructure has lessened the economic performance of most African cities and towns.

There is evidence that Africa's urban growth takes the form of slum growth with increasing inequalities. Because of a lack of institutional, financial and political resources to deal with increasing urbanisation, more than half of urban dwellers in SSA cities will still be living in informal settlements or slums in the coming years. Should the current urban growth trend continue, the situation in Africa will be particularly critical, as more than half of its population is expected to live in urban areas by 2050 (UN Department of Economic and Social Affairs, 2008).

Sub-Saharan Africa is expected to account for more than 60 per cent of urban population by 2050 (compared to 66 per cent for Asia and 88 per cent for Latin America). Richer African countries are more urbanised than poorer ones, and coastal countries are more urbanised than landlocked states (See Table 6.1).

In SSA, an estimated 42 per cent of the total population live in extreme poverty, whereas 72 per cent of the urban population live in slums. Great variations are also observed across the continent. Whereas North Africa has a high urbanisation level (52 per cent) and a low percentage of slum dwellers (28 per cent), SSA has a lower urbanisation level (35 per cent) but a very high proportion of the urban population living in slum conditions (72 per cent).

As the landscape of most African cities is changing rapidly, many have been characterised by high levels of extreme poverty. In sum, African cities are facing the following key urban development challenges: low rates of economic growth and increasing urban poverty; inadequate infrastructure; slums proliferation; weak urban–rural linkages; marginal role of local or municipal governments; weak capacities of municipal authorities; environmental challenges; and climate change issues. If well managed, rapid urbanisation can be a force for greater prosperity. However, it could also be a source of chaos and poverty if the necessary conditions are not met. Appropriate policy reforms or government strategies are necessary in order to better address urban development challenges in the continent.

158    *Nadège Désirée Yaméogo, et al.*

*Table 6.1*    Income and Urbanisation in Africa—2008

|  | Urban Growth | | Urbanisation Rate | |
| --- | --- | --- | --- | --- |
| Income Level | All Africa | All Africa | Coastal | Landlocked |
| Low Income | 4.1% | 33.8% | 40.1% | 20.6% |
| Lower Middle Income | 2.4% | 53.1% | 55.7% | 38.9% |
| Upper Middle Income | 1.5% | 62.9% | | |

*Source:* UN-HABITAT. (2008). *State of the world's cities 2008/2009: Harmonious cities.* London: Earthscan.

On the basis of the previous chapters, this part underlines the main challenges that are yet to be addressed by African countries for them to benefit from urbanisation. Therefore, this part summarises policy reforms and observed outcomes, wherein an assessment of a number of programmes in the context of urbanisation policy is undertaken. This is followed by the role of development partners in the urban development programmes in Africa. Subsequently, this chapter examines the important future role of the AfDB in the urbanisation process. Lastly, concluding remarks are reported.

## POLICY REFORMS[2] AND OBSERVED OUTCOMES: SOME EXAMPLES

In most African countries, urban policy reforms have not been implemented with success. Chapter 3 discussed how the inappropriateness of countries' urban development strategies has contributed to the proliferation of informal settlements and slums. Indeed, most African governments continue to operate without any explicit national urbanisation strategy. For instance, policy efforts to implement decentralisation measures have in general underperformed, mainly because of fiscal backing and lacklustre support from national leaders.

Moreover, the division of functions between different levels or spheres of government has been problematic, causing intergovernmental conflicts, misalignment and inefficiency in many African countries. For instance, decentralisation has contributed to the strong shift towards corporatisation, privatisation and public–private partnerships. But the main institutional problem associated with decentralisation is the division of powers and functions between central and local governments. Not enough power has been assigned to sub-national governments, especially local governments.

Issues arise especially when it comes to paying basic services, such as water and sanitation infrastructure, electricity supply, waste removal, health care and education fees. Local governments depend on unreliable central government grants, which are often not adequate to finance their projects.

Yet, local governments are constrained by lack of financial resources coming mainly from central government transfers and grants.

Therefore, as stated in Chapter 4, central governments end up disproportionately controlling local governments, making the former less responsive to their local needs. Thus, appropriate institutional reforms should be accompanied by an important support to local governments and authorities. One of the errors that must be avoided is to create a uniform system that assigns powers and functions to lower levels of government. It is in fact necessary to differentiate the categories of local governments according to their capacity, revenue-raising potential, and their population size and density. It is also important to focus on democratic enhancement tools that foster state responsiveness, legitimacy, accountability and enrolment of civil society and citizens in development programmes.

On the other hand, several factors have contributed to the proliferation of informal settlements in SSA and other developing countries. These factors include inappropriate policies and weak legal and institutional capacity. Most African countries lack clear urban development strategies at the national level. They lack clear policy guidelines for managing slums and preventing the emergence of new slums.

Slum programmes were quite popular in the 1970s, but in the mid-1980s, a shift away was observed with the implementation of Structural Adjustment Programmes (SAPs) imposed by the IMF, the World Bank and other donors. In the 1990s, the World Bank strongly encouraged many developing countries to adopt "enabling markets." However, low and mid-income households were marginalised by such programmes because they couldn't afford them. Consequently, informal settlements have sprawled. In fact, these programmes drastically reduced government interventions that targeted the most vulnerable populations. They failed in taking into account sensible policies, such as targeted subsidies. The enabling markets approach had worsened the living standards of many African cities and towns by increasing the number of urban poor. The following subsection summarises the outcomes of SAPs in African countries and in Tanzania in particular.

## IMPACTS OF THE STRUCTURAL ADJUSTMENT PROGRAMMES ON URBAN DEVELOPMENT

The objective of SAPs was to stabilise the external and internal balances of developing countries by reducing fiscal deficits, increasing economic efficiency and encouraging privatisation and export-oriented production. In the 1980s and 1990s, most countries in Africa were forced to implement these measures as a pre-condition to aid and loans from the IMF and the World Bank and other donors. For instance, some measures consisted of reducing public spending, particularly in unproductive sectors, such as

## 160 Nadège Désirée Yaméogo, et al.

introducing user charges in education and health care, withdrawing subsidies, and retrenching workers. Governments had to abandon their role of housing producers and adopt the role of managing the entire housing sector (World Bank, 1993). Furthermore, as mentioned in Chapter 3, the implementation of SAPs was often associated with decentralisation.

However, these reforms negatively impacted the living conditions in many urban areas in Africa. The quality of life in urban areas depends on the availability of social services, which include health, education, recreation facilities, water and sanitation, electricity, ICT and transportation infrastructure. Therefore, cutting public spending on unproductive sectors impeded the living conditions of urban households. Indeed, several years after implementing these measures, the living conditions in most African countries had worsened with a decline in households' real income and deterioration of social services.

## THE CASE OF TANZANIA

After several years of implementing SAPs, Tanzanian cities and towns deteriorated into chaotic infrastructural, social, and economic states. For instance, the majority of the urban population had difficulties to access clean water, adequate shelter, health care and other basic services. The number of slum settlements grew tremendously to accommodate the majority of urban poor who had been marginalised by these economic reform policies. In contrast, some parts of the cities were showing evidence of development efforts through the explosion of new commercial, transportation, and hotel infrastructure.

The SAPs had therefore increased the gap between rich and poor. By reducing government spending on social services, SAPs negatively impacted urban development in Tanzania. Insufficient public budget made it difficult to finance urban projects, such as adequate housing. Other public services provisions were also seriously impacted by SAPs. They included waste management, water and sanitation infrastructure, electricity supply and health care facilities. For instance, Lugalla (1997) carried out an in-depth study to show how SAPs had negatively affected the living environment and health conditions among the urban poor. In sum, SAPs exacerbated hardships and enhanced poverty in Tanzania.

## COMMUNITY-BASED TENURE REFORMS IN KENYA

One of the most important land reforms in the post-independence period in Africa was carried out by the government of Kenya. The objective of these reforms was to replace indigenous tenure with individualised freehold and lease-hold titles, inspired from the Western freehold land tenure system.

Kenya went through three basic responses to informal settlements: eviction or demolition; relocation sites and services; and *in situ* upgrading (Ogero, Omwando, & Basset, 1992). But all three policy reforms had very limited success. Indeed, the first response, involving demolition of slums, did not eliminate the need for housing. Residents who were evicted simply erected other shelters elsewhere. Most site and service projects intended for the poorest ended up in the hands of the middle class or the rental market. The best example was the Dandora sites and services in Nairobi, funded by the World Bank. Finally, because of illegal and informal transfers of properties, the *in situ* upgrading projects also did not reach the objective of providing security of tenure to the poor.

The relative economic success in Kenya in the 1990s was attributed to this land tenure reform. But it was also blamed for the escalation of family disputes, property rights concentration in the hands of a minority, growing landlessness, rural–urban migration and limited access to land by women. To address the question of land tenure, the Small Towns Development Project (STDP) was initiated. Its objective was to consider alternatives to individual leasehold title for informal settlements upgrading. The idea was to adapt the American community land trust model as a tenure form for providing access to land to the poor urban households in Kenya. This project was first experimented with in Voi and extended to other cities in Kenya. The results were quite positive (Basset & Jacobs, 1997).

## URBAN WATER SECTOR REFORMS IN SENEGAL

In 1995, the government of Senegal launched reforms in the urban water sector. These reforms aimed to dissolve the state-run company and create a new asset-holding company that owned all the government fixed assets. The company was also mandated to manage the sector, while another entity was designed for the production and distribution. A private operator was assigned the duty to run the system. Eight years after these reforms, the following results were observed: About 20 per cent increase in the amount of water supply; 35 per cent increase in the number of customers connected; better service delivery in terms of response time to complaints and hours of service; and better water quality. In addition, the water utility was better run with lower water losses and higher bill recovery. The main factors that contributed to the success of these reforms include appropriate form of contract, strong political will, good governance, flexibility and innovation. These reforms had positive impacts on the poor because of the nature of the operator incentives and because of the government policy of subsidising connections in low-income neighbourhoods. However, issues related to tariff inequities and poor targeting subsidies still remain (Brocklehurst & Janssens, 2004).

## HOUSING SUBSIDIES SYSTEM

In developing countries, housing subsidy conditions vary significantly. The first issue concerns the lack of adequate resources under which the subsidy instrument works well (for instance, competitive supply of housing services). The second relates to difficulties in reaching the poorest populations due to the size of the informal job and housing sectors. Consequently, the poor populations are generally excluded from the benefits of instruments targeting their needs. Third is the lack of information on households living in slum settlements. Because the informal sector is very important in developing countries, public policies should assume that the government cannot observe informal wages and capital income. This informational problem often complicates the process of identifying and selecting poor households that could benefit from subsidy programmes.

## The Case of Morocco

In Morocco, housing subsidy programmes have drained lot of resources, with a yearly spending of about 2.6 per cent of the GDP. However, most of these subsidies are implicit. The housing subsidy system includes income tax, deductions of mortgages interest, tax breaks to developers, and land subsidies to public developers. Reduction in local taxes for homeowners is the most important subsidy, but it is not applicable to renters. Consequently, as in many other developing countries, this kind of subsidy does not target necessarily the poorest populations. In Morocco, it appears that overall, housing subsidies have insufficiently targeted the poor population and are not sustainable in the long term. In fact, the World Bank has been actively supporting this country in improving the economic efficiency of their subsidy systems (Spence, Annez, & Buckley, 2008). In the majority of developing countries, even if housing subsidies are often an important share in public spending, their efficiency could be improved by better targeting of low-income households.

In conclusion, policies and programmes that have contributed in reducing urban poverty are those that promote macroeconomic stability, define property rights, present good investment climate, attract foreign direct investment and give broad access to social, educational and health care facilities among other basic infrastructures, such as water, sanitation, electricity and transportation. Countries that have reduced or stabilised slum growth in the last two decades are those that have undertaken nationwide approaches to deal with slum proliferation. South Africa and Tunisia are examples. The reason for success is the political commitment at the central government level, large-scale slum upgrading and service provision for the poor through implementation of legal and regulatory reforms on land policy, regulation programmes and inclusive policies.

## ROLE OF DEVELOPMENT PARTNERS

Africa faces enormous urban development challenges characterised by slum proliferation, poor access to essential services and infrastructure and growing insecurity and poverty. In order to help African cities to address their urban development challenges, development partners in this area need to play a catalytic role. Over the last decades, a number of development partners have supported several urban development initiatives in Africa. They included the World Bank, UN-Habitat, Cities Alliance, the Swedish International Development Cooperation Agency (Sida), Agence Française de Développement (AFD), Municipal Development Partnerships (MDPs) and Shelter-Afrique.

## The World Bank

The World Bank has supported African urban development issues for almost four decades. So far, this institution is the only one that provides urban development finance on a large scale across Africa. Its programme covers virtually all types of urban investments (especially in water supply in SSA). Thanks to its long experience in Africa, the World Bank is able to develop appropriate financing instruments. More recently, it adopted a new urban and local government assistance strategy to focus on cities and economic growth, city management and governance, urban poverty and slum upgrading, urban planning, land and housing, intergovernmental fiscal relations and municipal finance, and urban environment and climate change. The organisation is piloting a new framework and analytical tool—urbanisation review—to assist countries to proactively respond to the urbanisation pressures they face. The World Bank's new urban strategy focuses on the following five areas:

- The cities management finance and governance business line: This line will assist cities and local governments to improve planning and financing of service delivery, and to strengthen urban governance. It will support a number of critical actions, such as the upgrading of legal and regulatory frameworks, building sound accountability mechanisms for local governments and utilities, and promoting a mix of financing strategies by segmenting local governments and utilities into those that are market oriented.
- The urban poverty and slum upgrading business line: This line is aimed at assisting cities and national governments to address urban poverty by expanding policy-based interventions and scaling up investments in services that are of benefit to the poor.
- The cities and economic growth business line: The goal of this line is to outline a range of strategies that cities can pursue to enhance

164 *Nadège Désirée Yaméogo, et al.*

their economic growth. They include improving the sub-national investment climate, analysis of competitiveness and private sector partnerships.

- The urban land, housing and planning business line: This line aims to intervene in areas where formal markets have failed to reach the poor and low-income households. One of its priorities will be to improve housing subsidies to the poor.
- The urban environment, climate change and disaster management business line: This line focuses on urban form and design to achieve gains, reduce a city's carbon dioxide footprint and take advantage of the co-benefits of climate change mitigation and adaptation.

## The Cities Alliance

Created by UN-Habitat and the World Bank, this institution is a multifaceted coalition of representatives of slum dwellers, local authorities, developing country governments (which include Ethiopia, Nigeria and South Africa), bilateral donors and multilateral organisations. The Alliance provides grants for technical assistance and implementation. It aims to support cities in preparing development strategies that link their economic growth with poverty reduction objectives. It focuses on the formulation of urban development strategies and the upgrading of slums.

Like the Asian Development Fund, the AfDB should formally join the Cities Alliance. This will give the Bank the opportunity to help set the Cities Alliance priorities in its agenda for Africa, to improve the AfDB's internal capacities, and to offer support to the Bank's regional member countries (RMCs) in the designing and co-sponsoring of their proposals related to urban development.

## The UN-Habitat

This institution is recognised as the global clearing house for "best practices" in urban development. It has an extensive technical cooperation programme in Africa. It manages the Global Urban Observatory, which is the most comprehensive source of data on urban conditions in the continent. AfDB has a partnership with this organisation in the water for African cities. The partnership can be extended to other areas. UN-Habitat has a broad agenda in shelter and urban development. The organisation is a strong advocate of slum upgrading and tenure security for the urban poor. It has helped to leverage urban development and to campaign for good urban governance, especially on sound political frameworks for decentralised local governments.

## Other Development Partners

Over the last two decades, a number of new development organisations have emerged. They include the Urban Management Programme (UMP),

The African Development Bank recognises that cities and towns are major drivers of economic growth. In 1992, the Board of Directors approved an urban development policy to guide the Bank's operations in the urban sector, to build foundations for dialogue with counterparts, and to promote cooperation with other development partners. This policy focused on the capacity of regional member countries (RMCs) to plan and implement investment programmes, to promote the private sector, to support decentralisation, to improve the living conditions of the urban poor and to upgrade human resources. For several years, AfDB has supported urban development by investing in public infrastructure, industry, and social, health and educational facilities. From 1967 to 2007, urban dwellers and enterprises benefited from about 15–20 per cent of the Bank's cumulative financing.

During the recent years, the Bank has supported urban decentralisation (as in the case of Mali), and several projects that have improved the living conditions of urban poor, such as the project of Urban Poverty Reduction in Ghana (See Box 6.1; AfDB, 2011). In the case of Mali, the Bank lent 5 million units of account (UA[3]) to support the government in strengthening the institutional, organizational and territorial governance framework of the decentralization.

---

**Box 6.1 Tackling Urban Poverty in Ghana**

In Ghana, particularly in the Central and Northern regions, urbanisation is increasing while urban poverty is worsening. An estimated two million urban dwellers in Ghana are classified as poor. As a pilot country, Ghana has benefited from the AfDB Group's urban poverty reduction project worth about USD 40.25 million. In Accra alone, since the 1990s, 45 per cent of the population were living in the poorest neighbourhoods with lack of water, sanitation and educational facilities.

The objectives of this project was to: (i) Develop urban settlements through participatory management, job creation and strengthened public-private partnerships and local governance and management capacity; (ii) improve living conditions in urban and peri-urban zones by increasing

*Continued*

## Box 6.1 *Continued*

access to basic quality services and socioeconomic infrastructure; (iii) facilitate access to income generating activities through capacity building and a strengthened urban small-scale enterprise sector.

The project covers 12 metropolitan, municipal and secondary towns of 4.45 million people. The expected benefits include improvement in the livelihoods of urban poor through better access to good socio-economic infrastructure, creation of 6,000 jobs for unemployed youth, and skills development training for at least 4,000 women. The project is expected to generate 350 and 50 urban and peri-urban socio-economic and environmental sub-projects, respectively (AfDB 2011).

## African Development Bank's Urban Development Strategy

The AfDB Group has recently developed a new urban strategy to enhance the effectiveness of its interventions in urban development in Africa. The main objective of the strategy is to boost the viability and competitiveness of African cities in order to help them to better perform their role as engines of growth and economic development. This new strategy will focus on three main pillars in alignment with the Bank's strategic orientations and core areas of intervention.

The Bank's vision of urban development in the continent is to make cities and towns healthy environments, competitive and bankable, and well governed. The urban strategy is based on the Bank's medium-term plan for 2008–2012 and the 2009 African Development Fund (ADF) mid-term review. Therefore, a great emphasis is put on infrastructure development, urban governance and private sector development. This strategy also helps in mainstreaming the key cross-cutting issues concerning all urban operations, namely knowledge generation and management, regional integration, environment, climate change, gender and empowerment of vulnerable populations. The strategy is based on the following major areas:

## Infrastructure Delivery

As basic infrastructure is an important enabling factor for economic growth, it is crucial to improve the welfare and inclusion of vulnerable populations, and to strengthen the competitiveness of urban areas. Accordingly, the Bank's assistance to RMCs will focus on the following issues: (i) Upgrading water supply, sanitation, drainage and solid waste management services; (ii) improving urban mobility; (iii) supporting energy projects (i.e. public lighting); (iv) promoting broadband connectivity within and between African cities and between them and rural areas, harnessing information and communication technology (ICT) to broaden socio-economic activity and enhance competitiveness; and (v) supporting the development of urban social infrastructure (i.e. health care and education). In terms of capacity building for infrastructure development and management, the Bank will particularly promote professionalism in cities management.

## Urban Governance

One of the most important areas of the Bank Group's intervention will be to support municipal and local authorities in their efforts to build and strengthen good governance and practices. To achieve this objective, the Bank's efforts will be oriented towards strengthening fiduciary controls, enhancing financial transparency and accountability and increasing fiscal self-sufficiency and sustainability of public investment in urban development. The Bank will focus on the following key priorities:

(i) Support fiscal decentralisation and related reform processes to ensure fair distribution of resources to all levels of government, as well as access to resources commensurate to their newly transferred responsibilities;

(ii) Assist municipalities to improve their systems of revenue collection (i.e. assess and improve tax base and tax administration);

(iii) Promote a culture of transparency and support central and local authorities in their efforts to establish anti-corruption strategies and systems;

(iv) Strengthen the capacity of municipalities to undertake their own urban planning and secure control and management of urban resources;

(v) Strengthen the existing municipality networks and broker new ones to foster synergy/solidarity and exchange of experiences and best practices among authorities facing similar development challenges.

## Private Sector Development

The Bank's goal is to support the private sector—from small enterprises to mega organisations—by improving the business climate and the development of small and medium enterprises (SMEs). For that, the Bank encourages a good investment climate through technical assistance to municipalities and other sub-national governments. This will help to reform their legal regulatory frameworks and to strengthen economic and corporate governance. It will also promote fiscal responsibility, transparency and accountability in order to provide incentives and reduce transaction costs for private business development.

The Bank will also aim to strengthen local financial frameworks through effective partnerships with other financial institutions and development partners acting in the urban development area. It will provide long-term financing through investment loans and grants, credit, guarantees and equity, and also offer technical support. Furthermore, the Bank will contribute to the building of competitive private enterprise and infrastructure through interventions under the infrastructure pillar and by participating

168    *Nadège Désirée Yaméogo, et al.*

in major investment programmes aimed at creating strong development bases in cities with strong economic potential for private investment and industrial development.

AfDB will further support the development of SMEs by increasingly promoting an enabling business environment for domestic private sector development, and by building capacity with special focus on home-grown SMEs. This will be done through training, provision of credit and the offering of marketing and financial services. The Bank will identify "world class" corporations that can become strong development partners through which it can derive significant economies of scale for development of SMEs.

## Cross-Cutting Issues

In order to achieve sustainable development, the Bank will address some critical cross-cutting issues. First, concerning issues related to environmental challenges and adaptation to climate change, the Bank will address threats emanating from unplanned urbanisation and unregulated development processes. Second, for issues concerning integration, the Bank will support regional planning, identification, prioritisation and financing of bankable urban-related regional infrastructure (i.e. airport hubs, regional port gateways and road/rail corridors). It will also support trade facilitation (i.e. regulation of transport services, simplification of trade procedures and custom modernisation). Third, for issues related to gender equality, the Bank's strategy will stress the empowerment of vulnerable groups, particularly women and the youth, and support regional member countries governance and policy reform related to such issues. Finally, the Bank will work to address issues related to urban–rural linkages. As the inter-linkage between urban–rural economies are critical for cities to serve as real engines of growth, the Bank will put important efforts in: (i) Supporting inter-municipal cooperation and regional development planning; (ii) improving marketing and storage facilities within urban areas; and (iii) supporting investments in agro-based industries located in urban areas.

## AfDB's Urban Development Implementation Strategy

The AfDB's urban strategy will exploit the Bank's existing financing instruments using the central governments' channel, which includes: (i) Loans and guarantees, mainly to middle-income countries (MICs), and private sector loans to MICs and low-income countries (LICs); (ii) loans and/or grants from ADF window to LICs and fragile states; and (iii) Trust Funds and other facilities. For sub-sovereign financing in the case of creditworthy municipalities, the Bank will invest in knowledge generation and lessons from other institutions concerned with this type of financing.

The following are the Bank's financing instruments:

The Way Forward   169

- For infrastructure delivery, the Bank's support will be mostly in the form of traditional project loans or grants for eligible countries. The Bank's instruments (loans, guarantees and equity) will be used to support private investments in roads, power supply, water supply, sanitation and other urban infrastructures. The Bank will also continue to support public investments that enable private sector participation through credit lines and credit support/guarantees facilities.
- Concerning decentralisation and municipal governance, the corresponding instruments will be policy-based lending. Adjustable programme loans will be used to support decentralisation programmes. The Bank will also contribute to capacity building for local governments through investment loans/grants or standalone technical assistance operations.
- For private sector development, the Bank will contribute to the provision of urban infrastructure. It will also provide technical assistance to municipalities and other sub-national government for reform of their legal and regulatory framework with the objective of improving business climate. The Bank will participate in major infrastructure investment programmes using its traditional instruments (i.e. equity, loans and guarantees). The Bank will use financial intermediaries to assist the huge number of SMEs across the continent. This assistance will be in terms of credit or guarantee facilities combined with grant resources for technical assistance and capacity building. In addition, the Bank will use non-financial instruments, such as advocacy and policy dialogue, knowledge development and management through research and economic and sector work, advocacy services and capacity building.

The Bank's capacity to deliver its urban development support to RMCs will be the key risk in the implementation process. Therefore, it will use a result-based management approach to monitor the implementation of each of its urban development operations. In addition, the Bank will develop and give importance to partnership and networking with other relevant development partners to maximise the benefits of their interventions.

## ENHANCING PRODUCTIVITY AND PROMOTING DEPOLARISATION OF ACTIVITY CENTRES

According to the agglomeration theories, urban areas can contribute to economic growth and social transformation. In fact, cities are essential for economic diversification toward higher productivity. Therefore, firms seek out localisation and agglomeration that can contribute to improve their productivity (Henderson, Kuncoro, & Turner, 1995; Rosenthal & Strange, 2001; Deichmann et al., 2005; Au & Henderson, 2006). For instance, urban areas can attract firms and industries by providing larger markets, information and technology sharing, knowledge resources and easy access to credit.

The physical concentration of workers is an important initial phase in the process of raising the level of productivity. However, there is no agglomeration theory that guarantees that the mere condensation of people and firms will automatically result into a well-functioning city. In fact, the agglomeration theory is based on the following three conditions: knowledge spill-overs, labour market pooling and inputs sharing. But these elements assume that cities, especially governments, are able to create environments where economic agents can meet and exchange easily, where workers can move among jobs and where productive inputs can efficiently move. It also requires that governments provide adequate public infrastructure services.

However, African countries face the enormous challenge of establishing a sustained economic growth through increased productivity as the necessary basis for reducing poverty. Contrary to fast-growing emerging economies, notably in Asia, whose economic expansion has been driven by manufacturing rather than the primary sector, Africa's recent growth has been commodity-driven. Manufacturing is known as a dynamic driver of economic development, but it has not yet served as a source of growth in SSA. From 2000 to 2010, there were 17 converging countries[4] in SSA. All of them were either oil exporters or mineral exporters. Whereas the developing countries' average share of world manufacturing value added rose from 19.6 per cent in 1995 to 33.6 per cent in 2009, Africa's share remained at only 1.6 per cent, with South Africa accounting for half of it.

The slow growth in manufacturing has been attributed to the premature de-industrialisation of the continent , partly triggered as a consequence of the structural adjustment policies that had tackled unsustainable industrialisation paths (Yumkella, Kormawa, Roepstorff, & Hawkins, 2011). Furthermore, the manufacturing and service sectors are dominated by small-scale enterprises, which use low skills and low capital endowments. Compared to low-income Asian countries, African industry factor productivity is much lower and the share of transaction costs is much higher, hampering firm competitiveness. Transportation costs are at least twice those of the typical Asian country. These factors impede the growth and competitiveness of cities.

Typical cities in middle- and high-income countries have reasonable assets of basic infrastructures, transport corridors, skilled workers and other basic necessities, whereas many African urban areas remain bereft of such requirements, even though they are facing rapid growth. Urbanisation in Africa has been characterised by slum proliferation, and increasing poverty and urban inequalities. Therefore, there is a huge need for African cities to invest in infrastructure and other basic services in order to attract firms and industries and enhance their competitiveness. Moreover, countries should diversify their economic activities by not relying only on commodity export revenues. For instance, agriculture remains the single largest source of employment and income, even though its productivity has not "taken off" since independence (ILO, 2004). This sector contributes about 15 per cent of GDP, about 64.7 per cent of total employment, and accounts for more than 75 per cent of domestic trade by value (Yumkella et al., 2011). But there is room for improving agricultural productivity and tapping into the agribusiness potential of the continent.

On the other hand, economic growth in urban areas should be sustainable. Because many African countries are dependent on climate-sensitive sectors such as agriculture, tourism and natural resources, green growth is an alternative paradigm that has gained momentum in the continent. The recent crisis in the horn of Africa has shown how climate change can negatively impact the living conditions of the population. Several countries, among them Kenya, Ethiopia and Djibouti, were negatively affected by severe food insecurity due to drought and high food prices (AfDB, 2011). Urban dwellers in countries like Djibouti suffered from high food prices and food insecurity (UN-OCHA, 2012). The pursuit of activities that are aimed at negating the effects of climate change, such as low carbon emission, could have a desirable effect on sustainable development. An urban development strategy should be oriented toward green economy, which could, in turn, help solve the challenges of climate change and alleviate poverty. This can be done, for instance, by harnessing cleaner sources of energy and developing drought-resistant, and higher-yielding crop varieties. A green city is more about consuming intelligently with less waste and low-carbon energy intensity (UN-Habitat 2010, 2011). Proper planning and well-designed green technology could help improve cities' productivity and achieve green and inclusive growth for the next decades.

## "GREEN" MASS URBAN TRANSPORTATION

The rapid urbanization in Africa has had profound implications on the overall structure of the transport sector in urban areas. When public transport is formally organized and planned, it can provide safe, sustainable and cost-effective mobility options. Public transport can contribute to sustain economic growth, reduce air pollution, mitigate climate change impacts and foster social inclusion. In 2000, one African in three lived in a city—by 2030, it will be one out of two. In addition, city expansion has increased travel distances between economic centres making it more difficult for urban dwellers to travel for their daily activities (jobs, hospital, schools, markets, etc.). It has also greatly complicated the task of planning, regulating and operating urban transport in many African cities (Kumar & Barret, 2008). Yet authorities have had difficulties in meeting the service demands of new urban dwellers, especially in public transport services. As a result, African cities

## 172    Nadège Désirée Yaméogo, et al.

*Table 6.2*    Shares of Various Modes of Transport in Use in 13 African Cities

| Country | Large Bus | Mini Bus | Private | | | | |
|---|---|---|---|---|---|---|---|
| | | | Taxi | Motorcycle | Car | Walk | Other |
| Abidjan | 11 | 19 | 29 | 0 | 18 | 22 | 1 |
| Accra | 10 | 52 | 9 | 0 | 13 | 12 | 4 |
| Addis Ababa | 35 | 20 | 5 | 0 | 7 | 30 | 3 |
| Bamako | 1 | 10 | 5 | 56 | 19 | | 9 |
| Conakry | 1 | 14 | 6 | 0 | 1 | 78 | 0 |
| Dakar | 3 | 73 | 6 | 6 | 11 | | 1 |
| Dar es Salaam | 0 | 61 | 1 | 1 | 10 | 26 | 1 |
| Douala | 10 | | 13 | 12 | 2 | 60 | 3 |
| Kampala | 0 | 41 | | 20 | 35 | | 4 |
| Kigali | 1 | 75 | 10 | 0 | 10 | 5 | 0 |
| Lagos | 10 | 75 | 5 | 5 | 5 | High | 0 |
| Nairobi | 7 | 29 | 15 | 2 | | 47 | 0 |
| Congo Dem. Rep. | 8 | 0 | | 58 | 14 | | 20 |
| Average | 7 | 39 | 9 | 12 | 12 | 35 | 4 |

*Source:* Kumar A., & Barret, F. (2008). *Stuck in traffic: Urban transport in Africa.* Africa Infrastructure Country Diagnosis (ACID) report. Washington, DC: The World Bank.

share common features which include: a growing population inadequately served by the transport system, declining standard of public transit, overlaps and conflicts between the public agencies in charge of the transport system, massive growth in the use of minibuses and private cars and inadequate and deteriorating transport infrastructure. The poor management of cities and towns has resulted in increasing road congestion, air pollution, road accidents and other transport-related climate change issues.

In most African cities, public transport is mainly dominated by mini-buses (8–25 passengers) as reported in Table 6.2. Whereas large buses are ideally the backbone of cities' urban transport networks, in most of the cities, large bus companies, initially state-owned, have not operated efficiently and most eventually went out of business. On the other hand, most small buses are provided by the informal sector and have proliferated during the last years to fill the gap left by large public buses. Mini–buses, however, present clear disadvantages which include: road congestion, reduced safety, higher CO2 emissions and unpredictability of schedules. Access to bus services is very limited in many cities, especially for the poorest populations. The low density of paved roads (see Table 6.3), poor road surfaces and narrow streets reduced the geographic access of these buses.

As alternatives to buses, the use of commercial motorcycles has grown very rapidly in cities such as Douala, Lagos, Lomé, Porto Novo and

*The Way Forward* 173

*Table 6.3*  Paved Roads in Selected African Cities—2008

| City | Paved roads (m per 1,000 pop) |
|---|---|
| Abidjan | 346 |
| Conakry | 174 |
| Dakar | 467 |
| Dar es Salaam | 150 |
| Kampala | 225 |
| Kinshasa | 63 |
| Lagos | 400 |
| Average sample | 318 |
| Average, developing countries | 1,000 |

*Source:* Kumar A., & Barret F. (2008). *Stuck in traffic: Urban transport in Africa.* Africa Infrastructure Country Diagnosis (ACID) report. Washington, DC: The World Bank.

Kampala. In cities such as Ouagadougou and Bamako, private motorcycle use is common. About 9%, 12% and 12% of the people use taxis, motorcycles and private cars, respectively. Small-scale suburban rail networks exist in a few cities such as Kinshasa, Lagos and Nairobi (Kumar & Barret, 2008). In sum, the evidence shows that there is a need for improving public transport in most African cities. Upgrading urban public transport would improve transport options and accessibility but would also create a better urban environment.

However, effective urban public transport networks require coordinated attention to urban planning, the construction and maintenance of infrastructure and the organization of transport services. Yet, public urban transport in African cities is characterized much more by weak regulation and planning, involving many institutions at all levels (federal, state and local). This has resulted in poor accountability and lack of coordination. The government's role should consist of enabling connections between urban and peri-urban centres at affordable costs. It is important to understand that the connection between urban centres will have an important impact on future options for climate change resilience. Therefore, for the near future, more and sustainable public transportation systems will be indispensable for African cities.

In recent years, there has been a growing interest in sustainable public transport that can address rising congestion and pollution in urban areas. In fact, each year, millions of people die or are unable to continue working or attending schooling because of exposure to air pollution from the transport sector or road accidents, and the poorest are disproportionately affected. By 2020, road fatalities will increase by 80% in low- and middle-

174  *Nadège Désirée Yaméogo, et al.*

income countries. The transport sector contributes to about 80% of the harmful air pollutants that cause 1.3 million deaths per year, mostly in developing countries (Replogle & Hughes, 2012). Estimations indicate that the economic cost of air pollution and road accidents ranges between 5–10% of GDP in developing countries (UNCSD, 2012). In addition, even though the current per capita transport emissions in developing countries are relatively low compared to OECD countries, about 90% of the increase in global transport GHG emissions is expected to come from developing countries, mostly from private vehicles and freight (UNCSD, 2012).

During the Rio+20 meetings (25 January 2012 and 20 June 2012), the international community highlighted the need for policymakers and development partners to invest more in sustainable urban public transport in developing countries. The eight largest multilateral development banks (including the African Development Bank) committed to invest USD175 billion to finance more sustainable transportation systems over the next decade. This implies a shift toward green public transport which provides not only environmental benefits (i.e. reduction in air pollution by reducing the use of private vehicles) but also non-environmental benefits (i.e. access to the transport network for low-income groups, reducing of road congestion, improvement in road safety). Therefore, in the coming years, the challenge for African governments is not only to improve the supply in public urban transport, but also to pay attention to its sustainability by investing in green technology.

The pace at which African governments can shift toward sustainable transportation systems remains a challenge. For instance, policy reforms are needed to discourage unsustainable transport options by removing subsidies for motor fuel (private vehicles, for instance) and redirecting them toward public transport. They can also invest in mass vehicles (large buses) or rail in high-demand corridors. For example, public buses can complement private mini-buses where the transport demand has not yet been met. Authorities can also encourage the use of green public buses by promoting or subsidising cleaner energy use such as liquid petroleum gas (LPG). Investments in paved roads are also required as this is a major concern for many countries. But, in addition to the choice of where to invest public money, governments will need to address issues related to the planning and regulating of urban public transport systems. This will require capacity building in the planning and management of the urban public transport network.

## CONCLUDING REMARKS AND RECOMMENDATIONS

Urbanisation has not helped African countries to seal the growth gap with other developing regions in the world. Instead, it has been characterised by slum proliferation and increasing poverty and urban inequalities. African governments have given little attention to sustainable urban development.

The Way Forward 175

Notably, national development plans and poverty reduction strategies have not given high priority to matters concerning urban development. Yet, urbanisation is not exclusively a challenge of cities or municipalities. The role of urban governance should be shifted from service delivery to strengthening location competitiveness by fostering production, investment and growth of the private sector.

Many poor cities lack the basic infrastructure and services necessary to attract business and foreign investment. However, if managed properly, African cities can become important drivers of domestic demand-led-growth, regional integration and technological innovation. The creation of economically dynamic national or regional centres should be central to the economies of African nations and to the future economic growth. As in Asian countries, these regions could serve as production centres of wealth and the cradle for innovation, trade and productivity. Creation of new economic hubs across regions in the national economy will certainly help in balancing distribution of population in the country. This is paramount for successful urbanisation.

Furthermore, African governments need efficient, multi-tiered coordination mechanisms to support their urban development processes. Development partners have been supporting the continent for several years. However, many of their interventions have not produced the expected outcomes. For instance, by adopting the SAPs, several countries ended up with worse living conditions for their populations. In addition, some policy reforms were not appropriately formulated by governments to target the most vulnerable populations, and consequently widened the inequality gap between the rich and the poor.

In order to contribute efficiently to the urban development process, development partners need to coordinate their interventions with the beneficiary governments and regional agencies. Their interventions should also target the main urban development challenges mentioned above in terms of governance, support to the private sector as an engine of growth, environment, gender equality and regional integration issues. In that context, the AfDB has defined a new urban strategy to help its regional member countries to meet their urbanisation challenges.

## NOTES

1. The distinction between urbanisation and urban population growth must be understood. The former is related to a phenomenon linked to structural economic change, whereas the latter is a measure of absolute change referring to urban areas, and has no reference to rural population growth (Pernia, 1993).
2. Housing policy regimes are a set of policies and government interventions that enable, motivate and constrain housing actions. According to Angel (2000), five different housing policy regimes can be identified. The first type is the property right regime, which defines the extent to which people are free to own or exchange properties, the transparency of the land registration

176  *Nadège Désirée Yaméogo, et al.*

system and the assignment of different rights in housing. The second type is the housing finance regime, which covers the development of housing finance institutions, mortgage insurance and banking regulations, prudential regulations and restrictions on capital flows. The third regime is the housing subsidies system. Another type of housing policy involves government spending on residential infrastructure, and the availability and quality of urban infrastructure services (i.e. public transit, water and sanitation facilities and social services). The last type of policy instrument is the regulatory regime that includes building codes, zoning and subdivision regulations, and delays in getting permits.

3. UA: the unit of account is equal to the International Monetary Fund's special drawing right (SDR), which is about 1.53 US dollars.
4. The 17 converging countries are either oil exporters (Nigeria, Sudan, Chad, Equatorial Guinea, and Angola), mineral exporters (Botswana, Ghana, Tanzania, Mozambique, Sierra Leone, Namibia and South Africa) or resource-based economies (Cape Verde, Mauritius, Ethiopia, Uganda and Rwanda).

## REFERENCES

African Development Bank. (2011). *The Bank Group's integrated urban development strategy: Transforming Africa's cities and towns into engines of economic growth and social development.* Tunis: The African Development Bank.

Angel, S. (2000). *Housing policy matters: A global analysis.* Oxford University Press.

Au, C., & Henderson, V. (2006). Are Chinese cities too small? *Review of Economic Studies, 73*(3), 549–576.

Basset, E., & Jacobs H., M. (1997). Community-based tenure reform in urban Africa: The community land trust experiment in Voi, Kenya. *Land Use Policy, 14*(3), 215–229.

Brocklehurst, C., & Janssens, J. G. (2004). *Innovative contracts, sound relationships: Urban water sector reform in Senegal.* Washington, DC: World Bank, Water Supply and Sanitation Sector.

Deichmann, U., Kaiser, K., Lall, S. V., & Shalizi, Z. (2005). *Agglomeration, transport, and regional development in Indonesia* (World Bank Policy Research Working Paper No. 3477). Washington, DC: World Bank.

Henderson, V., Kuncoro, A., & Turner, M. (1995). Industrial development in cities. *Journal of Political Economy, 103*(5), 1067–1090.

International Labor Organization (ILO). (2004). *World employment report 2004–2005.* Geneva: ILO.

Kumar, A., & Barret, F. (2008). *Stuck in traffic: Urban transport in Africa.* Africa Infrastructure Country Diagnosis (ACID) report. Washington, DC: The World Bank.

Lugalla, J. L. P. (1997). Economic reforms and health conditions of the urban poor in Tanzania. *African Studies Quarterly, 1*(2), 19–37.

Ogero, B., Omwando, Z. P., & Basset, E. (1992). *Background paper on the Kenyan experience in urban upgrading.* Kenya: Ministry of Local Development, Urban Development Department and GTZ Small Towns Development Project.

Pernia, E. (1993). *Urbanization, population distribution and economic development in Asia* (EDRC Report Series, No. 58). Manila: Asian Development Bank.

Replogle, M., & Hughes, C. (2012). *State of the world 2012: Moving toward sustainable prosperity.* Washington, DC: The Worldwatch Institute.

Rosenthal, S., & Strange, W. (2001). The determinants of agglomeration. *Journal of Urban Economics 50*(2), 191–229.

Spence, M., Annez, P. C., & Buckley, R. M. (2008). *Urbanisation and growth: Commission on growth and development.* Washington, DC: World Bank Group.

UNCSD. (2012). *Sustainable, low carbon transport in emerging and developing economies.* Rio 2012 Issues Briefs 13. New York: United Nations Conference on Sustainable Development.

UN-Department of Economic and Social Affairs. (2008). *World urbanisation prospects, the 2011 revision.* Retrieved from http://esa.un.org/unup/ (accessed 7 February 2014)

UN-Habitat. (2002). *The global campaign on urban governance.* Nairobi: UN-Habitat.

UN-Habitat. (2008). *State of the world's cities 2008/2009: Harmonious cities.* Nairobi: UN-Habitat. Retrieved from: http://www.unhabitat.org/pmss/list-ItemDetails.aspx?publicationID=2562 (Accessed 7 February 2014).

UN-Habitat. (2010). *The state of African cities 2010: Governance, inequality and urban land markets.* Nairobi: UN-Habitat.

UN-Habitat. (2011). *State of the world's cities 2010/2011—Cities for all: Bridging the urban divide.* Nairobi: UN-Habitat.

United Nations Office for Coordination of Humanitarian Affairs (OCHA). (2012). *Horn of Africa crisis* (Situation Report No. 31). Nairobi: OCHA.

World Bank. (1993). *Housing: Enabling markets to work* (a World Bank policy paper). Washington, DC: World Bank.

World Bank. (2010). *Systems of cities: Harnessing urbanisation for growth and poverty alleviation.* Washington, DC: World Bank.

Yumkella, K. K., Kormawa, M. P., Roepstorff, M. T., & Hawkins, M. A. (Eds.) (2011). *Agribusiness for Africa's prosperity.* Vienna: United Nations Industrial Development organization (UNIDO)

# Contributors

## EDITORS

**Steve Kayizzi-Mugerwa** is Director of the Research Department at the African Development Bank, where he has also been Regional Director for East Africa, Director for Policy, Lead Economist and Head of the Extended Mission to Zimbabwe. He was previously Project Director at the United Nations University, World Institute for Development Economics Research, in Helsinki, and Senior Economist at the IMF. Before that he was Associate Professor at Gothenburg University and external examiner at Handelshogskolan, Stockholm; University of Lund; Dar es Salaam University; and University of Cape Town. He earned his PhD at the University of Gothenburg and has published on macroeconomic policies, institutions and development in Africa.

**Abebe Shimeles** is Manager of the Development Research Division, African Development Bank. Previously he has worked for the World Bank, United Nations Economic Commission for Africa, ACTIONAID, and taught at Addis Ababa University. He is a Resource Person at the African Economic Research Consortium. His recent research interests include labor market integration, migration issues in Africa and impact evaluation of policy interventions. He holds a PhD in economics from the University of Gothenburg, and an MSc from the Delhi School of Economics.

**Nadège Désirée Yaméogo** is a Senior Research Economist at the African Development Bank, where she focuses on the economics of urbanization and development. Before that she worked for Analysis Group Inc., a Canadian consulting firm. She has also taught econometrics, macroeconomics, international economics, and environmental economics at Laval University and at the Panafrican Institute for Development in Ouagadougou. She holds a PhD in Economics from Laval University.

180 *Contributors*

## CONTRIBUTING AUTHORS

**Albert Mafusire** is Senior Country Economist at the African Development Bank and is based at its Southern African Resource Centre in Pretoria. Before that he was program coordinator at the Zimbabwe Economic Policy Analysis and Research Unit. He has lectured and undertaken research at the University of Zimbabwe and worked as a consultant for Zimbabwean and international organizations. His research interests are mainly in the areas of trade and economic development more broadly. He holds a PhD in Economics from Queensland University.

**Beacon Mbiba** is Senior Lecturer and Program Leader, Urban Planning in Developing Countries and Transitional Economies, Oxford Brookes University. He is a member of the Royal Town Planning Institute, and has lectured at the London School of Economics and Political Science; University College, London; and the University of Reading; and co-ordinated the Urban and Peri-Urban Research Network at London South Bank University. He has been a consultant for the United Nations-HABITAT and expert evaluator for the EU Research and Innovation Directorate, and as a policy analyst for Blair's Commission for Africa. He has researched on impacts of globalisation on urban and peri-urban transformations, diaspora entrepreneurship and development. He holds a PhD in Town and Regional Planning from the University of Sheffield.

**Solomon Mulugeta** is Associate Professor in Urban and Regional Planning, College of Social Sciences, Addis Ababa University, where he has lectured, supervised theses, and served as Chair of the Department of Geography and Environmental Studies, Dean of the College of Social Sciences and member of the University Senate. He is also member of the editorial board of the Journal of Ethiopian Studies. Additionally he participated in the drafting of the national urban development policy of Ethiopia, and official reports on the Millennium Development Goals and informal settlements in Addis Ababa. He holds a PhD in Urban Planning and Policy Development from Rutgers, New Jersey.

**Mthuli Ncube** is the Chief Economist and Vice President of the African Development Bank, and supervises the Research and Statistics Departments and the African Development Institute. Before joining the Bank, he was Dean of the Faculty of Commerce, Law and Management at the University of Witwatersrand (Wits) in Johannesburg, and before that Dean and Professor of Finance at Wits Business School. During his tenure, the Wits Business School rose in rank to among the best 45 business schools globally. He has also been an investment banker, serving as Chairman of Barbican and Selwyn Capital. Within the public sector, he has served on the boards of several agencies, notably as member of the South African Financial Services Board, Chairman of the Board of the African Economic Research Consortium, in Nairobi, Governor of the African Capacity Building Foundation, and Chairman of the Global Agenda Council on Poverty and Economic Development of the World Economic Forum. He earned his PhD in Mathematical Finance from Cambridge University and has written widely in the fields of econometrics, finance and economic development.

**Edgar Pieterse** holds the South African Research Chair in Urban Policy at the National Research Foundation, directs the African Centre for Cities, and is Professor in the School of Architecture, Planning and Geomatics, both at the University of Cape Town. He serves on the Research Advisory Boards of various research centres such as: the Indian Institute for Human Settlements, LSE Cities, the Low Carbon Mobility Stakeholder Board at the University of Oxford, and the Gauteng City-Region Observatory. He is also a Senior Fellow with the University of Cambridge Programme for Sustainability Leadership. He holds a PhD from the London School of Economics and Political Science.

**Warren Smit** is Director at the African Centre for Cities, University of Cape Town, where he co-ordinates the Healthy Cities and Urban Flooding Citylabs and is a member of the Global Research Network on Urban Health Equity. He holds an MA in City and Regional Planning from the University of Cape Town.

**Ivan Turok** is Professor and Deputy Executive Director at the Human Sciences Research Council, Pretoria, South Africa and Honorary Professor at the Universities of Cape Town and Glasgow. He is also Editor-in-Chief of the journal *Regional Studies*. He has a PhD in Economics, MSc in Planning and BSc in Geography. His fields of expertise include spatial economics, urban regeneration, labour markets and economic development. He is an expert adviser to the United Nations, OECD, European Commission, SA Government, UK Government and African Development Bank.

# Index

Note: Page numbers ending in "f" refer to figures. Page numbers ending in "t" refer to tables.

## A

administrative decentralisation, 54, 70. *See also* decentralisation
*Africa Infrastructure Report*, 68
African Development Bank, 3, 77, 165–169, 174
African Economic Outlook, 49, 77, 138
African Ministerial Conference on Housing and Urban Development (AMCHUD), 165
African Network of Urban Management Institutions (ANUMI), 165
*Africa's Infrastructure: A Time for Transformation*, 9
Agence Française de Développement (AFD), 163
agglomeration: benefits of, 18–19, 22, 36; dynamics of, 10, 18–19, 62, 68–69; economies of scale and, 18–19; framework of, 26–27; importance of, 2, 10, 14; theory of, 18–19, 169–170; urbanisation and, 14–19, 22, 26–27
agricultural production: improving, 51, 156, 171; policies on, 51, 156; rural poverty and, 20–21, 143; urban agriculture, 29–30

## B

basic infrastructures: for economic growth, 27–29, 68–69, 162, 166–175; investment in, 67–70; lack of, 8–10, 9f, 47, 68–69, 132–133; strategies for, 67–70, 166–175. *See also* infrastructures
bureaucratic barriers, 22–23, 55, 106

business development, 31, 38, 167. *See also* firms

## C

capital developments, 84, 114–116, 119n15
'cash cow' debate, 114–116
centre–local relations, 81–87. *See also* urban development
cities: driving development, 14–38; economic trajectories for, 28–32; migration to, 2, 6–11, 15–16, 20–22, 35–36, 134, 142–143, 156; upgrading settlements in, 124–154. *See also* urban areas
Cities Alliance, 112, 139, 147, 152, 163–165
Community-Led Infrastructure Finance Facility (CLIFF), 151–152
crime rates, 2, 5, 16, 127
cultural advancement, 17–21, 64, 124

## D

decentralisation: administrative decentralisation, 54, 70; deconcentration and, 54; democratic decentralisation, 51–54, 70, 75; efforts in, 51–61; experience of, 43, 76–77; explanation of, 54; fiscal decentralisation, 54, 167; government role in, 55–60, 169; implementation of, 43, 54–55; infrastructures and, 52–53, 52t; institutional reform and, 60–61, 70–76; issues with, 55, 70, 158; local government and, 57–60; policies for, 70–76; political

184 *Index*

decentralisation, 51–54, 70, 75; reform and, 60–61; strategies for, 70–76; urban development and, 42–77
deconcentration, 54
democratic decentralisation, 51–54, 70, 75. *See also* decentralisation
development challenges: future of, 156–158; national strategies for, 64–65; reform and, 61–64; scale of, 43–50
development crisis, 42–43, 50–53, 76
development partners, 12, 158, 163–169, 174–175
development policy: debate on, 14–16, 21, 26, 35; implications regarding, 36–38; processes of, 64–67; for promoting cooperation, 165–166
development trends, 2–10. *See also* urban development
division of labour, 15, 18, 21, 26, 28, 31

**E**
economic development: advancement of, 17–21; cities driving, 2–3, 14–38, 52–53; foundation for, 27, 29; impeding, 75; infrastructures for, 27, 29, 52–53; innovation and, 2, 140, 161, 175; overview of, 1–13; stages of, 27–29; technology and, 2; theories of, 36; urbanisation and, 15–20. *See also* urban development
economic growth: drivers of, 156–157, 165; foundation for, 27, 29; future of, 163–171, 175; infrastructures for, 27–29, 52–53, 68–69, 162, 166–175; poverty reduction and, 12, 156–157; progress in, 14–18, 21–22, 26–36, 77; rates of, 32, 43, 156–157; stages of, 27–28; supply and demand for, 28, 31–32, 104–105; sustaining, 171; theories of, 36; urbanisation and, 14–27, 163–171
economic trajectories, 28–32
economies of scale, 15, 18–19, 28–30, 168
education services, 18–22, 37, 63–64, 70, 104, 114

enclave economy, 10, 34

**F**
finance: global financial crisis, 43, 61–63; for housing, 90, 117, 139, 175n2; for infrastructures, 104–105, 109–112; for intervention, 91–93, 102–105, 112–117; market financing, 90–91, 90f, 104–112; pricing strategies for, 105–109; for urban development, 81–119, 89f; for utilities, 104–105, 109–112. *See also* urban finance
finance gap, 83, 93, 109, 117, 160, 174–175
financial markets, 90–91, 90f, 105–110
firms: attracting, 169–171; benefits for, 18–19; business development for, 31, 38, 167; in cities, 18–19; competition between, 19, 30, 52, 167–168; domestic firms, 34–38; improving productivity of, 169–170; informal enterprises, 29–30, 37; innovation and, 18–19, 30; investment strategies for, 26–27; manufacturing industries, 4, 26–30, 170; medium enterprises, 26, 167; private firms, 42, 102; producing goods, 29–30, 34–35; shared services for, 18; small enterprises, 26, 31, 111, 139, 166–167, 170; staff development for, 18–19, 54
fiscal decentralisation, 54, 167. *See also* decentralisation
Foreign Direct Investment (FDI), 29, 32, 162
foreign investment, 14, 16, 29, 32–35, 118, 162

**G**
GDP growth rates, 136–137, 136t, 150
global financial crisis, 43, 61–63
globalisation dynamics, 18–21, 30–33, 60–67, 149
Goal 7, Target 11, 149–150, 153
governments: bureaucratic barriers, 22–23, 55, 106; centre–local relations and, 81–87; functions of, 71–76, 72t–73t, 74f; interference from, 11, 22–23, 55, 81, 106; levels of, 55–60, 58t,

*Index* 185

158–159; responsibilities of, 55–60, 58t, 158–159; revenue for, 59–60, 59t, 83–89; role of, 26, 55–60, 67, 70–76, 72t–73t, 74f, 109, 156, 169; strategies for, 82, 163–167, 175
green jobs, 67
green mass transportation, 171–174
green technology, 171–174

## H

health services, 19–22, 63–64, 70, 104, 114
housing: development of, 81–82; financing, 90, 117, 139, 175n2; land for, 93–94; need for, 93–94, 124–125; property rights regime, 175n2; public housing programmes, 70, 77n4, 147; regulatory regime, 175n2; residential infrastructure, 175n2; subsidy systems for, 162, 164, 175n2
human progress, 14, 36. *See also* progress

## I

income inequality, 1, 8, 43, 50, 62. *See also* poverty rates
income levels, 157–158, 158t
industrial development, 38, 167–168. *See also* urban development
industrialisation, 14–15, 23, 27, 31, 170
inequalities: income inequality, 1, 8, 43, 50, 62; structural inequality, 9, 26, 31, 47–48; urban inequality, 8, 47–53, 63–64, 76–77, 170–175
informal settlements: basic services in, 130–133; characteristics of, 125–133; defining, 125–127; future of, 156–162; government intervention in, 143–146; growth of, 6, 131–143, 156–159; health issues for, 131–133; housing in, 129–131; inappropriate policies on, 139–142; infrastructure in, 67–70, 103–105; migrants from rural areas, 142–143; Millennium Development Goals for, 149–150, 153; orderly living in, 131–133; population of, 7f, 131, 133–138, 135t, 136t; poverty

rates in, 1–3, 43, 127–128, 133–139, 136t, 138t, 149–153, 156; proliferation of, 131–143, 156–159; quality of life in, 2, 43, 125–135; reasons for, 131–132; rural connections to, 142–143; trends of, 125–127; upgrading approaches, 148–149; upgrading benefits, 146–148; upgrading programmes, 150–154; upgrading strategies, 143–154; urban growth rates and, 133–136; urban poverty and, 136–139; vacant land for, 128–129; weak institutional capacities, 138t; weak policies on, 139–142
Information and Communications Technology (ICT), 31, 33, 160–161, 166–167
infrastructures: basic infrastructures, 8–10, 9f, 27–29, 47, 68–69, 133, 162, 166–175; decentralisation and, 52–53, 52t; delivery of, 60, 103, 166–169; development of, 8, 67, 95, 110, 166–167; differences in, 47; for economic growth, 27–30, 52–53; financing, 104–105, 109–112; investment strategies for, 61–63, 67–70, 165–167; network infrastructures, 8–10, 46, 53, 62–63; on-site infrastructures, 95, 98, 104–105; paved roads, 173t; physical infrastructures, 37, 52; public infrastructures, 9, 20, 47, 60–63, 165–167, 170; residential infrastructure, 175n2; role of, 52–53; social infrastructures, 19–20, 63, 165–167; spending needs for, 50, 50t; supporting, 43, 88, 95, 157; transport infrastructures, 22, 24t, 35–37, 160, 172–174, 172t, 173t; in world regions, 19–23, 24t, 26–29
innovation: economic development and, 2, 18–19, 30, 140, 161, 175; facilitating, 18–19, 35–36, 95, 116–118; need for, 10, 18–19, 27–30
institutional reform: agenda for, 61–77; decentralisation and, 60–61, 70–76; development challenges and, 61–64; investment

186   *Index*

strategies for, 67–70; operational strategies for, 70–76; sound platforms for, 65–66; urban development and, 61–65; for weak institutions, 38, 43, 139–142

International Drinking Water Decade, 99

investment strategies: for firms, 26–27; foreign investment, 14, 16, 29, 32–35, 118, 162; for infrastructures, 61–63, 67–70, 165–167; lack of, 36, 156; reform for, 67–70

**K**

Kayizzi-Mugerwa, Steve, 156, 179
Kessides, Christine, 150
Kisumu Slum-Dwellers Association (KSDA), 152

**L**

labour: division of, 15, 18, 21, 26, 28, 31; skilled labour, 37; urban labour markets, 20–22, 37, 134, 139, 170

land: availability of, 85, 86t, 116–117; community land, 95–96, 161; consolidating, 94–96; development of, 81–82, 88–93; information on, 86t, 88, 116–117; management of, 81–82; need for, 37; pooling, 94–96; public ownership of, 95–96; supply of, 37, 93–94; tenure reforms, 91, 160–161, 164

landlords, 94–96, 128

**M**

Mafusire, Albert, 1, 180
manufacturing industries, 4, 26–30, 170
market finance: capital developments and, 114–116; donors for, 81, 96–104, 111–113, 112t, 152, 159–164; strategies for, 105–109; for urban utilities, 104–105, 109–112

mass transportation, 171–174
Mbiba, Beacon, 11, 12, 81, 180
Millennium Declaration, 149
Millennium Development Goals (MDGs), 17, 61–62, 87–88, 93, 149–150, 153

mortgage markets, 90–91, 90f

Mulugeta, Solomon, 11, 12, 124, 180
Municipal Development Partnerships (MDPs), 163

**N**

Nairobi City Water and Sewage Company (NCWSC), 106–108, 112t
National Slum Dweller's Federation (NSDF), 151
National Water and Sewage Corporation (NWSC), 99, 101, 106, 109, 111, 112t
Ncube, Mthuli, 1, 156, 180–181
network infrastructures, 8–10, 46, 53, 62–63. *See also* infrastructures
"New Economic Geography," 22

**O**

Office National de l'Eau et de l'Assainissement (ONEA), 85, 99, 107, 111, 112t
on-site infrastructures, 95, 98, 104–105. *See also* infrastructures

**P**

physical infrastructures, 37, 52. *See also* infrastructures
Pieterse, Edgar, 10, 11, 42, 181
political decentralisation, 51–54, 70, 75. *See also* decentralisation
political interference, 11, 22–23, 55, 81, 106
population: growth in, 1, 3–10, 14–17, 35–37, 42–44, 45t, 133–138, 135t, 136t; of urban dwellers, 3–10, 4f, 4t, 44, 124–125, 129; urbanisation and, 175n1; of world regions, 24t, 134
poverty increases: rates of, 1–3, 15–16, 136–139; reasons for, 43, 149–153, 156
poverty rates: future of, 156–157; income inequality and, 1, 8, 43, 50, 62; in informal settlements, 1–3, 43, 127–128, 133–139, 136t, 138t, 149–153, 156; reducing, 12, 149–153, 162, 165–166; rise in, 1–3, 15–16, 136–139, 136t; rural poverty, 8, 20–21, 48t–49t, 50, 62, 134; urban poverty, 1–3, 43–50, 48t–49t, 136–139, 149–153
poverty reduction: accelerating, 23; economic growth and, 12,

156–157; programmes for, 149–153; urbanisation and, 15

pricing strategies, 105–109

private sector development, 166–169

private sector participation (PSP), 81, 91–95

productivity enhancement, 169–171

progress, 14–18, 21–22, 26–36, 77. *See also* economic growth

prosperity, 14–23, 26–28, 157

public housing programmes, 70, 77n4, 147

public infrastructures: for economic growth, 20; explanation of, 47; industrialisation and, 170; investing in, 61–63, 165–167; lack of, 9, 60–66. *See also* infrastructures

public–private partnerships (PPP), 92–99, 104, 117

## Q

quality of life: improving, 19–20; in informal settlements, 2, 43, 125–135; in urban areas, 2, 19–20, 129–131, 160

## R

reform: decentralisation and, 60–61, 70–76; development challenges and, 61–64; institutional reform, 61–77; investment strategies for, 67–70; operational strategies for, 70–76; sound platforms for, 65–66; tenure reforms, 91, 160–161, 164; urban development and, 61–65; for urban utilities, 96–106

rural poverty: agricultural production and, 20–21; migration and, 15–16, 134; urban poverty and, 8, 48t–49t, 50, 62

rural-to-urban migration: discouraging, 16; informal settlements and, 142–143; population growth and, 6–11, 35–36, 156; poverty rates and, 15–16, 134; quality of life and, 2; urban labour markets, 20–22, 134

## S

scale, economies of, 15, 18–19, 28–30, 168

settlements. *See* informal settlements

sewage utilities: community involvement with, 103–104; financing, 104–105, 109–112; governance reform on, 99–101; management of, 96–99; models of, 96–103; ownership of, 96–99, 96f; price-setting strategies for, 106–109; reform for, 96–106, 100t; tariffs on, 106–109, 107t, 108t

Shelter-Afrique, 163

Shimeles, Abebe, 156, 179

slum dwellers: eviction of, 146; improving lives of, 153; organisations for, 66, 77, 151–152; population of, 2–3, 7–9, 7f, 44–50, 46t, 129, 157; resources for, 147. *See also* informal settlements

Slum Dwellers International, 66

slum landlords, 128

slums, definition of, 44, 125–127

slums, indicators of, 44, 46

Small Towns Development Project (STDP), 161

Smit, Warren, 11, 42, 181

social development, 11, 16–21, 72–75. *See also* urban development

social infrastructures, 19–20, 63, 165–167. *See also* infrastructures

Society for the Promotion of Area Resource Centres (SPARC), 151

SONEDE, 99, 112t

squatter settlements, 125–127. *See also* informal settlements

*State of the World's Cities 2010/2011*, 43

Streetnet, 66

Stren, Richard, 53

Structural Adjustment Programmes (SAPs): enforcing, 56; impacts of, 159–160; implementation of, 55–56, 159–160

structural inequality, 9, 26, 31, 47–48

supply and demand, 28, 31–32, 104–105

Swedish International Development Cooperation Agency (Sida), 152, 163

## T

technology: economic development and, 2; facilitating, 36, 166; green technology, 171–174; need for, 11, 20, 25, 28–33

188 *Index*

tenure reform, 91, 160–161, 164
tenure security, 129, 146, 164
tenure systems, 22, 160–161
tourism, 19, 21, 30, 56, 171
transport infrastructures: costs of, 23, 24t; for economic growth, 160; investing in, 37; lack of, 22–23, 35–36; modes of transport, 172–174, 172t; for rural areas, 36–37. *See also* infrastructures
Turner, J. F. C., 144–145
Turok, Ivan, 10, 11, 12, 14, 181

**U**

UN-Habitat, 91, 102, 106, 112, 130, 136, 163–165
United Cities and Local Governments of Africa (UCLGA), 165
Universal Declaration of Human Rights, 124, 147, 152–153
urban areas: crime in, 2, 5, 16, 127; driving development, 14–38; economic trajectories for, 28–32; migration to, 2, 6–11, 15–16, 20–22, 35–36, 134, 142–143, 156; quality of life in, 2, 19–20, 129–131, 160; upgrading settlements in, 124–154. *See also* cities
urban crisis, 50–53, 82–87
urban development: centre–local relations and, 81–87; challenges of, 156–158; cities driving, 2–3, 14–38, 52–53; community involvement with, 10, 102–104; decentralisation and, 42–77; development partners and, 163–165; economic trajectories for, 28–32; examples of, 158–162; finance challenges for, 87–118, 89f; finance gap in, 83, 93, 109, 117, 160, 174–175; financial markets and, 90–91, 90f, 105–110; financing, 81–119, 89f; foundation for, 27, 29; future of, 156–176; housing subsidy system and, 162, 164, 175n2; infrastructures for, 27, 29, 52–53; institutions and, 42–77; local government and, 81–82; models of, 91–105, 92f; national strategies for, 64–65; opportunities for, 10–12, 26–28; outcomes of, 158–159; overview of, 1–13;

policy reforms for, 158–159; private sector and, 166–169; productivity enhancement for, 169–171; programmes for, 142, 146–148, 153–154, 158; reforms and, 61–65, 158–161; stages of, 27–28; strategies for, 61–76, 166–167; sustaining, 52–53, 61–66, 63f, 76–77, 174–175; tenure reforms and, 160–161; trends in, 2–10; urban crisis and, 50–53, 82–87; urban governance and, 167–168; water sector reforms and, 161. *See also* economic development
urban development challenges: future of, 156–158; scale of, 43–50; strategies for, 61–76, 166–167
urban development programmes, 142, 146–148, 153–154, 158
urban dwellers, 3–10, 4f, 4t, 124–125, 129. *See also* informal settlements
urban dynamics, 10–12, 26–28
urban economies: opportunities for, 10–12, 26–28; prospects for, 32–35; trajectories for, 28–32; views on, 32–35. *See also* economic growth
urban finance: access to, 109–112; capital budgets, 84f, 87; centre–local relations and, 81–87; challenges of, 82–91; donors for, 17, 81, 96–104, 111–113, 112t, 152, 159–164; finance gap, 83, 93, 109, 117, 160, 174–175; market financing, 90–91, 90f, 105–110; for on-site infrastructures, 104–105; pricing strategies for, 105–109; revenue collection and, 105–109; salary expenditures and, 84–85, 84f; tariffs and, 105–109. *See also* finance
urban governance: bureaucratic barriers, 22–23, 55, 106; centre–local relations and, 81–87; functions of, 71–76, 72t–73t, 74f; levels of, 55–60, 58t, 158–159; political interference and, 11, 22–23, 55, 81, 106; responsibilities of, 55–60, 58t, 158–159; revenue for, 59–60, 59t, 83–89; role of, 26, 55–60, 67, 70–76, 72t–73t, 74f, 109,

# Index 189

156, 169; strategies for, 82, 163–167, 175; urban development and, 167–168

urban growth rates, 3–10, 133–137, 135t

urban inequality: level of, 8, 47–48; rise in, 63–64, 76–77, 170–175; trends in, 48–53, 174–175

urban labour markets, 20–22, 37, 134, 139, 170

urban management: characteristics of, 56–57, 56t; decentralisation and, 54; governance and, 55, 139; impacts on, 54–55, 139; model of, 56t; problems facing, 60–61, 67–68; reform for, 60–61, 75–76

Urban Management Programme (UMP), 164–165

urban poverty: rate of, 48t–49t, 50, 62; rise in, 1–3, 136–139; rural poverty and, 8, 48t–49t, 50, 62. *See also* informal settlements

Urban Poverty Reduction, 165

'urban transition,' 15

urban utilities: financing for, 104–105, 109–112; models of, 96–103; reform for, 96–106. *See also* utility models

urbanisation: agglomeration and, 14–19, 22, 26–27; discouraging, 16; economic development and, 15–20; economic growth and, 14–27, 163–171; external forces on, 50–53; importance of, 17–26; industrialisation and, 14–15; progress and, 14–18, 21–22, 26–36, 77; prosperity and, 14–23, 26–28, 157; rapid urbanisation, 11, 15–16, 23, 25,

157; scale of, 43–50; trends in, 2–10, 4f

utility management, 91–93, 92f

utility models: community involvement with, 103–104; finance for, 104–105, 109–112; governance reform on, 99–101; key performance indicators, 102; management of, 96–99, 96f; privatisation structure of, 123t; successful models, 101–102. *See also* urban utilities

utility ownership, 91–93, 92f, 96–99, 96f

## W

Water and Sanitation Urban Programme (WSUP), 69–70

water utilities: community involvement with, 103–104; cost of water, 47t; financing, 104–105, 109–112; governance reform on, 99–101; management of, 96–99; models of, 96–103; ownership of, 96–99, 96f; price-setting strategies for, 106–109; reform for, 96–106, 100t, 161–162; revenue from, 114–116, 115f; tariffs on, 106–109, 107t, 108t

World Bank, 21, 50, 57, 91, 98–99, 144–145, 159–164

World Development Report (WDR), 15, 21–26

## Y

Yaméogo, Nadège Désirée, 1, 156, 179

## Z

Zimbabwe National Water Authority (ZINWA), 85, 114